*Bigger than My Body*

# BIGGER
## THAN MY
# BODY

*A Mother's Memoir About the
Love, Loss, and Legacy of Two Rare Boys*

NATALIE K. WATSON

COPYRIGHT © 2025 NATALIE K. WATSON
*All rights reserved.*

BIGGER THAN MY BODY
*A Mother's Memoir About the Love, Loss, and Legacy of Two Rare Boys*

FIRST EDITION

ISBN    978-1-5445-4932-3    *Hardcover*
          978-1-5445-4931-6    *Paperback*
          978-1-5445-4930-9    *Ebook*

*For William and Hamish, my beautiful boys, my greatest teachers. Thank you for showing me how to love beyond language, beyond fear, beyond the physical. You changed me forever, and this book is for you.*

*You are my biggest inspiration.*

*I love you.*

*Thank you.*

# CONTENTS

PREFACE: A BROKENHEARTED LEGACY ................... 11

1. THE MEN IN BLACK ................................................ 15
2. THE GOLDFISH AND THE BIRD ................................. 21
3. LAST BIRTHDAY .................................................... 29
4. TORN FROM SOCIETY ............................................ 41
5. WHITE PUPPIES .................................................... 57
6. THE DIVA IN THE DELI MEETS THE SCOTSMAN ........ 75
7. BABY NUMBER TWO .............................................. 85
8. THE DIAGNOSIS OF A RARE PARENT ...................... 95
9. STATUS EPILEPTICUS ........................................... 113
10. RUNNING FOR MY LIFE ....................................... 127
11. THE COST OF CARING ......................................... 141
12. THE HORSE WHO BOLTED ................................... 151
13. CAPTAIN RESILIENCE .......................................... 161
14. ART FROM THE HEART OF RESILIENCE ................ 183
15. BIGGER THAN MY BODY ..................................... 199
16. REST IN PEACE .................................................. 211
17. WELCOME TO GRIEF ........................................... 225
18. MY GRIEVING BRAIN, MY HEALING HEART ........... 233
19. A GRIEVING HEART'S WISDOM ............................ 245

EPILOGUE: A LEGACY STILL UNFOLDING ............... 259
ACKNOWLEDGMENTS .......................................... 265
ABOUT THE AUTHOR ........................................... 271

*Bigger Than My Body* is a memoir based on the author's personal experiences and opinions. It is intended for storytelling and informational purposes only.

Names and identifying details have been changed to protect privacy. Some dialogue has been recreated, and certain events dramatised for narrative clarity.

References to specific organisations or authorities do not imply endorsement. The author is not responsible for the content or changes to third-party websites mentioned in the text.

This book includes personal experiences with Adenylosuccinate Lyase Deficiency. The author is not a licenced healthcare professional. Nothing in this book should be considered medical advice. Always consult a qualified provider before making changes to your health or lifestyle.

This book is provided "as is." The author and publisher make no guarantees about the accuracy or completeness of its content and disclaim all liability for any outcomes resulting from its use.

Thank you for approaching this story with care, curiosity, and personal responsibility.

*Preface*

# A BROKENHEARTED LEGACY

THE WORDS TO "A BROKENHEARTED LEGACY," A POEM I LATER credited to my eldest son, William, first came to me in 2015, somewhere high above the clouds on a flight from Melbourne to Broome. I was watching a YouTube video of Simon Sinek's TED Talk, "Start with Why: How Great Leaders Inspire Action," when that single, powerful question settled in my chest: *Why?*

At the time, it felt like everyone was chasing their purpose—asking what they were here to do, what gifts they had to offer, how they could make a difference in the world. The question was everywhere: *What's your Why?*

But for me, it became deeply personal.

*What were my boys' Whys?*

Boys who couldn't speak.

Boys who couldn't explain themselves to the world in the usual ways.

I put my phone down and gazed out the window. The sky was endless, soft, and silent. And then the tears came—uninvited, but honest. I asked the question again, this time through sobs I didn't expect: *What were my boys' Whys?*

At that moment, the urge to write overwhelmed me. Words began to pour out of me, as if they'd been waiting there all along. Waiting for me to ask. I believe they came from my eight-year-old son, William, who was back in Melbourne, staying at a hospice with his younger brother.

This is what came through. This is his voice. His reply. His reason. His Why.

*I am the child who cannot talk.*
*I am the child who cannot walk.*
*I am the child who is detached from the ego.*
*I am the child whose body doesn't cooperate with the material world*
*but my energy is miraculous.*
*I am the child who is here to say, "Slow down, people, live in the*
*moment and find happiness in just being with those you love."*
*I am the child who communicates on a different level.*
*I am the child who will keep you conscious and living deliberately.*
*I am the child who is here to inspire and create*
*unconditional love with all that know me.*
*I am the child who can, without saying a word, spread*
*unconditional love and acceptance.*
*I am the child who hears you cry at night and wants*
*you to know you're going to be okay.*
*I am the child with disabilities and I am here to inspire action.*
*I am here to be your greatest teacher.*
*I am here to help YOU achieve your highest potential.*
*I am here to tell you to let go of your excuses and find acceptance.*
*When we connect, accept and care for each other*
*the world will be a better place.*

*Embrace our time together.*
*Your understanding of life and your life's purpose will be found in me.*
*This is my legacy.*
*Namaste.*

I was amazed at how effortlessly the words poured onto the page, as if William was answering me from thousands of miles away—not through speech, but through something deeper. It felt almost telepathic, like his spirit had reached across the sky to respond to my aching question: *Why?* I would later shape those words into a fuller poem for my blog, but even then, I knew they carried a meaning far beyond me. From that moment on, I began to sense that we shared a purpose—one greater than our bodies, greater than this physical life.

Ten years after writing these words for William, my friend, who also had a severely ill child, messaged me. "Hey, Nat, how are you? You've been on my mind a lot lately, how are you holding up?" she asked.

"I'm better than I was yesterday," I replied.

We chatted back and forth for a while before I said, "Here's a question for you. If I were to write a book, what's the one thing you would want to know?"

Her reply was swift and firm. "All of it. I just want to know all of it. I'd want to know chapter by chapter details of your journey with your beautiful boys, from infancy to now, and what you have done to keep on going. Your inspirations—the people who helped you get through it—what those people did or said. Even saying what didn't help! I think that's helpful too. A book reflecting on your beautiful boys and who they are and the wisdom and profound gifts they have given you just by being them. I want to know how you got through the tough days. I want to know how you found purpose again, after all that loss."

Sinek says, "When you know your Why the How becomes clear." Not necessarily easy, but clear. When you know Why, you can discover a purpose to pull you through the tough days. I guess what got me through was the words and sentiment in Will's poem. I had to believe that something good could come from all the sorrow and pain.

My boys chose me for a reason. What was it? Why them? Why me? When William's poem took shape on that plane far above the wide horizon of Australia, I instantly felt a calling from within that was relentless. I would serve their legacy. Looking back on that moment now, I can see that something bigger was at play.

William's "A Brokenhearted Legacy" is my Why, and this book is my How. They became my purpose and the reason I'm still here today.

To protect the privacy of others, I've changed some names and the details of my story. I still worry that the topics and ideas I write about, as well as my perception of some of the people who touched my life, will upset some readers. But I realised I was still trying to play Mum and protect others' feelings instead of giving my own a voice through the sometimes-harsh reality of raising two rare boys. I thought getting my often-untold story out into the world would help more than harm, so here I am. It was vital for me to have a legacy that confirmed that my boys were here! That what we experienced together mattered! And will always be of value, no matter the dark moments.

So that's what this book is about. All of it. All the joys. All the sorrows. How I felt. How I processed. How I grieved. The rawness at the time of the events and the reflections after putting myself back together later. Not all of it is pretty—some of it even makes me feel ashamed—but I know from experience it is important for parents in similar situations to have permission to feel and do all they need to get through.

Like these messy emotions and processes, the chronology of this book can feel a little messy, too, mainly because many events happened simultaneously, and some events stand out more starkly in my mind and heart than others. I've also tried to balance the good and the bad, so readers never have to stay down in the pits of darkness for too long. I hope you will find something helpful here, or at least some solace.

My story starts with William's death and the Men in Black.

*Chapter 1*

# THE MEN IN BLACK

IT WAS AROUND EIGHT THIRTY ON A COLD, RAINY WINTER'S night in July and our family doctor had just left our home. My husband, Scotty, and I were standing outside the front of our home in Bendigo saying goodbye to my sister and her husband. We barely noticed the rain. It was then that it all became so surreal.

A black Mercedes van seemed to morph out of the wet, shiny bitumen of the road at the end of our street and silently pull into our driveway. The driver and passenger were silver-haired, dressed in spotless white shirts, black trousers, black coats, and black ties, and the 1997 sci-fi movie *Men in Black*, starring Will Smith and Tommy Lee Jones, about government agents managing alien visitors to Earth, instantly came to mind. I reluctantly hugged my sister goodbye. The Men in Black exited the vehicle and walked over to my husband and me.

"Good evening, Mr. and Mrs. Watson," they said politely, introducing themselves like any other new visitor to our home.

"Good evening, gentlemen," my husband responded. I don't remember if I even replied. Unlike with other new visitors, our expressions didn't lift with this normal greeting and the mood remained sombre.

"We're sorry you had to come out in such horrible weather," Scotty continued, falling back on old social niceties.

One of the men replied, "It's nothing compared to what you're going through right now. We're sorry for your loss."

The Men in Black were from the funeral home. They had come to collect our nine-year-old son William's body.

The Men in Black unloaded a shiny, robust trolley out of the van. On top of the trolley was a black zipped bag. I remember noting its quality: the thickness of the black vinyl, the double-stitched seams, and the size of the black-coloured zip that matched the colour of the bag. They wheeled the trolley into our home. The wheels did not make a sound in the rain.

The men were deeply respectful with a comforting air of assertiveness about them as they guided us through the next steps. They followed us down the hall to our son's bedroom where he lay peacefully, as if still only sleeping.

The Men in Black then left my husband and me in William's bedroom. They wanted to give us privacy. They told us, "Please, dress him in what you want now, or you can bring his clothes to the funeral home tomorrow morning when you come to complete the arrangements." They did not say, *Put him in the clothes you want him to be buried in.* They were too courteous and respectful for that.

I began fumbling through William's wardrobe to find his new shirt and trousers. Two weeks earlier, I'd taken Will shopping to buy him a nice set of clothes for his ninth birthday dinner. I thought he needed some nice going-out clothes so he could look his best at dinner, something other than the casual tracksuit pants or pyjamas in which he spent the majority of his time.

Gazing at William's body, so motionless on his bed, I asked my husband, "Should we put him in the new clothes we bought for him for his birthday?" William hadn't gotten his chance to wear the new clothes. He'd been too unwell on his birthday to go out, so we'd had a quiet dinner at home. They hung in his wardrobe with price tags still attached.

I didn't think, when I went shopping with Will, that these were the clothes I'd be burying him in.

"How about we put him in his dressing gown?" my husband suggested. I glanced at the brand-new clothes still on their store hangers in my hand, and put them back in the wardrobe. He was right, William would be much more comfortable in his dressing gown.

William spent a lot of time in his cosy, navy blue polar fleece dressing gown. It was two sizes too big for his small frame. As the boys got older, I was more inclined to buy clothes at least one to two sizes bigger so they could get another season out of them as they grew. It would have hung down just below his knees if he stood up in it. William's frame had grown thinner and more fragile over the last few weeks. Beneath the gown he still wore a pair of his favourite pyjamas. The top was made from the soft flannel common in children's sleepwear departments. The matching fleece trousers were grey with sunshine yellow robot heads all over them, a character from the musical kid's show *Yo Gabba Gabba!* They were the clothes he was most comfortable wearing. The clothes that felt most natural. The clothes that were William.

The clothes he would have wanted to wear for his last adventure in this body, if he could have said so. We'd say goodbye to him in his pyjamas—that was enough for us.

While one part of my brain reasonably decided on William's last outfit, another part was running in circles. I never imagined I'd be standing over my son's body discussing what clothes to put his precious body in. These are details you never consider.

We began to dress our first-born son together for the last time. My husband and I stood on opposite sides of his bed, and taking one arm each we gently, respectfully, almost ceremonially, began to dress him. We wrapped his cosy dressing gown around his body, over his pyjamas, and tied a single looped belt around his waist. We then each took one of his feet and pulled his handknit woollen socks up his legs. We placed his favourite teddy in his arms upon his chest, a well-worn stuffed Tigger from Disney's *The Many Adventures of Winnie the Pooh*, and respectfully gave him a kiss goodbye on the forehead.

My husband then carried William's body out of the bedroom and placed him onto the awaiting trolley in the living room. The body bag was now unzipped and ready to hold the mortal remains of our son.

"Are you ready for us to take him?" the Men in Black asked. We reluctantly nodded, and they began to zip up the body bag, stopping the black zipper halfway, at his chest.

"Do you want to kiss him again?" they asked. "Do you want to say your final goodbyes?"

What I really wanted to do was hold my son! I began wailing uncontrollably but only from within, all that energy and emotion bottled up inside my body.

We each kissed him again. I took the teddy out of my son's arms and I pressed it against his lips for the teddy to have a kiss too. I then kissed the teddy's lips, as if to take another kiss from my son.

At that moment, impulsively, I decided to reclaim the teddy as my own. Originally, I'd planned to send Tigger along with William to his final rest, but faced with being left with nothing, I instinctively clutched the stuffed tiger in my arms. Tigger's fur had grown soft with washing and much handling by William, who'd spent many hours holding onto the pale orange teddy, flinging it about, feeling the sensations of floppy weight and fur. I didn't think of this history when I grabbed the teddy back. My only thought was that Tigger was the closest thing to Will. He'd been in his bed day and night. The teddy was the only piece of William I had left. Tigger was now the substitute for all William's cuddles.

Our kisses still fresh on William's lips, the Men in Black zipped up the body bag the rest of the way so it covered his delicate face. I couldn't watch William's face get covered. As the heavy black metal tab zipped slowly, respectfully towards his chin, I looked away.

The Men in Black wheeled our little boy, just a small lump now in the thick black body bag, through our home, down the long hallway, and out the front door to the waiting black Mercedes van and loaded him into the back. The sound of the van's boot slamming made me startle. Then the Men in Black, in stately fashion, got into the front seats of the dark Mercedes and drove off, seeming to morph back into the black bitumen road from where they came.

I wanted to scream at them to come back. I wanted to run after them. That van had my son in the back of it! All alone. In the dark. I'd never see him again. Instead, I stood frozen, speechless in my grief. My husband placed his arm around me to comfort me. We stood there in the cold rain, holding each other in numb silence.

Scotty was the first to break that silence, his voice coming to my ears as if from the bottom of a well. "We gave him the best life we could. We couldn't have given him a better life. Poor wee guy. He was robbed."

Still staring down the road and somewhat dissociated, I remarked, "I wish they were the real Men in Black from the movie, and one of them would hold up a Neuralyzer to zap my memory of this day away." But this wasn't a science-fiction movie about extraterrestrial experiences. The memories of our son's suffering and death could never be erased. We knew it was the end of William's pain, yet the beginning of a whole new unimaginable pain for us. The pain of grief.

William had been our whole world for nine years, and now that world was gone, his life taken by the complexities of a rare disease. He had never learned to crawl, walk, jump, or play unassisted. He was unable to communicate effectively. Yet, simply put, he was our world. He was and always would be our hero.

*Chapter 2*

# THE GOLDFISH AND THE BIRD

TOGETHER MY HUSBAND AND I WALKED BACK INTO THE HOUSE. The time showed it was 9:00 p.m. Had it been only five hours since William had passed and half an hour since the Men in Black arrived and left? Scotty went to check on our youngest son, Hamish, who by now was sound asleep. My destination was different. I went back into Will's room. I needed to reflect.

William's goldfish still swam in its five-gallon rectangular tank next to his special bed. I bought the tank for his fourth birthday. It was big enough to have a filter that bubbled away all day and night, the water forever circulated and siphoned back into the tank. It had its own light, also left on all the time, that lit up the medieval castle at the tank's centre and the colourful fake plants that waved serenely in the slight current.

There had been a few fish to occupy the tank over the years, but the current resident was about three years old, so old I didn't think goldfish lived that long. His colour was the classic orange-gold and he had the googly eyes that seemed to look permanently towards the surface of the water, and his tail was a long double fan. He was beautiful, but he was also massive. A real monster. I don't think he had a name, we just called him the Orange One. All I knew was that I couldn't add any small goldfish to enrich his habitat and social life because he ate them. So he swam solo under the tank lights, a bulbous shadow that broke up the dim glow in the darkened room as he swam back and forth, unsure whether to stay in his dark castle home or come out and give me an eyeful. Weirdly enough, this fish only lived about three weeks more than William, even though I took care of him the same.

Next to the tank, William's favourite oil burner diffused a nurturing, comforting blend of lavender, sweet orange, and frankincense, the same scents I'd rubbed on William's skin only days before. I tipped a drop of each oil into my hands and breathed them in while observing the stillness of the room.

I turned on William's magical mood lighting that shone stars onto his ceiling and chased away a little more of the nighttime darkness, and I laid down on his bed to watch the calming light show. His pillow said "Brave Bear" and sat on top of the matching duvet and sheet set. The bedding still felt warm from where William lay only five minutes earlier. Across the room, I could make out the gray silhouette of the timber rocking chair I'd bought for William before he was born.

In the coming days, when my grief got overwhelming and I needed to calm myself, the only thing that gave me comfort was lying in his bed and nuzzling into his pillow, every inhale breathing him into me. Or I'd sit in his rocking chair cuddling Tigger. William's scent, distinct from the oil fragrances that lingered in the air, surrounded me. Every night for two weeks I would cry myself asleep in the bed, cuddling the teddy I'd stolen back from Will's arms so it could fill mine.

This first night, moments after losing him, I was emotionally exhausted but my mind raced with memories of my son's short life with us. Why had we lost our son? What was the reason for his short life?

I couldn't bring myself to move. I wanted to be around William and all his favourite things a little longer. But try as I might, as the hours dragged on, all I could see was that black van driving away with my son. Finally, no longer able to feel or think as everything drained out of me, I fell asleep.

At 3:00 a.m., almost twelve hours after William had taken his last breath, I began to wake. Suddenly, fully awake, my eyes shot open in horrific panic. The events from the day before shuffled into my conscious mind like a card deck as I struggled up from the fog of a nightmare. I had dreamed that William had woken in the cold, dark funeral home and was calling out for me. I felt his fear. He had never been anywhere on his own; he has always had someone with him. The reality of my little boy being alone out there in the spirit world, or not knowing for sure if what I felt was or wasn't him, was, and still is, traumatic. My worst fear was for my son to be lost—alone and afraid; I was living my nightmare.

I lay there, trying to process the nightmare and get my heart rate back under control, when I began sensing William. Not his physical body, but him as a small ball of energy spinning around in the corners of his bedroom. He was like a bird trapped in a cage. He zoomed around his room erratically, from one corner to the other. I could sense he was terrified. William was pure innocence in the physical world and now he was pure innocence in the spiritual world, too, now only as free-flowing energy. Energy that felt like a baby who didn't know what this new form was—and his panic was unbearable to witness.

I had never felt such true panic for my child—I felt powerless. I was here, lying in his bed, and he was over there, on the other side, close to me and so far apart at the same time. I wanted to reach out and hold him, but instead, I hugged his Tigger, patting the teddy as if it was William, saying over and over, "Shhh, it's okay, Will, Mummy's here."

I wanted to protect him. I just needed to hold him again, if only for a moment, to show him it would be okay. I wished I was dead so

I could stop the pain—our pain, of being torn away from each other. Almost simultaneously with this thought, I found myself detaching from my physical body so I could take my spirit to him, to reconnect on the spiritual plane. I couldn't physically hold my baby but I could feel him—he was still here with me; his body may have been at the funeral home but his spirit was with me. My instincts took over and I felt a calmness come over me. We were mother and son, separate beings, but in so many ways we were one. And why wouldn't he be? He was created inside my body. He was of my DNA. So on a cellular level I was him and he was me. I nurtured every part of his being right to the end. I was there when he took his first breath and there when he took his last.

William seemed to recognise me as our energies intertwined. It was like coming home and being greeted by your adorable puppy that has missed you all day. We had found each other again. I could feel his positive energy buzzing all around where my body lay. When we touched in the spirit world, I finally felt at peace with my son. I accepted him in his new form, I soothed him—and let him go. He was free from pain, and for the first time in our life together I felt nothing but joy for his miraculous energy. He was no longer a terrified bird trapped in a cage, he was finally free to fly.

I lay there in the darkness of William's room, holding his spirit in mine, and asked for loved ones that had gone before him to show him the way towards the light. I asked them to teach him how to use his newfound free-flowing energy and help him understand what will happen next. It was a mixed bag of souls. William had never met Uncle Nori, but I knew the man had had a big heart. There were our old neighbours, Don and Noeline, who helped care for William as a young baby. Then there were my dad's mum and my mum's mum. "Please," I pleaded, "take William and look after him because he is new to this world." I didn't know if my call to these distant, departed relatives and friends would help William. I wasn't sure if it was possible for him to connect with them, as wouldn't they have found their own new physical bodies too? Or could they choose to remain a spirit and meander through our lives, earning the name "angel" and provoking wisdom within each of us for generations to come?

William's now-comforting presence was enough to reassure me that he was now in safe hands and at that moment there was no question if I should go back. I did what I did just in that moment, and when it was done, I was pulled back into my body.

Suddenly, I was willing to believe there was more out there, something bigger than our bodies. A life energy, made up of an energetic world and a physical world. How or why it existed I didn't know, but in the moment I felt William's immense loss and panic, I wanted to help his spirit find its way to a new physical body, one that was accepting of his beautiful innocent soul. I didn't have to think to make this energetic connection, it just flowed naturally through me. It wasn't something I was taught. I'd been exposed to religion as a child, but years ago curiosity and logic had led me to become agnostic towards organised religion to favour a broader spiritual awareness. After my experience with my boys, I now believe that our soul is essentially who we are for eternity. Yes, forever! At our essence we'll all have our time to experience the physical realm in a body and then have our time in the nonphysical realm as something like a spiritual guide or guardian angel. I believe we are all multidimensional. Regardless of which religion we follow.

But living the hard day-to-day of life makes it difficult to pay attention to our immortal souls. After we're born it's almost like we detach from that spiritual plane. In some cultures, this detachment feels more severe than others. We focus on the experience of the physical body in our day-to-day lives, but then all of a sudden that becomes challenged. Whether it be triggered by a traumatic accident, sudden illness, hospital operation, or profound grief and desire to be with the loved one that's passed, there is sometimes a moment where an intervention occurs between life and death. If you've seen the light and come back safe again to your body, it seems you can't return without a whole new connection to the other side. Most call this a near-death experience. I call it a moment of being reborn.

At William's passing, I'd yet to fully explore my connection to the nonphysical. Afterwards was a different story. I'll never forget that feeling of connection and the wave of comfort that came over me. It was an absolute out-of-body experience, one which I both experienced and observed. This…spirituality…was innate. It took hold of me like something primal, like childbirth. Something I didn't know was in me.

It was hard for me to decipher the imaginary from the real at that harsh moment of waking, or perhaps I was still asleep and it was all a very lucid dream. But dream or not, the recollection of what I felt was very real. I desperately tried to work out exactly what had happened and which side of sanity I was on. I thought I'd never share that experience with anyone so they wouldn't think I was crazy. But the times "they are a-changing," and as I get older and wiser it no longer appears so strange. In fact, it's an experience that provides solace and connection in times of profound grief and despair.

In life, William may not have been able to speak or walk, or move his body consistently with intention, but his caretakers at his school called him George Clooney because he was still somehow charming and sweet. His energy seemed boundless, even as it was directed into nonverbal vocalising and bouncing in his seat.

Whenever someone would take photos of us together, I'd say, "Look at the camera!" but William would never look at the camera. He'd always keep looking at me. It used to get me frustrated. "Why can't you look at the camera? In every photo you're always looking at me!" I'd sometimes say in exasperation. And now one of the fondest memories I have is going through all my photos and seeing him gazing up at my face in every one, as if he was trying to say, "No, Mum, I want to look at you."

William looking at me

The presence in Will's bedroom felt like that. Like William was looking at me even as I looked at the mirrored screen of my phone's camera. It's like when you think someone's in the room with you, but no one's there when you turn around. Or like when you're in a shopping mall and your husband comes up behind you while you're looking at the shoes. You haven't turned around yet, but you feel him, as a familiar presence, and you feel comforted even before you look to see him. Sometimes I think I see something out of the corner of my eye and nothing appears when I try to focus on it. But I know I felt something in William's room that night. My senses told me there's something there. I can't see him; but the essence of him was still there. Our body's nervous system remembers the energy we receive from others, both good and bad.

For a few weeks after William's death I felt him very close by, and then at times I couldn't feel his presence at all. It was as if he had flown away to visit other loved ones; my mum said she felt him while she was out in the garden; my husband said he felt him during the final kilometres of a marathon he was competing in. Even years after his death, many of William's loved ones have felt him visit. I take comfort in the thought that he wants to explore the world with all his newfound freedom. So through my moments of immense grief and pain, a strange euphoria comes over me, because I know this little guy and I am a part of his journey, both in this world and the next.

*Chapter 3*

# LAST BIRTHDAY

SIX MONTHS BEFORE WILLIAM PASSED, I HAD PLANNED A SPEcial ten-day holiday with William's younger brother, Hamish. It was actually Hamish's Make-A-Wish holiday to swim with dolphins. But as the departure date drew closer, William developed a cold and so we decided to change our plans and keep William at home with his dad. William's good days had gotten fewer and farther between. It was obvious to everyone, especially his school, as his attendance fell off because he was unwell so often, sleeping more often than not. He was too unwell to travel.

On July 3, 2016, William turned nine. I made a special birthday dinner for the whole family complete with roast vegetables, roast pork with the best pork crackle I think I have ever made, along with applesauce and gravy. I remember the boys crunching away on the crackling and the look of sheer delight in all that there is about pork crackle. They loved their food and even when Will was sick he never refused a meal. We made it a tradition in our house that birthday cakes be a lamington cake, which is basically a freshly baked soft sponge cake soaked briefly in a chocolate sauce and then rolled in desiccated coconut with a fresh cream and jam centre. My friend who owned the local bakery would make it by special order in a large rectangle cake pan. And it was superb!

After we finished dinner, Scotty took the lamington cake out of the fridge, he lit the sparkly candles and the number nine candle at the centre, and we all sang "Happy Birthday" to William. As we sang his face lit up, as this was one of Will's favourite songs. We helped him blow out his candles and Grandma began cutting his cake.

Literally moments before Will took his first mouthful of birthday cake he began to have a seizure; Scotty wheeled William away from the table and into his bedroom for privacy. When the seizure stopped he got him out of his wheelchair and laid him down in his bed where he could sleep and recover comfortably. Later that night William woke up, and despite the late hour my husband fed him his slice of birthday cake. "There y' go, mate, a wee slice of birthday cake for you." Maybe Scotty knew, in his heart of hearts, that this would be Will's last birthday.

William frequently had seizures and had been quite unwell with another cold. Often when William was unwell he would become more susceptible to seizures even though he took various medications in the hope to help control them.

Two days after his birthday, William's cold developed into a nasty chest infection. He started to have a persistent fever. We called in the doctor for a home visit and she prescribed penicillin. Perhaps William had inhaled a small portion of his dinner, which could have caused the lung infection. But the medication didn't seem to help. He continued to get worse and his seizures had increased in frequency.

After twenty-four hours the doctor returned and we admitted William to the hospital for some further tests and to insert an intravenous line to administer fluids and an even-stronger type of penicillin, one that was used to treat things like meningitis.

William had spent a lot of time in and out of hospital over the past two years and we had a plan with the palliative team that whenever we could, we wanted to care for him at home.

Later that night we had the patient transport drive William and me home from the hospital. Throughout the night he continued to have low-grade fevers with seizures every hour or so. My husband and I were very concerned for him; William had had many episodes similar to this, and he would usually turn the corner after five days and start getting better, making almost a full recovery. The relentless fever, however, was new, and worrisome.

The nurse came to our home and administered penicillin via IV each day for the next couple of days as his seizures became more and more frequent. Every hour became every half hour, and then the seizures became nonrespondent to our regular emergency seizure medication. We called an ambulance, and his frequent seizures became one continuous seizure, or what doctors call "status epilepticus."

Scotty stayed home with Hamish until Aunty Catherine arrived to mind Hamish, and then meet Will and I at the hospital.

The emergency room nursing staff all knew William from previous visits to the hospital, always for extensive seizure management. Scotty and I gently held William's hands and feet while we sat on his bed watching him continuously tremor all over and moan in discomfort.

I knew my son was dying when I saw the brownish, foul-smelling discharge from his nostrils and mouth. It seemed like a lot. "It looks like old blood. Sometimes children bite the inside of their cheeks or tongue when they have a seizure," the doctor attempted to reassure me, but this didn't look like regular dried blood. I didn't know it at the time, but this was a sign of something called "bacterial pneumonia." Knowing what I know now, I wonder if it could have been Golden Staph, an especially vicious staph infection that's resistant to common antibiotics. Even without this knowledge, in my heart, I knew it didn't look good.

William had now been sick for a fortnight, and on the heels of the noxious discharge, a rattling sound developed in the space between his chest and throat. I desperately hoped it was the chest infection, and not what they call "the death rattle." His lung X-ray was clear and there was no sign of infection that they could treat. The doctors now believed the fevers were from his body's regulatory system shutting down. In fact, he was slowly dying right before our eyes.

The doctor stood on one side of the bed and my husband and I stood on the other side of the bed with William lying between us hooked up to oxygen and IV drivers releasing a building dose of phenobarbitone, Keppra, and midazolam. They had begun to sedate him for comfort. The doctor didn't have to say anything, really, we already knew this was the worst we had seen our William. By this stage, he had been seizing for four hours straight, despite being loaded up with emergency seizure medications. We were very aware of how distressed William's body was. He was lying in his bed completely unconscious, yet his heart rate was running at 185 beats per minute and only momentarily dropping back down to 130 beats per minute. The average resting heart rate for a nine-year-old child is between 70 and 110 beats per minute.

While standing over our son, we talked through our medical options to help make him comfortable without putting him on life support. We were relocated to a private room in the children's ward overnight and we each took turns sleeping alongside William in the hospital bed, singing "Twinkle, Twinkle, Little Star" and other lullabies to help settle him. Lucky for our boys, Scotty and I were somewhat gifted when it came to singing and William was easily soothed. It was like an on/off switch. If Will started to get distressed while getting his blood drawn or IVs inserted, all I had to do was sing "Twinkle, Twinkle, Little Star" and he would stop moving and crying to listen. "My God, that's a gift!" the nurses would say.

We knew and were very respectful of the fact that William was still capable of knowing what was going on around him, even when sedated, and we didn't want to leave him for a minute without him knowing how much he meant to us. He continued to tremor alongside our bodies for a few more hours until the medication had been completely infused into his body. He slept peacefully for a few hours without a seizure and for a moment he was conscious enough to respond with what appeared to be an appreciative moan as my husband and I sang to him again and told him how much we loved him.

We thought for a moment he looked a little better, but slowly the seizures came back again. Hopelessness set in. After nine years of struggle, William's tired little body was giving up. We felt his surrender.

It was excruciating to watch our son being slowly tortured by seizures. He hadn't eaten since his birthday almost three weeks before. Life support was pain relief and some fluids through a nasogastric tube. As soon as he became awake enough to eat, he'd seize.

We had two choices going forward. First, we could sedate him even deeper to stop the seizing so a mechanical ventilator could be inserted to take over his breathing. He would remain in hospital on life support until we decided, as his parents, to let him go and turn off the artificial life support. A little over a year earlier, we'd faced a similar situation with William and had chosen this route. Now we knew what this choice would do to him physically and emotionally and had vowed never to do it again. So we made a formal complex care plan with the doctors that if William got that sick again, we wanted him comfortable and pain free and at home with us, not on life support in a stark hospital room 150 kilometres away from our family, friends, and home.

So we went with our second choice. We'd take William home and, with the support of a palliative care team, care for him in his final days and hours in the place he loved.

For us, we knew we couldn't keep William like he was any longer. It was just too cruel. So we'd follow William's lead and surrender to the disease, but we'd make that surrender as peaceful and pain free as possible. We'd worked hard to give him a beautiful life since his birth. We wanted to give him a beautiful death too.

"We'll take him home," we told the doctor and the emergency registrar as we met in an empty room a few doors down from William's.

"Then you know what that means," he said solemnly.

"Yes, we know what that means," Scotty responded.

"Doctor, what about organ donation?" I barked anxiously, strangely excited by the potential of my son's death benefiting another child's quality of life. I felt somehow it would help me with my grief if I knew we could help another family by donating William's organs.

"I'm sorry," the doctor said, "when we consulted with the metabolic team, they said William isn't a suitable candidate. We can't take the risk of the organs being rejected because of the Adsl Deficiency." Meaning, they didn't want to risk the loss of a second child to William's disease.

This news shattered me. I wasn't expecting this additional blow to hurt so badly. "Can't they even take his eyes?" I knew corneas could help cure blindness.

The doctor shook his head slowly, a pained look on his face. "No, I'm sorry, they can't take anything, not even his eyes."

I understood—but it made me furious. Never before have I felt so insulted for someone else. William's body was perfectly formed. Other than the metabolic condition, he was healthy. Yet his organs could not even save another child's life. This final rejection of his body for organ donation gave us the permission we needed to take William home to pass peacefully.

We had been told to make plans for his care at home. While we knew this day might come, we were never quite ready for it. Modern medicine has the power to keep the human body alive long past the point when it would have reached a natural end. There is no obvious line in the sand anymore concerning what's a good fight and what's prolonging the inevitable. We want children, especially, to live to grow old, so we fight fiercely for their lives. However, we must look at what kind of life we're forcing them to live.

There is a point for every parent of a child with a life-limiting disease or injury where the switch occurs, from fighting to surrender. But this isn't warfare, it's life, and as much as we struggle against it, death is a natural part of it, and doesn't always play fair. Scotty seemed to accept this long before I did. It was much harder for me to accept. I was prepared to keep William here at all costs.

I came to realise that acceptance didn't mean I was giving up. It meant I could turn to embrace the journey. I could let go of the resistance that offered me a peaceful life. I needed that peace in William's last days.

Parenting a child with disabilities and a life-limiting condition often feels like navigating uncharted terrain; each day brings unexpected challenges, shifting emotions, and moments that test your strength. In this journey, acceptance isn't surrender or weakness; it's a courageous act. It's choosing to meet reality with open eyes and an open heart, even when it hurts. There's a delicate balance between fighting for your child's needs and recognizing what's beyond your control. Acceptance helps us hold both—advocating fiercely when it matters, and softening into surrender when needed.

For me, it's been helpful to believe that every experience, and every soul who crosses our path, carries purpose. Sometimes, those who need the most love and care teach us the deepest lessons. When we find meaning in our struggles, we're better able to carry them. We stop resisting life and start trusting that—even in hardship—there's growth, grace, and the promise of brighter days. Acceptance doesn't mean we let go of hope. It means we move forward with compassion—for our children, and for ourselves.

No one knew how many days or weeks he had left with us. So I notified our friends and loved ones that he was now terminal and under palliative care at home. I invited our closest friends to come visit William, most possibly to say their last goodbyes.

My sister, who was very close to my boys and loved them like her own, was travelling around Australia with her husband in their caravan. She was at least a two days' drive away when she got my call to come home. They began the long drive back to say goodbye to Will.

"Stay with us, Will," I pleaded to his still form as he breathed shallowly in his bed. "Stay with us until Aunty Catherine's come back." I knew she would be devastated if he went while she was away, especially since she'd been worried about leaving to go so far away weeks earlier when he first fell ill.

It was Monday morning, four days after coming home from the hospital, and we were not sure how the day would progress in caring for William, so we decided to send Hamish to school on the school bus and carry on as normal as possible. I was numb when I received a call from the school.

"Hamish had a seizure on the bus when it arrived at school," the staff person told me. "He needed emergency medication to stop the seizure. We called the ambulance to attend to him."

I felt sick. For a moment, I thought, *Jesus, I could lose both of my boys today!* How much more could we cope with? Defeated, all I could say into the phone was, "Okay, I'm on my way, I'll come get him."

I left Scotty at home with William, and I arrived at the school to see Hamish on the floor with a cushion under his head and an oxygen mask over his face. The school, a special developmental school that specialised in children with complex care needs, and the paramedics understood our family's circumstances with William and so after they ran all the appropriate health checks they released Hamish to go home so I could care for him instead of taking him to the hospital. I wanted us all to be home with William. I drove home with one of William's teachers monitoring Hamish in his wheelchair in the back of our van.

My husband and I made the special effort to put aside our own grief and let those that had cared for Will over the years at kinder, at school, and at home to come and share what we now knew to be his final hours with us in our home. The palliative care nurse visited at lunchtime and assisted in keeping him comfortable and pain free. He would still seize at the slightest sudden noise, but for the most part he was very peaceful and calm, perhaps because we'd done our best to make his room so calm and peaceful too. Warm lights lit the space. He had his favourite aromatherapy oils burning and soft, peaceful music played in the background. His pet goldfish swam ceaselessly in the fish tank beside his bed. And Tigger was by his side.

He was also surrounded by the people he loved most. We'd shut the doors to extended friends and only allowed those closest to Willian to continue to stand vigil, as he had grown ghastly thin since he'd stopped eating altogether two weeks before, either because he couldn't, or wouldn't, eat. A nasal gastric tube through his nose provided William's only hydration for those last weeks.

In the final days and moments before William's death, our close-knit group all shared special time together with him by his bed: his father, his little brother, his nana, his aunty, and his two favourite carers, Karlie and Carly, who shared our lives for the past four years. They would remain by his side all the way through the last minutes of his life.

A few days before William passed, I was giving William a massage after his shower when Scotty walked into William's room. "Here, I'll give you a hand," he said. We each stood on opposite sides of William's bed and began massaging him together. We started by each taking an arm and gently massaging sweet almond and lavender oil into his hands. We both looked at Will and we could see a subtle smile at the corners of his mouth, probably because he had our undivided attention. I like to think he was also enjoying the massage, too! It was reassuring to see some pleasant response because in those final days the pain medication left him unresponsive most of the time.

We took him outside into the warm winter afternoon sunshine (August is winter here in Australia, and we were blessed to have some beautiful sunny afternoons) and set him in his big comfortable beanbag to warm his frail body. His face tilted towards the sun and the pain wrinkles eased. Looking back, that was the last time we saw William smile.

It was around 3:40 on a Monday afternoon, July 18, 2016, exactly fifteen days after his birthday and about the time Will would have been dropped off by the school bus on a normal school day. Scotty had just left the house to get some fresh air and to collect a parcel from the post office. My mum went home to feed her dogs. We didn't know how close William was to dying. He was dying so peacefully right before our eyes, even as we spoke to him. Gently sedated in his bed, he hardly moved. But the sedation was better than watching him suffer in pain.

I was taking a beautiful video of Hamish lying alongside his big brother, stroking his arm, with Will's two carers looking on. I think Hamish knew more than all of us that his brother was about to pass. I approached Will ever so quietly in order not to startle him and trigger another seizure. The room was peaceful with the afternoon winter sun beginning to shine through the window. Yet, the air of anticipatory grief weighed heavily on our hearts. Even Hamish, who shared the same communication challenges as his older brother, seemed concerned as he patted his brother's arm. Will, however, didn't seem anxious at all. He looked at peace already.

Carly picked Hamish up off the bed and we all walked out into the kitchen. Karlie stayed with Will for a few extra minutes and then joined us. We'd barely settled when William called out with a strange gasp, the only noise he'd made all day. We had never heard that sound before. We all looked at each other and instantly knew that he had died, that call was Will's last breath. It was 3:48 p.m. We ran back into the room and it was obvious that he had died. He looked…soulless, the last glimmer of life fading from his eyes as we walked back into the room. I've read since this moment that it's a common occurrence that a dying person takes their last breath when their loved ones leave the room. It's thought that the dying person's soul is so delicately attached to the body that it can't help but want to be with the souls it loves, and so follows them out, resulting in one last big sigh as it leaves the physical self behind, never to return.

We all took a moment and wept as we consoled each other as we sat with Will for a little while longer, stroking his hair and loving him. Catherine rang my mum and I rang Scotty. He answered the phone and instantly knew…he had just walked into the post office. He'd only been gone for five minutes.

Once Scotty returned I left the room to ring the palliative care team and William's doctor. Two hours later, once they had attended and completed the formalities of noting time of death, Scotty rang the funeral home to make arrangements.

Death is the ultimate test and duty of parenthood: to be able to watch and hold your child as he dies and make that dying as kind and loving as you can.

Many times in the days before his death, we talked to William about what was to come. For my part, I believe in both heaven and reincarnation, so that's what I went with. For others, this conversation might be different. Some parents want to hide the unpleasantness of dying from their children, but I couldn't. I wanted William to know what was happening to him, and reassure him it was, finally, okay to let go and die.

In a soft and gentle tone, I'd say, "One day soon you'll wake up and all this pain will be gone. You'll become a new baby and begin a new life without seizures. You'll learn all sorts of wonderful things when you can read. You'll go and explore so many new places when you can walk. Your new body will learn to dance and bounce without being held up by support aids. You'll run fast like Daddy. Laugh and play like all the other children. And you'll sing like Mummy and Daddy with your own voice. You'll be able to sing your favourite John Mayer song, 'Bigger Than My Body.' Then you'll get your licence and drive a car. You'll have a girlfriend. Maybe, one day, you'll have your own babies too." I wanted him to know everything. All the possibilities that he'd been robbed of.

Most of all, I repeated over and over, "You're my Brave Bear, Will. You can go any time you're ready. Just don't be scared, Will. Don't be scared." And in the end, he wasn't. I couldn't give my son any of those other things in this life, but I could give him that. I could give him the level of love and acceptance that allowed him to live and die on his terms.

*Chapter 4*

# TORN FROM SOCIETY

BEFORE CHILDREN, I SPENT MANY YEARS AS A CAREER WOMAN, chasing opportunities to develop and grow as a business leader and rising to the challenge of my management roles within a male-dominated industry. Recently promoted to a new job role I was excited and proud to achieve at only thirty-three years of age, I felt my future was looking bright.

Up until this age, I'd had no desire to have children. I was happy with my four-legged fur babies (my boxer dogs) and I promised myself that one day I'd own a horse and dreamed of owning my own Friesian horse as a substitute for children. Friesians are those big, coal-black horses with the flowing manes and tails and hair like feathers around their hooves that look majestic, like they galloped right out of a fantasy novel carrying knights in shining armour—except it would be me holding the reins.

I loved animals, and in my early teens I wanted to become a vet, but I never really pursued that overwhelmingly rigorous academic path. I also loved writing as a teenager, particularly poems and song lyrics. I discovered I could sing at around seventeen years old and studied music for a year after leaving high school. Quickly, I realised that I needed to work in order to pay for my own education and life, and as everyone knew, babies made financial and professional goals harder, not easier. When I had conversations with other parents, they'd laugh and say, "Don't have kids, parenting is so overrated," or "Skip having kids and just have grandkids. They are much more fun." So for many years, I continued to work long hours to pursue a management career and didn't think of much else.

Scotty's brothers were a lot older than him, a similar situation to mine. They also didn't want children, so Scotty was the last chance.

Eighteen months into my new job role, however, I chose to take time out from my career to start a family. The male-dominated company I was with didn't offer the best environment for me, so stepping back to part-time and leaving them to it was an easy decision. I was also thirty-four now, and I knew my biological clock was ticking. I felt a strong pull towards making the choice of having children or forever holding my peace.

I also wanted to provide grandchildren for our parents to dote on and, quite frankly, I felt I was too focused on myself and my career and wanted to nurture someone else. I was ready and willing to share the rest of my life with a "mini-me" or three as a stay-at-home mum. Scotty and I carefully set ourselves up financially so I'd be able to do this, so by the time the babies came along, we felt we were ready.

Two years into my marriage to Scotty, I chose to honour my maternal instincts and start a family. I rarely made decisions without a lot of thought, planning, and/or a spreadsheet. Having children was no different than any of my other "projects," right down to creating my own ovulation spreadsheet so I could increase my chances of a winter baby.

It turned out I didn't need to plan that much. I thankfully fell pregnant on our first try! When I became pregnant I stepped joyfully into my new role of Mum. I felt a new connection to society as I would be bringing someone new into it. Though, to be honest, I felt a little awkward with the new attention on my pregnancy, especially as a female business leader. My day-to-day life was no longer about leading a team, driving performance, sales results, and key performance indicators. Instead, all I could think about was nurturing this special gift I had growing inside of me. It was my greatest responsibility and role ever, to create and love another life that would be linked to me in an eternal bond. That's all any of us really want, isn't it? To love and to be loved in return?

I embraced all of it. Even the long list of foods I should and should not eat. For the first three months I continued to run to stay healthy, but intentionally toned down my exercise as I got bigger. I had the baby's room all set up when I was only sixteen weeks' pregnant. I bought a lovely secondhand timber rocking chair from eBay, my first purchase on the auction website, in the style you might see on someone's front porch. An Ikea white chest of drawers and a beautiful white Boori cot made up the other furniture. I put matching cushions on the chair and soft blankets in the cot. I had four newborn outfits for the hospital, two blue and two pink, because we wanted to be surprised if the baby was a boy or girl. We picked out three names for each gender, and would decide on the final name once the baby was born. I tried to do everything that I was supposed to do to nurture the life inside me. I read all the books so I knew what to expect at each stage of my pregnancy. We passed all our tests and scans handily, with one scary exception.

On Christmas Eve my doctor rang me with the results of a nuchal translucency (NT) test that looked for common chromosomal and genetic defects that caused conditions like Down syndrome and spina bifida. She asked me to come in and see her that afternoon.

"I'm concerned about your pregnancy," she started with a limited preamble. "Your NT results came back significantly high with abnormal results." She hesitated, as if searching for gentler words but not finding any. "You may want to consider terminating the pregnancy."

Terminate? As in abort? I couldn't do that! Not when the test couldn't even tell us what was wrong!

"I want to do more testing to double-check the results," I said, protectively putting a hand on my belly.

The doctor nodded right away. "Yes, we'll run some more tests and see what those results show, but I wanted to prepare you for what may come." Then she referred me to get more testing done.

I waited seven days before we could speak to a genetic counselor who reported that the results I had received were incorrect. There'd been a typo in the baby's crown-to-rump measurements, which compromised the final result. The baby was actually in the normal range. Reassured and relieved by this amended risk figure, Scotty and I declined further diagnostic testing. But for approximately ten days over the Christmas and New Year's holidays, I thought I was going to have to terminate my baby at approximately seventeen weeks old. It was the longest ten days of my life.

After that fearful snag, it was smooth sailing. On the third of July, 2007, I gave birth naturally to our gorgeous son, William, at 5:55 p.m.

I remember walking for days before I went to the hospital to get checked. My stomach was huge and I felt so uncomfortable. I was ready! I just wanted to meet this shiny new human I'd carried around for nine months. I was going to be a mum! "Today's going to be the day!" I crowed to the world.

"Yes," the nurses agreed, smiling, "keep walking."

Scotty and I walked around the hospital grounds for what felt like another few days but was only hours before we got tired of it and went home. We weren't at home very long before the contractions increased and we went straight back to the hospital. It was 4:20 p.m. The pain was sudden and intense so I sucked on as much nitrous oxide, or laughing gas, as I could. Everything became a bit hazy and euphoric. I could hear another woman across the hall giving birth and then her baby's first cries. "Oh wow," I said between my gulps of gas, "she had her baby! Oh, that's so beautiful!"

Meanwhile, the nurse tried to get me to focus. "Yes, it is beautiful.

Natalie, now concentrate on delivering *your* baby." I couldn't listen to this serious person. I was off with me fairies on me happy gas.

"You're ready, Natalie, start to push!" I heard the doctor say from my nether regions. I was ready alright, and with three pushes…

"Okay, he's out!" I heard as I felt the urge to push vanish. I congratulated myself on having a natural birth. Well, not a hundred percent natural, my mind corrected lazily as I started to fall asleep because of the gas. I can't even remember being stitched back together. I remember seeing Scotty, off taking pictures of our new son as he weighed in at 3.7 kilograms and was checked over. "All clear, Nat, he's perfect!" he crowed, then Scotty turned around and took photos of me half asleep in the hospital bed, sending them to his family and friends. "Congratulations!" they sent back. "Welcome to the world, William!"

William Fergus Watson was a peaceful little guy. He barely cried and was very sleepy, like his mum. Immediately after his birth, he slept for a solid six hours. The nurse came in and told me to wake. "Natalie, you need to feed your baby."

"But he's sleeping! I thought you should never wake a sleeping baby," I protested.

"Yes, but he's sleeping way too long and can become weak if he doesn't eat." I felt reprimanded and guilty for taking my own rest while my son was going hungry.

William struggled to coordinate his sucking reflexes, which made breastfeeding him difficult and distressed us both. I spent three nights in hospital with William because of his feeding difficulty. We needed assistance from a lactation nurse, as he was initially regarded as failing to thrive since he'd lost instead of gained weight. The maternal nurse suggested I express my milk ASAP to keep my flow going while William wasn't suckling as much. Scotty went out and bought a breast pump so I could start giving William his feedings in a bottle. Gradually, over the next six weeks, I reverse weaned from the bottle so I could completely breastfeed him. "I've never seen a baby do that!" my maternal nurse said. "Usually, once the baby has a bottle they won't go back to the breast at such a young age." Her words had me glowing. This was a proud Mumma Bear moment I could brag about with other mothers one day.

Then there was the social aspect of having a new baby. During our antenatal classes at the hospital my husband and I connected with two other families with whom we maintain contact to this day. There were six of us mums in our parenting group and we all met when our babies were four weeks old. As a family unit, Scotty and I began to feel a new connection to the community. Along with the other mums and dads, we became more comfortable in our new roles as parents. We shared a kinship as we watched our tiny babies growing together.

When William turned seven weeks old, I booked my baby boy into our family's first photography session. But there was a shadow present at what was supposed to be a happy milestone. William had his vaccinations the day before and kept falling asleep throughout the photography session, which was within the realm of normal, but he also appeared to use only his peripheral vision to make eye contact. We struggled to get a photo where both his eyes were looking into the camera. The photographer mentioned that some babies can be a bit off after vaccinations, but I thought it was a little strange that she mentioned doing eye swaps in photoshop because William wasn't making eye contact. I would later learn that this eye condition was called "strabismus" and it was the first symptom that something was different in William than the other babies in our group.

At eight weeks old I took him to the community nurse to get him weighed and measured to see if he was hitting his developmental milestones. "He's not making much eye contact," she mentioned. "You need to do more there. Try sitting him in your lap and bringing him forward so he's looking at you a few times a day."

I immediately thought, so you're saying I have to teach him how to look at me? Shouldn't babies do this naturally? My thoughts then started to go inwards. Maybe there was something wrong with him? Or, maybe there was something wrong with me? What am I doing wrong? What could possibly cause these symptoms? Is it my milk?

Now alarmed, I asked the other mothers in my parenting group if they could see what the nurse saw too. I desperately wanted reassurance that my maternal alarms were false, and I had nothing to worry about. I was rightfully proud of how gorgeous my little man was and the other mothers reassured me that maybe he just needed more time to develop, since all babies go at their own pace. However, I couldn't shake the feeling that something was very different about William from the other babies that were smiling, laughing, and staring adoringly into their mothers' eyes.

A few weeks later, I took William to our family doctor for another set of vaccinations. He was looking healthy and drinking better from my breast, gaining another five hundred grams, so I crossed my fingers that everything was fine. As the doctor started to examine William, I told her about his lack of eye contact. "All babies follow their own timing," she said, thumbing through his blue book, the maternal health journal that recorded his development. Her words echoed the mums in my group. She was a mother of six children as well as a doctor, so I figured she knew what she was talking about.

As the appointment progressed I tried to relax, but I felt anxious as the doctor grew more quiet and more intrigued with William's eyes. She held a pen torch up to his eyes and I noticed he didn't track the light. I felt sick. "William's staring at the lights on the ceiling," she observed, "and he hasn't once looked at our faces for reassurance during the whole appointment." She immediately referred William to an ophthalmologist to assess his eyes and check for tumours or something else wrong with the optic nerve. William was about four months old. I told Scotty and we both agreed not to panic until we saw the eye specialist.

The ophthalmologist's findings determined the optic nerve was perfectly healthy, but that William had cortical visual impairment (CVI), where the optic nerve is intact but the connection to the brain is disrupted, like a TV channel with faulty reception. He didn't need glasses, as CVI is a brain-based visual impairment. It's a disability of access. The eyes can see, but the brain struggles to interpret the visual world. CVI has become the leading cause of visual impairment in children in developed countries. For William, this meant that on some days he'd see well and make eye contact and track objects more easily, and other days he would struggle to focus visually and was often super sensitive to light.

Other appointments soon followed to figure out what was causing the visual impairment. We had appointments with a neurologist for brain scans, lumbar punctures, and copious blood tests, all of which came back inconclusive to any particular genetic disease or illness. At around six months the doctors diagnosed William as having severe developmental delay with cortical visual impairment and referred us to a specialist early intervention team.

I knew therapy was absolutely necessary to give him any chance at a quality of life. William began falling behind in all his developmental milestones. The other babies at my mothers' group were all starting to crawl, while William could barely hold his head up during tummy time. He could barely roll over without any assistance. He didn't seek out toys nor was there any motivation to obtain a toy in the distance. I became obsessed, looking for therapies that could give him a better chance at life. I kept remembering the motto I'd heard in my infant and child CPR class: The earlier help is given the better the outcome. I knew therapy worked this way too.

William's eyes were tested again, and this time the diagnosis was conclusive. He was declared legally blind, which made him eligible for specialist support from the Royal Institute for Deaf and Blind Children (RIDBC). So twice a week we had an occupational therapist (OT) attend our home to help William learn to use his eyesight better. A physiotherapist was added to the team to teach him to sit up and bear weight on his legs so he could develop a walking gait.

So at six months old, William began with early intervention therapies and various visits to specialists to try to obtain a diagnosis—something that could explain all his challenges—in the hope of some kind of treatment or cure. My weeks became packed with appointments. The community nurse, the family doctor, the paediatrician, the ophthalmologist, the neurologist, the physiotherapist, the occupational therapist, the speech therapist, the vision specialists, the pathologist, the genetic counselors, and the metabolic specialist.

I took what the specialists and therapists recommended and made it my duty to give William every chance to gain normal body functioning. Every day we sat on the floor playing eye-tracking games, and I'd encourage him to roll from side to side and lay on his tummy on the floor so his brain would develop on both sides of the vestibular system and his neck would develop the strength to hold up his head. The vestibular system is a sensory system in the inner ear that controls balance and spatial orientation. It also helps with eye movements and coordinating posture and movement. He needed both balance and movement to attain independent movement.

The OT from RIDBC, who taught daily living skills, and the physiotherapist, who focused on physical development, had both worked in that field of disability for about thirty years and had never seen anything like William. "Whatever he has is rare," the OT said. This set me off on a quest to learn as much as I could to help William. I went to the library and borrowed as many books as I could find on early childhood development and sensory processing disorders to fill in the gaps in my understanding of my son.

Possibly one of the best things I did for William's health was take him to the chiropractor every fortnight for the first three years of his life. When William was unwell you could see the changes in his eyes, but the chiropractic visits seemed to help with his eye strabismus. Before we arrived at his appointment I'd notice his eyes turned upwards and outwards and that he'd be looking up at the lights a lot more than usual. Then afterwards I'd put him back in his car seat to drive home and look at him through the rear-vision mirror and see that his eyes had converged back to normal by the time we arrived home twenty minutes later.

Then I had my own appointments to see a psychologist, because I needed one. My anxiety was through the roof. I found myself in a constant state of panic for William. He was in need of a lot of help from so many people to develop the skills necessary to live an independent and fulfilling life. I knew we had only a small window of time to help him develop these skills. I liken my panicked feeling to hauling my drowning child out of the water, only to realise he wasn't breathing. It was like I was standing over his small body, screaming for people to come help me resuscitate him, knowing that every minute that went by without treatment or intervention could make his condition worse. The longer I waited, the more atrophy was done to his brain and body. There was so much work to do, so many opportunities to help William have the best quality of life, but I'd needed a lot of help.

Nothing had prepared me for this. This wasn't what we planned. What happened to watching him grow into an active, cheeky little boy? What happened to the secret pleasure of chasing after him through a playground as he attempted to chew on sticks and rocks? Of locking all the kitchen cupboards and drawers before he had the chance to pull everything out? I had looked forward to seeing which mum gained first bragging rights to crawling and walking, but now I could barely get my six-month-old to sit up.

Trying to seek out some maternal companionship, one day, I bravely took William to a new playgroup in our area. I was hopeful socialising him with other kids would help him progress. All the mums had their gorgeous, "perfect" babies and I knew that they knew there was something different about mine. I saw the looks and heard the whispers.

Some days, going out in public was really tough. I'd put on my brave face and refrain from yelling out to staring eyes, "Yes, I know there's something wrong with my child! I'm fully aware of it. I don't know what's wrong, but I'm trying to fix it. I'm trying to make it right!" The intense feelings of shame and guilt were unavoidable and forced me to do my own cognitive behavioural (CB) work with a psychologist in the months that followed.

It's worth acknowledging that the language around disability and inclusion has evolved significantly over the past sixteen years—thankfully, for the better. But even with more well-intentioned terms, there's still a gap between language and lived experience. As a parent, I've learned that using the "right" words doesn't always match the complex, messy emotions I felt—especially in those early days. Back then, I didn't see my child as "special" in the way the language encouraged me to. I thought something was wrong—something was broken and needed fixing. Words like "handicapped," "disabled," "special needs," "differently abled," or "neurodivergent" try to soften the reality, but they couldn't soften the grief or fear I was carrying. No matter how we reshape the vocabulary, the sting of difference still hurts—especially before understanding and acceptance have had time to grow.

Watching William in the new playgroup, it became very clear to me that he had fallen so far behind that we were now being left behind and excluded. When people in your playgroup avoid talking to you, and the organiser comes over and speaks to you privately and sympathetically offers you an early childhood intervention flier, as well as a flier for a playgroup specialising in children with disabilities and learning difficulties, you know you don't belong. This was the beginning of our exclusion. I felt like an outcast. Turned away from the village and shunned.

I don't think any of those mothers meant to exclude, they just didn't know what to say to me, and they were too polite to ask questions. No one ever said anything outright mean or did anything specifically to exclude us. At the end of the day, people don't really care about your problems as they are too involved with their own. Truth be told, I didn't quite know what to say to them, either. I didn't know how to engage, or what we'd even talk about. We were living in two different worlds—one was for normal babies, and one was reserved for babies who were "not normal."

Fast-forward to William's first day of preschool, another little boy noticed Will had a walking aid and that he moved differently. "Mummy," he chirped, pulling at his mum's coat, "what's wrong with that little boy?"

The mum shushed him. "Don't be rude. Don't ask questions," she scolded.

But on my end of things, I would have loved the questions. I would have loved to introduce Will to this little boy and help him understand how my son was different. Different, but not scary. Not bad. Not wrong. Just different. I know other parents with special needs kids might disagree with me, but I'd encourage others to err on the side of compassionate curiosity and, by all means, ask questions (after checking in with the parent to see if it's okay first) to learn as much as you can about who those kids are and how their lives might be different than your own.

When you are torn from society because your child doesn't fit in, there is grief that goes along with that loss. When I said I wanted my baby to be special, I didn't mean this! I don't know of any parent who wishes their baby to be born with a disability. It hurts on every level.

When you are a parent of a rare child, the feeling of discomfort follows you. Like you've done something wrong as a parent to make your child this way. Over time, I learned how to be comfortable with being uncomfortable. I had to act the part of the tough mum, with an attitude of, "My baby's cool. We've got our shit sorted." It took me years but I eventually learned to suck it up and put on a brave face so Will could attend those social activities with other children even though the sting of difference was still there in my heart and I was full of anxiety for our future.

I remember coming home from one of those first community playgroups and crying uncontrollably over the phone to my girlfriend. It was no surprise to her, as she knew something was different with my William, too, but couldn't quite put her finger on it, or have the heart to be the first one to ask or say anything.

I felt so at fault, so much so I started apologising to my husband when he came home from work later that day. "I'm a failure as a mother," I wept. "I don't know how to fix this. I don't know how to make William better!" I didn't know how to fight this fight, and I felt so alone.

Scotty took it all in stride. He was concerned, but didn't take others' behaviour as personally as I did. "It's okay, Nat, you can handle this. You're a great mum," he soothed.

For the next two years, Scotty and I worked hard to help William with his therapies and reach his fullest potential, or at the least prevent further decline of skills already learned. William couldn't learn through copying or mirroring the way other babies did. There was no poke my tongue out at you and you poke your tongue out at me. It was hard, focused, intentional work.

The physiotherapist and OT left me toys that were very reactive, such as a toy with a big red button that made the toy light up and play music. I'd have brightly coloured ones, too, set up on a black mat so he could see them better with his visual impairment. Sometimes, it would almost seem like he was following the toy I held up for him, but I could never be sure.

Every day, I would sit there on the lounge room floor with William, trying to teach him what seemed to be a simple skill to us: to reach for a toy, or even look at one. Putting a shaped object into a matching hole, a milestone peers his age were doing, was beyond his capability. I felt like *I* was trying to put a square peg in a round hole, most days. Hours and hours we spent together, just me and William and my little therapy bag full of his special toys, waiting for him to do something on his own, waiting for him to reward me with just a smile or eye contact. Never did I experience patience in the truest sense of the word more than at those times. He'd flap his arms and hands incessantly as he swung his head about, moving closer to the toy with his body as he tried to get it in focus and make his hand reach out to touch it. If he did, or even made a gesture in the toy's direction, my excitement would spike. "Yes, William! Such a good boy!" I'd praise, like he'd just won a race. Except for crying, most of the rudimentary forms of communication young babies use to express pleasure or curiosity was denied to us. His verbalizations, if he did them at all, were seemingly random. With minimal eye contact as the icing on the cake, I never knew if he understood why I was happy, but I continued to praise him anyway. I was slowly learning his difference was okay.

I tried everything that might counteract his challenges. I thought sign language might help, since it can be taught to babies. I'd wear a black top so he could better see my pale fingers in contrast. Again, since he didn't have any fine motor control, for all the days spent on signing he only half learned a few words, though he seemed to understand more signs than he could make as he got older.

From about eighteen months old, Will began using a Mulholland gait trainer, a fully supported walking frame. I worked with the physiotherapist and OT to strengthen and coordinate his muscles. But something was off. Being visually impaired also meant that his coordination and proprioception were significantly compromised and he always needed assistance with mobility. I padded the floors in the lounge room, a rug on top of a foam pad so he wouldn't hurt himself when he fell, which was inevitable.

At two years old, a year into his intensive therapies, William had some of the skills of a three-month-old baby. I'd be loving, calm, and gentle on the outside as I went through William's regimen of exercises, but on the inside I'd be screaming, "Please do something! Give me a sign that you understand! Oh, God, help me help him!" I didn't even know if William understood what I was trying to get him to do, or why it was important. I had to look hard for the wins in those days to give me a glimmer of hope that what I was doing was the right thing. Some days, it felt like I was banging my head against a brick wall.

My isolation from my old friends only increased my feelings of loneliness and despair. I had a friend named Sammy. We'd met through our husbands a couple of years before having children and by the time we were pregnant, just months apart, we were close. We'd shop together, talk endlessly about our pregnancies and birthing plans, and share our dreams for the babies we were about to welcome. I even bought the same Boori cot she had—I loved her style, her wit, and the way she evolved as a mum.

She had her little girl. I had William. Though just months apart, her daughter quickly outpaced him—until those months felt like years. Sammy was the mum I thought I'd be: calm, organised, nurturing. She and her husband were a great team. Their kids were polite, energetic, cheeky—everything I wished for William. What any parent probably wishes for their children. It was nothing my friend Sammy ever said or did that made me pull away from her, it was purely the pain of it all on my end. She had what I desperately wanted, and I couldn't face it. I needed to be able to love and nurture the child in front of me and not compare him to other children.

I knuckled down. Much of William's therapy was done in a standing frame to try to train his body to walk. It supported him from the waist through the trunk down to his feet. At one stage, I had William going in a posterior walking frame. He looked like he was doing well with the movement and walking pattern, but he didn't watch where he was going. He didn't get that bit, or couldn't do it. He'd look back at us, walk into walls, and fall. This would make me laugh. William had a great sense of humour and I wonder if he did it on purpose for the laughs he'd get.

While I couldn't give up on William's potential, Scotty was more black-and-white in his thinking. "Seriously, Nat, do you really think he's going to talk to you? Walk for you? Sometimes you have to face reality and pick your battles and meet him where he's at."

In this case, I'd come to agree with the Scotsman, at least in terms of walking. William was getting bigger, and the chubby baby falls were turning into more serious crashes. "You'll just have to stay in your wheelchair, mate," I told William. But I'd have him still stand in the frame for a few hours every day to let his joints and bones get properly aligned as he grew. I'd eventually resort to propping him up with big weighted padded blocks that couldn't fall over, and he'd stand in between them and watch television. I wanted him to be able to shift position so he wasn't sitting all the time, and I felt the walker, with all its straps and bars, was too restrictive. Here in this standing position he could bounce freely along to his favourite *Wiggles* DVD.

There was no end to his care and therapies. We still had to feed him and change him at two years old. At nine years old he knew what it meant to be on the toilet, but we'd still have to get him there. He could eat solid food, but we had to put it in his mouth. He could sign a thumbs-up and clap his hands, but for the most part we had to guess at his desires and his illnesses and pain by changes in the sounds he made and by his body language, since he didn't have any words to talk to us.

Despite all of this, though, William was happy. He was a gentle, caring little soul. And he loved music. I gave him a keyboard, which he could manage to touch while he was in his standing frame. He could press the coloured buttons which could change the tempos and produce funny sounds. He could be at that play station for an hour and not get tired of it. All those toys, and he only ever played with a few: his teddies and his instruments. They were enough for him.

Accepting is very different from giving up. It's like the difference between forcing a round peg into a square hole, and then realising no matter how hard you force against it, the round peg will never fit into the square hole. Once you accept this is the shape of things, you soften your approach and revise another way. There came a time I had to stop for my own preservation. How much pressure did all these therapies put on him and the family? At some point, I needed to accept that this version of himself was him. It wasn't Will that needed to change, it was me. How could I change my own limiting beliefs, to learn, adapt, and grow in order to give him his best life? Not the life I wanted for him, but the life he wanted. To be accepted as he was—perfectly different.

I lost count of how many times I told William that I loved him and that I'd always be there for him. I don't know how much of all of that he understood or believed, either, but at the very least I hope he always felt that my intent was kindness and love.

The ability to feel unconditional love for another human is perhaps William's greatest gift to me—one I couldn't have learned any other way than by being his mum. As a child, that kind of love came through the animals who offered quiet companionship and asked for nothing in return. They taught me that *love is a verb*—something you show by doing, by being present and returned energetically by an eternal connection. They also taught me that I loved caring for others. Maybe my childhood quietly prepared me for this kind of love all along, as there were many times I had to choose love over heartbreak.

*Chapter 5*

# WHITE PUPPIES

I WAS FIVE YEARS OLD WHEN I GOT MY FIRST MEMORY OF DEATH.

I'd only just started primary school in a new city after my parents' divorce. My older sister Julie, fourteen years my senior, was living with Mum and me at the time. She bought me a little tabby kitten. She felt bad about the divorce and bought me the kitten so I could have something to love and cheer me up. I loved all kinds of animals and they always made me feel better.

I don't think I had the kitten for more than three days before it met its fate in the jaws of our Samoyed dogs. You see, I had returned home from school with my sister Julie to find the kitten wasn't inside the house where I had left it that morning. So I went looking for it. It appeared to have escaped out the kitchen window and into the fenced backyard where Mum's four Samoyed dogs lived. I remember trying to figure out what the dogs were playing with so I went out into the backyard. I followed the trail of blood just outside the back door where the dogs would sleep and found the kitten's head just outside the back gate. I screamed and started crying. The dogs were still playing tug-of-war with its remains. Pieces of the kitten were all over the yard. My sister grabbed the last of the remains from the dogs, beating them over the head to make them let go. Through my tears, I hit the dogs too. We buried the pieces in a different part of the backyard in a small funeral, but the dogs dug them up again.

I cried for a long time after that. "Stop crying! It was just a cat. Plenty more where that one came from," the adults around me would say. It didn't feel like only a cat to me. But not my sister Julie, she knew my pain and empathised with me deeply. It was horrible to witness.

Animals never judged me. They loved me no matter what I looked like, or where I lived, and I could love them without fear of my love being rejected. They cared for me and I cared for them. The relationship was clean, simple, the exact opposite of my relationships with people. Which may have been why I gravitated towards them so strongly. Especially horses.

When I was very young and my parents were together, we lived on a horse property in the country, surrounded by animals. The horses were always my favourite. All my four siblings had horses and learned to ride. They were all much older than me. Catherine and I were fifteen years apart, Julie was fourteen years older, my brother was twelve, and Linda nine. I was so much younger and smaller, I was like my sisters' doll. Apparently, from the age of two, I'd follow them around the farm, nagging them to lift me up onto the backs of their horses to take me for a ride. I was horse mad from then on. But by the time I was old enough to start to learn to ride at four, my parents' relationship, which had been sliding downhill for years, imploded. My siblings would only half joke that it was my fault: "We were fine until you came along," they'd often say, especially my sixteen-year-old brother. I know now, as an adult, that he was hurting, too, but the words were a harsh blow to my four-year-old heart.

After my parents separated, my father sold the horse property and moved to Melbourne and remarried within a year of the divorce.

Almost from the moment he settled in with his new wife, my dad started building a boat in his backyard. Not a little dinghy, either, but a forty-two-foot yacht. You could see it grow and take form from the highway above the houses. He worked on it for over over thirty years before successfully getting it in the water. It was his labor of love, achieving something by chipping away at it day after day. The backyard was full of his little projects, but the boat was his baby.

Dad was a carpenter and builder by trade, who became a teacher and taught trades to high school students. He later worked as a construction manager on building sites. I remember he worked long hours. When I went to stay with him on weekends he'd usually be working, leaving me to play dolls with my very maternal stepmother, my stepsister, and two younger half-siblings. She even bought me a doll baby so I could practise dressing it and changing its nappy, while she changed the nappy of my infant half brother. The few hours of daylight when Dad was home, we'd go out into the yard and work on his boat. Or he would. I'd usually tinker around below the boat playing horses on my hobby horse or playing with the pet rabbit of the moment (strangely, the rabbits seemed to escape quite often and there'd be a different rabbit to replace the last one the next time I visited).

My brother and three sisters decided they didn't want to live with either parent. My brother and two sisters moved to Queensland while still teenagers while my eldest sister travelled overseas. It was a whole new state for a whole new start. At seventeen, my brother had just gotten his licence so they drove as a group with all their possessions and found individual places to live. My brother, a young apprentice carpenter by trade, found work instantly and lived in a caravan park while he got settled and met his future wife, whose parents also owned the caravan park. My sisters Julie and Linda lived with each other for a while before moving in with their own future husbands. Within a few years they all had two children each and I was an aunty to my nieces and nephews at the age of eight years old. My brother became an award-winning builder and my sisters specialised in real estate and equestrian sports, particularly dressage. I loved visiting them during the Christmas school holiday. Queensland is warm most of the year and my sister Linda had a pool at her property so I'd spend most of the Christmas holidays swimming and riding horses.

I was about eleven years old when my sister gave Carly to me as a school holiday project. The mare had been saved from the knackery and being turned into pet food. She'd ended up at the doggers because she was quite dangerous, lashing out to bite and spontaneously kicking with both legs if you went anywhere near her back legs. My sister bought her and her brother for thirty-five dollars each. She was thirteen-two hands and steel grey. I felt sorry for her and spent the whole six weeks of the school holidays befriending her and riding her bareback around her yard. Eventually she trusted me enough to put a saddle on her back. I visited my sisters only once or twice a year and so I only ever rode her a few more times. But she was the first horse I loved and we had a beautiful bond.

Me and my horse Carly

I couldn't ignore the fact that my sisters owned horses but I couldn't. Not in the city, in our little Richmond flat over my mum's clothing boutique where I lived with her. Every Christmas I'd ask for a horse. It was all I ever wanted, to open up the door to my backyard on Christmas morning to a pony grazing on the lawn. Everyone laughed about it, but it was my vision of heaven, so I kept asking for a horse, trying to will it into existence. Vaguely, as a young child, I knew Mum didn't have a lot of money to spare and Christmas was always a modest affair when it came to presents. But a child's dream is hard to crush, and on Christmas Day every year, I'd check the backyard, and every year it would be empty.

One school holiday, when I was twelve years old, my older sisters tried to "kidnap" me to live with them in Queensland permanently. I loved the idea, of course, since it meant I'd finally be with family and have a chance to have my own horse, but of course when my mum found out she was pissed, to say the least, and demanded I come home to Melbourne at once. Her anger might have had something to do with the fact that my dad also supported the idea without consulting her. No matter the cause of her resistance, I had to come back home to the city and live in what a country girl at heart would describe as a "little flat." In reality, it was a shop with a dwelling above. My bedroom was upstairs and overlooked the neighbouring roofs. Its walls were plastered with posters of horses, and my favourite pop stars at that time—Culture Club, A-ha, and Madonna—which surrounded me while I spent my day dreaming about horses until the next holiday to Queensland.

Meanwhile, my mum tried to make her own dream happen by running her business. She had one big room in the flat set out where she'd design and make the clothes for her shop. She'd go out and sell them at markets and other shops around Melbourne. As a designer, she was always very descriptive about clothing: the textures, colours, fabrics, cuts. When she and my eldest sister, Catherine, who still lived in Melbourne, would talk about an outfit they had seen at their favourite boutique in Melbourne, Feather's, Mum was all about the detail and she'd describe the garment in the most beautiful way: "It's an over jacket that trails past the knee in an emerald green jacquard satin…" If I was going to describe the jacket to someone it would be more like: "It's, um, really nice." I struggled to find the descriptive words that came so naturally to my mother.

The shop was two doors up from the Judy Banks School of Television and about a hundred meters from the Johnny Young Talent School, where young entertainers would take classes in singing or dancing for the stage. Starting in 1971, they'd broadcast a show every week on a Sunday night called *Young Talent Time*. It was one of Australia's most-watched shows and I was a big fan. I often dreamed of what it would be like to attend classes there as I'd watch members of the Young Talent team walking past my mum's shop on their way to school for rehearsals. Sometimes they'd stop and come in and browse my mum's designs. I'd see Tina Arena, Dannii Minogue sometimes with her sister Kylie, and Vince and Karen Knowles.

The fame and fortune all around us didn't seem to penetrate our little world, though. Things were tough financially for us in the 1980s. We barely had money to pay the bills, and to make budgeting worse, Mum still kept four demanding Samoyeds who were kenneled in the small garage behind the shop.

Then there were those unexpected expenses that always seem to find you when you're struggling. I vividly recall how parking was hard to find without risking a parking ticket, as it was mostly two-hour parking around the shop (no local residence permits back in those days). I'm sure those parking rangers earned commissions for how many fines they dished out. Meanwhile, since Mum was often the only person in the shop, moving the car meant closing the shop. There was the garage, but her dogs were in it. Poor Mum always seemed to have a glove box full of parking fines that accumulated and multiplied in interest weekly.

In 1985 things got really bad. Sometimes, my mum didn't have enough money to keep a car, so she'd hire a used car from Rent-a-Bomb so we could go driving on the weekends, either to a dog show or just to escape the city for a while. Things were tough but my mum, always the eternal optimist, still held hope and dreamed of owning a property again where she could have her breeding kennels not cooped up in an inner-city backyard. We'd often drive around looking for her next dream home which seemed to cheer her up and motivate her to keep working on her dreams despite our current financial situation.

Those tight finances also made food scarce in the flat. We always had a big jar of Vegemite in the fridge but hardly any bread and no milk. When I went to my dad's for the weekend, I'd stuff my face with all the yummy treats my stepmother had stocked the pantry with. I'd inhale everything I could when I stayed with my grandmother, my mum's mum, who was a fantastic cook and would often bake sweet treats for when I'd come to stay. The problem was I was only ten years old, and I could easily eat a whole fruit cake over the course of a weekend. My grandma was often left in shock at how much food I had eaten, commenting to my mum about my weight when she came to collect me at the end of the weekend. My other siblings, after not seeing me for a few months, would also comment when I'd arrive. "Look at you, you're so cute and chubby!" Switching my nickname from Natles to Fatles, they'd tease. "Stop eating so much, Fat Nat! You need to exercise more." According to the scales I was bordering obese for my age, so I wasn't really that big, but I was definitely softer and rounder than kids who had more space to run around in than I did in the city, and who didn't binge eat whenever they got the chance.

My mum didn't say much to me specifically about my weight at first, but she modeled strict control over appearance. She was always dieting and very exacting about having the right body size, which was par for the course in the clothing design industry. When I was twelve I'd often model dresses she sold in her shop. One photo that ended up in a local newspaper had me in a beautiful formal dress down to the floor. Then, after I turned thirteen, I stopped being able to fit into the dresses.

Young me in dress

When I was twelve, I joined my new best friend Kate's family for one of their weekend holidays at the surf beach in Torquay, Victoria. Kate's parents both had the cool job of graphic designer and lived in a small, chic terrace in South Yarra. Kate had white-blonde hair and was very thin and tall. I most definitely wasn't. I couldn't fit into her spare wet suit. I couldn't even fit into her dad's wet suit. They had to ask around the caravan park for a bigger one. When they finally found it, I squeezed myself into it and struggled to pull the zipper all the way up. I could barely move. Kate's younger brother laughed at me: "You look like a whale!" he cackled.

"Davey, stop it! Don't be rude!" his mum yelled as his father looked on sternly, but the damage had already been done. Embarrassment and shame, as only a twelve-year-old girl can feel, filled me. That moment haunted me for years and I started getting anxious when hanging out with people, wondering when they'd comment on my weight.

My constant hunger turned out to be the least of our worries, though. Those unpaid parking tickets didn't go away no matter how many times my mum changed cars, and one day the city came to collect.

It was 1986. I was fourteen. And my mum's business went bankrupt. I remember coming home from school to find a sign on the shop's front window saying:

Hi Nats,

Shop's closed. Go to Cathy's place.

Mum XX

Cathy worked for my mum but she was like a sister to me. She was twenty-three years old and dressed like Madonna, with full-on '80s blue eye shadow, dark blush on her cheekbones, and big hair. I used to love Friday nights because it was late-night shopping and Cathy would work late. We'd get fish 'n' chips from the takeaway shop on the corner, turn the radio up, and dance around Mum's shop.

There was no dancing to be had that afternoon. I looked in and the shop was being emptied by people I didn't know—all our furniture, my bed, even my doll's house. Everything! It was all gone. The debt collectors took whatever they could sell.

Devastated, I turned away from this scene and started walking up Lennox Street, past the JY Talent School, to the Victoria Street high-rise housing commission apartments where Cathy lived with her mum. I stayed there with her until Catherine came to pick me up and took me back to Grandma's place where Mum was now staying. Mum cried for days and days after that, and I never saw Cathy again.

Mum, her four Samoyeds, and I lived with Grandma for a little while until Mum eventually rehomed her dogs, including my favourite, Kyslo. We moved into a small flat on the other side of the Yarra River in Prahran closer to where I went to high school and we lived in the area until 1991.

I left home at sixteen after a huge fight with my mum's boyfriend, Arthur. We moved in with him shortly after Mum closed the shop. One day, I was on the phone with a guy I really liked. We had met at a party the week before and he'd given me his number. I had only just plucked up enough courage to call him. We had barely cut through the awkward initial small talk when Arthur stormed in.

"Get off the phone, girl, I need to call my bookie!"

"Hold on," I said, "I'm right in the middle of something."

Arthur's call was urgent, apparently. "Get off the phone! Now!" he roared, grabbing the phone out of my hand.

Indignant, I punched him in the chest. "Give it back!"

In response, he punched me in the face. "Get out," he snarled, and then hung up on my potential boyfriend who heard it all. Embarrassed and humiliated, I never called that guy again.

I took Arthur the Arsehole at his word, as I never wanted to see him again, either. When I told my mum what had happened, her reply was, "It's his house and phone and you were being rude."

A few days later, my dad helped me move in with a friend, who was a year level higher than me in school, and her dad in Prahran. My dad lived on the other side of Melbourne and didn't have a spare bedroom for me. My friend's place was still close to my school and only a block away from where my mum lived, if I needed her.

I always thought my mum loved her dogs more than me. Mum's bred Samoyed dogs for over sixty years and has devoted her whole life to them. They were big, white fluffy dogs with pointy ears and plumed tails that curled over their backs. They were beautiful when their coats were all brushed out and glistened in the sunshine. My mum studied the various breed standards and became a qualified judge of not only Samoyeds but many other breeds. She judged at dog shows both locally and internationally. While I lived with her, we often attended dog shows. That was the highlight of our week, travelling long distances to show off the progeny from the bloodlines that she had meticulously bred. Hopefully the judge would also see the quality of her dogs and award them points towards gaining their Australian champion title; sure we'd win prizes, which were mostly trophy ribbons and bags of dog food. It was all for the glory of breeding good "stock" with the title of champion. Then we'd go back home to start all over again the next week. To her, the quest for the perfect Samoyed is never-ending and even at eighty-six years old, she continues her obsession.

I, however, always wanted boxer dogs, ever since meeting Kate's red boxer dog, Robbie, in my first year of high school. Robbie was a big joker and always full of energy. I loved how he stood so proud. Somehow the breed reminded me of an Arabian horse, and if I couldn't have a horse then I'd have a boxer as my substitute. I was twenty-one when I moved out to live with my then-boyfriend and we bought our first boxer dog, Rosie. She looked just like Robbie. I'd been working since I was twelve, delivering newspapers to start, then I got a job as a cashier at Bi-Lo when I was old enough, and now I was a retail manager in the deli department. I'd saved my money and had a steady, modest paycheck to make it all work. It was liberating.

Me at twenty-one and Rosie

My partner and I had only just settled into our first grown-up home together for a couple months when we came home one night to find Rosie gone. Somehow, she'd gotten out of the yard. We went out driving to find her. When we turned down the main road, my dread escalated. At the intersection, we could see another car with its hazard lights on further down. As we slowly approached in our car I could see headlights shining on a lump on the verge. It was a dog. My dog. Her body was still intact but the angle at which she lay made her broken back unmistakable. We rang the vet and they said they'd take the body for a $300 disposal fee. "Wrap the body in a tarp," they said, "to catch any bowel release from rigor mortis." So we wrapped Rosie in a tarp, put her in the boot of the car, and took her to the vet. I wanted to get her ashes but couldn't afford them, so we said goodbye and left her at the clinic.

Despite this tragedy, I still thought I could become a breeder. I knew I could make some extra money by showing and selling the puppies of my boxer dogs. I knew that world from my mum and thought it would be a smart way of affording the animals I loved. In four years I had accumulated four beautiful boxer dogs. I had my preferred type from champion bloodlines and was busy planning my next litter before the first one was even born. Everything had a plan. How you do one thing is how you do all things, right? So everything about their care was immaculate. They were fit, healthy, well-socialised, and trained. They ate the best dog food and took the best supplements. Most days they lived better than me. My whelping room was a warm, spacious spare bedroom with clean lino flooring, set up weeks in advance of need so the bitch could get used to it. I put a little tent up over the whelping box so it felt like a cosy, private little cave. I now had to just wait and let nature take its course, fingers crossed our plans agreed with each other.

The nurturing part I had down pat, but I wasn't exactly prepared for the moral burden that was the other side of the coin of breeding animals. As with most dogs, it's recommended that puppies have their dewclaws surgically removed, which is a little vestigial side digit on most dogs' front and sometimes hind legs. It's no longer functional for most dogs. The procedure is usually done within the first few days of life and it's supposed to keep the claw from getting caught on fencing or clothing and tearing off. The safety reason was easy enough to accept for that one.

Docking the tails was a little more morally circumspect, though it also had its roots in trying to keep boxer dogs from breaking them against door frames or table legs. It normally required another surgical procedure where a vet cut the tail off at the required length and cauterised it. Some breeders did this procedure themselves the old-fashioned way; when the pups were only a few days old they'd band the tails to cut off circulation until the end of the tail rotted and fell off about a week later, like they do with certain breeds of sheep. I couldn't quite justify removing the tail from a perfectly happy and healthy four-day-old puppy and would have another experienced registered breeder assist me with this process. I felt ashamed and always questioned the rationale of removing something that was designed to be there. I guess it would later support my decision to refuse circumcision for my own sons. Years later, I was relieved to hear that the Australian National Kennel Council (ANKC) banned tail docking in all breeds of dogs for cosmetic reasons.

Removing appendages was bad enough, but it was nothing compared to the problem of white puppies. White was not acceptable as a colour variation for boxer dogs. Registered breeders with the boxer dog club signed a document saying they'd never take money for white puppies. If they chose to give away a white puppy, the breeder had to disclose to the new owner that the puppy could have more health problems. They could be deaf, or blind, or more prone to skin cancer because their albinism gave them pink skin that could be more prone to severe skin allergies and sunburn. White puppies were always spayed or neutered as part of an ethical breeder's dedication to ensure the breed standards were maintained into the future.

More often than not, though, in this breed white fur was dealt with quickly and ruthlessly. Breeders chose not to put time and money into a puppy who would never live up to breed expectations, so any white puppy in a litter was put down. I was horrified to learn that there are a few ways to do this. The vet, of course, but that cost time and money. Then one breeder told me, "If you see a white puppy in the birth sac, don't open it. Don't let the bitch open it. The bitch may be too distracted with the others in the litter to notice anyway. Just quietly take it away and the pup won't take its first breath."

Killing puppies wasn't exactly what I'd signed up for as a breeder. "Please," I begged each time my bitches gave birth, "please, don't have any white puppies!"

Breed enough dogs, have enough litters, and eventually your luck runs out. In four litters, I had a total of three white puppies. With two, I'd followed another breeder's advice to have them put down within days of being born. The mobile vet left the pups with me to dispose of. I wrapped the newborn pups in newspaper and put them in the freezer. On the next bin night the tiny frozen body went out with the trash. The third white puppy, I let live. The bitch only had two pups. I told myself that was why I couldn't go through with it.

Aside from the cruelties dictated by breed standards, there was also the risk inherent with birth itself. I remember one of my bitch's litters had ten puppies. She was a champ and delivered all of them naturally, all alive. But a few days in, the puppies started wasting away, and one by one, they died.

It was eventually determined the litter had what was known as "fading puppy syndrome," which more accurately meant they'd contracted sepsis. I was never sure, exactly, where the infection came from. It could have come from their mum. She produced a lot of milk to feed them all and because her pups were sick, not all of them suckled properly to drain her teats. She got mastitis, an infection in the mammary glands. Her mastitis led to a breast abscess that eventually burst, and I'll leave it to the imagination how foul it was. I had to apply fresh cabbage leaves every day to draw out the infection so she could heal. The puppies could also have contracted an infection through the belly button. When puppies are born, the mum usually chews each one out of the birth sac, eats the sac (not wasting that precious nourishment), and chews away the umbilical cord, crunching the last bit to detach it, which flattens and crushes the ventricles, sealing it. But with a large litter my bitch didn't have the energy to do this for the last puppies, so I helped by cutting the cords with clean scissors. This method can spare the mum in the short term, but it can also leave the cord ventricles open enough for bacteria to enter. I believe that's another reason why doctors will clamp a baby's umbilical cord first, before they cut it. I'll never know if the sepsis was of my doing or would have happened anyway, but I can't shake the guilt.

By the time the vet diagnosed the issue, it was too late for the puppies. The antibiotics the vet gave me didn't seem to work at all. Four died in quick succession. I took each fading little puppy to the vet to be humanely euthanised. I was devastated. How could this happen? What was the cause of the infection?

The fifth puppy took longer to die. Early in the day, I noticed the bitch pushing it to the corner of the whelping box. Every time I picked up the whimpering puppy to put it back by her teat, she'd push it away again. She could sense it was sick. In fact, she sensed her entire litter was sick. She kept trying to get out of the box, refusing to nurse her dying puppies, which I'm sure was the cause of her mastitis as her milk went unexpressed. I had to hold her down in the whelping box between my knees so the puppies could feed. Meanwhile, the sickest pup she'd pushed away didn't attempt to nurse even when I held him up to a nipple; he just kept crying in my hand. By late afternoon, I put the puppy on a hot water bottle in a shoebox, intending to take it to the vet the next morning. The incessant crying was unbearable because I couldn't do anything more for him. By then, I knew he was dying, as I'd seen his sisters and brothers die. That night, I put him, his hot water bottle, and his little box in a wardrobe at the other end of the house so I couldn't hear him cry as I tried to fall asleep. In the morning, when I went to check on him, he was dead. When the sixth puppy started fading fast, I took him to the vet straightaway. I couldn't listen to another puppy cry to death.

After that, the vet gave the remaining puppies a stronger antibiotic, which did work. Three weeks after birth, I now had four healthy puppies out of ten and a bitch recovering from an ugly bout of mastitis.

I was twenty-six when I decided I didn't have what it takes to be a dog breeder. After that devastating litter where so many puppies died, I realised this wasn't my dream—it was something I'd inherited, passed down from my mum's passion. I'd been a registered breeder for five years, but I no longer wanted to tie my self-worth to whether or not I produced a champion. I still appreciate the beauty and structure of purebred dogs, but I couldn't be the one to decide a puppy's fate simply because it didn't meet breed standards. For a while, I continued to show my boxer, Sassy, other people's Dobermans and rottweilers, and occasionally my mum's beloved Samoyeds—but that chapter of my life as a breeder had come to a close.

Australian Champion Rosadene Sarsaparilla—Sassy 1999

Sometimes I wonder if I set myself up from the start by trying too hard. Was I so afraid of loss that I tried to outpace it—holding on too tightly, planning too carefully, hoping that control might protect me from heartbreak? Maybe my fear of things going wrong made it harder for anything to go right.

I don't carry resentment for my childhood, but I can see now how those early losses—of animals, home, love, and belonging—shaped me. They influenced how I would mother, how I would love, and how I would grieve. When I was offered a job in Sydney, I made a decision to start fresh, to focus on my career. I rehomed my other dogs and kept only Sassy. It felt like a clean break—but in truth, it was just another chapter in a lifelong pattern of learning how to hold on and when to let go.

*Chapter 6*

# THE DIVA IN THE DELI MEETS THE SCOTSMAN

IN JULY 2000, I ACCEPTED A NEW JOB OPPORTUNITY AS A DELicatessen specialist. Sassy was about five years old when I was offered the job in Sydney to help set up several pilot stores for an up-market food retailer. I was so excited for the opportunity I packed up my house as quickly as I could and relocated from Melbourne.

I knew no one in Sydney. On the weekend before I was scheduled to move, I got to talking with one of my friends who was a police officer. He told me his best mate, who was a security guard, had also recently moved to the same Sydney suburb where I planned to move. He gave me his security guard mate's number and I scheduled to meet up with him when I arrived in a week's time.

I had been in Sydney for only two days when I agreed to meet with the security guard. It turned out he lived with a couple of friends in an apartment literally around the corner from where I was staying in my temporary accommodation. They invited me over for pizza and told me they'd come pick me up. I waited for them out the front of my apartment and they drove past and stopped. A passenger in the front seat wound down the window and asked, "Are you Natalie?"

"Yes," I said cautiously.

"Well, get in!" he joyfully called.

Now, riding in cars with strangers was something my mum warned me never to do, but I trusted the fact that these were friends of a friend and I had messaged my sister, back home in Melbourne, moments before to tell her what I was doing and where I was going. There were four people in the car including the security guard: another guy named Phil and two girls in the back seat about the same age as me holding a pile of pizza boxes. It looked safe enough. It was a new adventure and I was looking forward to meeting new friends and exploring a new city.

We all went back to their place around the corner and had pizza and a few drinks. They all made me feel so welcome and invited me to a mutual friend's joint thirtieth birthday party that was being held the following weekend. I didn't know the mutual friend, either, but they called him Scotty and told me they'd pick me up next Saturday night to take me to the party.

There must have been about seventy people at the party. Within a few minutes I was introduced to everyone except Scotty. Who was this guy that everyone was talking about? I found out he was out the front with his mate warming up their bagpipes. Yes, bagpipes!

You see, Scotty was a boy from Glasgow who had migrated to Sydney ten years earlier. In fact, the couple that hosted the party had previously employed Scotty and had sponsored him to work and become an Australian citizen. They were like his adopted Aussie family. When Scotty and his mate started playing those bagpipes, it took the party to the next level as the dueling pipers played "Scotland the Brave" and "Black Bear," his piper mate playing in harmony (seconds or thirds) as a highland dancer kicked up her heels between the pipers. Then everyone began dancing in ring formation like a traditional Scottish *ceilidh*, or dance party.

I'd never experienced anything like it. The energy and emotion of those pipes and everyone dancing was like nothing I had ever felt. This wasn't just my introduction to new friends and birthday bagpipes, but also my introduction to Scotty, the Boy from Glasgow, a.k.a. "the Scotsman." Phil introduced me to Scotty but I could hardly understand a word he said as his accent was so broad, so Phil acted as an interpreter for me. Of course, I didn't know it at the time, but this piper would be my future husband.

Over the next few months, Scotty and I became good friends and started dating. It's funny, because at first I didn't think he liked me in that way, as I felt my constant requests for him to repeat what he had just said and "to speak more Australian" may have extinguished any spark he had for me. But that wasn't the case, and pretty soon, I no longer needed Phil to translate his Glaswegian accent and our appreciation for each other grew.

Within a few months of moving to Sydney, I quickly realised that I would need to sell my home back in Melbourne as my tenant was behind in his rent and this in turn put me under considerable financial strain. I realised that if I wanted to keep Sassy I'd have to share my space with people I didn't know, or get a second job so I could afford to live in a house with a dog-friendly backyard. For a moment I was torn between moving back to my home in Melbourne or rehoming my dog, so when Phil told me he was looking for a new flatmate I knew what I had to do. I rehomed Sassy and moved in with Phil while Scotty and I continued to date.

I really began to admire Scotty's exuberant attitude towards life. His sense of humour. Like most Brits, Scotty came to Australia to enjoy the warmer weather and the beautiful beaches, and that he did. We'd always be on some kind of adventure around Sydney, but we especially loved spending time around Sydney's northern beaches. He was like my very own Sydney tour guide, knowing all the colonial history of the early settlers, the best scenic lookouts of the harbour and its beaches, and the best pubs and cheap eats at the local RSLs. I had never really experienced pub culture before but I quickly learned. Like a taxi driver, he knew all the backstreets, dodging traffic to get from West Sydney to the beach suburbs quicker than anyone I knew. It was thrilling to be with him, and I loved that he loved my home country more than anyone else I knew.

Scotty had an uncanny way of working to live, not living to work. He ate well, had some weights and a sit-up bench in his lounge room, and would go running three to four times a week no matter how hot it was. His older brothers had struggled with weight all their lives, so he was determined to not let his get out of hand. He did what made him feel healthy and took his guilty pleasures in moderation.

This self-control filtered into all aspects of his life. Since he'd migrated such a long distance, he didn't have much furniture in his tiny, two-bedroom flat in Parramatta, or any of the knickknacks that tend to accumulate when someone's lived in one place for a long time. In fact, you could call his aesthetic rather…sparse…if you were being kind. Just one television set on an overturned cardboard box and two secondhand recliners for him and his Pommy backpacker flatmate. He saved every penny he earned.

I was…not this. I liked my creature comforts.

At this time in my life, I was a smoker and still very body conscious, a leftover from my childhood weight issues. I still struggled with my weight. As much as I didn't want to be like her, I turned into my mum when it came to yo-yo dieting. My New Year's resolution every year was to lose ten kilos before I'd start any exercise regime, which sounds like putting the cart before the horse but I wanted to feel comfortable in my activewear. A quick crash diet that mainly consisted of starving myself to shed the weight, but it always came back and then some by year's end. Going to the beach in my bathers sounded like a great idea to Scotty, but the thought filled me with dread as it gave me flashbacks from my early teens and that awkward Torquay beached whale experience. Before I'd moved to Sydney I had attempted to start running a few kilometres a couple of times per week with Sassy, but aside from that I wasn't active at all, and my diet, while not the worst, wasn't the best.

With Scotty it was different. I somehow got the spark to get out of my body shame and take action. Every weekend, we would go for walks around the harbour and eventually we started running together. There's no quicker way to give up smoking than to start running! I quickly realised how much smoking affected my lungs, and funny enough, as I cut back on the cigarettes my ability to control my breath when running got better. I started with only the short length of a soccer field, then the long length, then I was able to run the whole loop of the field.

"Come on, Nat, you've got this!" he coached, running backwards up a hill in front of me as I struggled to run it forward. "Focus on your breaths! One more kilometre to go! Nice and steady!"

"Alright! Just shut up and let me run!" I puffed, half annoyed, half laughing.

As I ran more and I lost weight, my confidence grew. I felt like I was achieving something. I got up to seven kilometres in one session, running with him. He coached me through my running the whole time, always my champion and never my judge. If there's one thing I'm grateful for, it's Scotty helping me find my eye of the tiger and encouraging me to take better care of my own mental health through physical activity.

It took me three years to give up smoking cigarettes completely; in the end hypnosis definitely helped me kick the habit for good.

Scotty also helped me face my issues around food. We would share desserts. I'm not sure if his reasoning was to help me control my weight or because he wanted to be thrifty—he never said—but it made it easier when we did it together. We would have pizza on Saturday night, knowing we were going to do a long run Sunday morning. Or we would do a long run and get a dessert with dinner that night as a reward. One of my favourite Scotty quotes was: "It's not what you eat between Christmas and New Year's, but what you eat between New Year's and Christmas that counts." He taught me you didn't have to go without, you just had to keep a balance.

We also loved music and singing together. He lived life on his terms and was full of bravado and could sing like no one was listening. A proud man, he didn't seem to care what anyone else thought. Those healthy lungs gave rise to a powerful singing voice. Singing was a talent that we shared. We would often sing duets in the car; one of our favourites was the theme song from Baz Lurhmann's 2001 romantic musical *Moulin Rouge*, "Come What May," sung by Ewan McGregor and Nicole Kidman. The lyrics seemed like a promise, projected at the top of our lungs, that we would love each other until our dying day, come what may.

Three years later, we married in the celebrant's office in Inverness, Scotland. We didn't want a big, expensive wedding—or to go through the headache of who we would and wouldn't offend if they couldn't come to a destination wedding—preferring to spend the money on a three-week whirlwind tour of Germany, Austria, France, and Italy. We'd do a big wedding party with family and friends at the Harbour Bridge Hotel when we returned to Sydney. The last stop on our tour would be Scotland, where we'd meet up with Scotty's parents, get married, and spend two more weeks there for our official honeymoon. I bought a dress that wasn't too expensive because I wanted to be able to replace it if it was lost during the three weeks of travel we planned to do before we got married in Scotland. Despite being only $320 it was lovely.

When we landed in Glasgow, Scotty's parents picked us up and we drove all together to a little seaside village just outside of Inverness called Clachnaharry. Two days later, on our wedding day, we scheduled a black Hackney cab to take us to the registrar's office in Inverness, then onto Inverness Castle for photos and Bunchrew House for our intimate wedding reception and accommodation. Scotty's parents went back after dinner to the accommodation in Clachnaharry and we continued our Scottish honeymoon. Bunchrew, built in 1505 by Alexander Fraser of Lovat, is a mansion on the shore of the Firth of

Beauly. It was a special place and made for beautiful photos. Then we spent the following two weeks travelling around Scotland as husband and wife.

My wedding photo

Now, when you hopscotch across the country, trying to do things on the cheaper side so you can see more, you always take a risk. In the Scottish Highlands, there's a classic old hotel called The Drovers Inn, established in 1705. This place took pride in being the oldest pub in Loch Lomond.

As you walk into the foyer, you're greeted by a massive brown bear standing on its hind legs. The pub downstairs sports a bar made from a big slab of dark wood probably cut down long before the first Jacobite rising. Sheep-sized, rough-edged stones form the foundation and walls. Then, as you go up the dark staircase to your room, every board creaking as if this was the year it was finally going to give way, a parade of taxidermied wildlife confronts you on every step with unblinking, dead, glass eyes. As I've since discovered it is renowned to be the most haunted pub in Scotland, and that famous Jacobite

Scottish outlaw and folk hero, Rob Roy Macgregor, reportedly stayed at the hotel back in 1716.

When I say "hotel" I use the term loosely. It's more an "accommodation experience," and oh boy, what an experience! I'm not sure if the inn was ever considered top-notch, even when it was first established a few hundred years ago. It lacked the modern conveniences one ignores in a modern hotel until they're missing. The bathroom was shared with the entire floor, so we had to fill up our room's washbasin (a washbasin!) if we wanted privacy to clean up. And the rooms were tiny, built for a time when heating cold Scottish nights was only provided by a fireplace and a few flea-ridden Irish wolfhounds. The fireplaces no longer worked in the individual rooms, but you could still smell the soot that had worked its way into the ceiling beams and floorboards over centuries.

We put our belongings in a side room and didn't actually make it to our bedroom until it was time to turn in. The bed was quite small to fit in the small room, maybe a full-size if we were being generous, and when we sat on the mattress that may have once hosted a few Jacobites, it dipped dangerously into the centre. It was a good thing we were married already because there was no extricating our limbs from each other as the dip in the centre of the bed funneled us together. Scotty had to curl awkwardly around me as the ancient mattress pushed us together. Then, despite the forced body warmth, we were cold. There was a draft like a stray banshee was breathing on us all night and we couldn't figure out where it was coming from. It wasn't until morning that we discovered the thin curtain was hiding a missing window pane from the casement windows, most likely put in the last time the building was upgraded in the seventeenth century.

The Drovers set a trend for our honeymoon. At another accommodation in Tobermory, we felt like we'd stepped into our own personal rom-com, except we were already in love and this was a test of our resilience as a couple. There was a radiator heater over the bed, of all places, but we didn't know how to get it working in the dark and again had to snuggle together for warmth. The accommodation actually turned out to be a backpackers shared house and we had only one tiny bedroom to ourselves and a communal kitchen, lounge, and shared bathroom. We waited somewhat disappointedly until 6:00 p.m. to see if anyone else was staying there. Lucky for us, no one else had booked the same two nights we had scheduled so we had the place to ourselves. And once we got the radiator working properly our dorm-like room was actually quite cosy.

Fortunately, just like those feel-good rom-coms, there was a lively bunch down at the village pub—full of charm, cheek, and stories as rich as the Tobermory whiskey itself. Between the local banter, seaside tales, and a dram or two, we found ourselves ending the day with a wee Highland jig at a real-life ceilidh being held in the town hall across from the fishing pier, and we were lucky to meet a very talented Canadian-Scottish composer and folk music DJ named Martyn Bennett. He and Scotty hit it off, talking all things bagpipes. We ended up having the best night in that seaside village on the Isle of Mull. What we thought was going to be a complete disaster turned into one of the highlights of my life.

One of the things I loved about Scotland, especially in its out-of-the-way places, was that it wasn't commercial. There were no big billboards or adverts at the petrol stations or along the roads. It felt… subtle. Humble. Courteous. People drove slowly down single-lane freeways and pulled over to wait patiently for another car to pass. Highland sheep slept along the roads. It all felt like an earlier, simpler time that tested your ability to cope and improvise with grace.

We thought our honeymoon was just a quirky beginning—two lovers laughing through drafty rooms and creaky beds—but perhaps it was the quiet rehearsal for the kind of love that endures the coldest nights, the darkest roads, and the greatest loss a heart can bear.

*Chapter 7*

# BABY NUMBER TWO

WILLIAM WAS EIGHTEEN MONTHS OLD WHEN I DECIDED TO send him to day care for one day per week. This allowed me a little bit of time to myself to go visit a friend, have some lunch, or go shopping. It was also an opportunity for William to have one day where he was around other children of a similar age and I was hoping that maybe he would start copying their behaviour, which would help his development. The whole "monkey see, monkey do" part of learning.

As mentioned before, we had created a wonderful early intervention team that gave William every chance at a better quality of life, but fulfilling all the learning tasks along with 24/7 care still challenged me as a mother because I honestly felt like I couldn't do enough to make him better. I couldn't fix this for him and I'd be damned if I was going to make it worse for him. I wanted him to have the best life he could, and that meant having a chance at a regular family.

Scotty and I began to plan a second baby, as we believed a brother or a sister for William would enhance all of our lives together, and we were heading up on the recommended time span between two children, when my own body would have healed and recharged fully from pregnancy and birth. I planned for a summer baby this time. I thought somewhere around Christmas would be nice, but not too close to the holiday, as I wanted Baby Two to have his or her own birthday and not have to share it.

We planned for our new baby even though we still didn't have a diagnosis for William. We consulted with genetic counselors to ensure there was no underlying genetic disease or disorders. They ran the standard tests, and while they couldn't pinpoint exactly what, if anything, had caused William's delays, they thought there was just a one in four chance of another child with such developmental delays. Scotty and I decided a 75 percent chance of a normal child was good, and within a few weeks I was pregnant again. My expected due date was the twenty-second of December.

While I was pregnant, I started looking into other reasons for William's condition. Maybe he'd had a birth injury? Maybe that's why he'd been so sleepy? I started the process of requesting my hospital file to see if perhaps something had gone wonky during delivery.

Maybe William's nuchal translucency test wasn't faulty after all, and they had got it wrong. And, yes, it appeared that he had been distressed, as his heart rate had been elevated. The birth had been slow, potentially depriving him of oxygen. There was evidence of meconium in the birth fluid, which is a key indicator of fetal distress. I had been so off my nut on the happy gas I'd been none the wiser at the time. But it couldn't be determined whether William's condition contributed to his slow birth, or whether the slow birth contributed to his condition, or whether they were related at all. There wasn't enough evidence to pursue any legal action, but I had a potential environmental reason for William's challenges.

Not surprisingly, I experienced extremely high anxiety while pregnant the second time. For someone who planned to avoid bad things happening at all costs, not knowing what would or would not make my baby healthy was torture. At one stage, I was overwhelmed with the thought that Baby Number Two would have the same condition as William, and I didn't know if my fear was just fear or my intuition.

I got myself so worked up I decided that I needed help to settle my nerves. I had some counselling and hypnosis to help visualise an easy labor and healthy delivery of this new baby. I began to learn through this process how important a positive mindset was to ensure a healthy birth outcome.

I also had several ultrasounds to ensure Baby Two was developing okay, as this baby also didn't move around as much as I thought it would. For a moment there, I was worried that my second baby wasn't moving much at all in the final weeks. The constant dread got to me despite my counselling, and then I felt guilty over my negative thoughts potentially hurting the baby too. I hated my second pregnancy. I just wanted to get it over with and meet this new human that Scotty and I had created.

At 8:45 p.m. on Christmas Eve, I started to have contractions and thought I better get to bed early because this baby will be here in the morning. A Christmas baby! Too bad about the joint birthday with Jesus and Christmas, kid, I thought sympathetically but happily. At 5:00 a.m., I woke up with my contractions intensifying. By 9:00 a.m. we presented to the hospital and by 11:57 a.m. our beautiful, perfect, robust little boy arrived just in time for Christmas lunch at the hospital.

The birth was natural. I felt I was taking back control of my body even as the hypnosis work took hold and I started to observe my body calmly. I went into primal mode as my natural stress response started pumping out adrenaline and endorphins. What a rush! The experience was the benchmark for the level of connection amongst my mind, body, and spirit I'd try to find later in life. So I fought it out. I refused to have the amount of gas I'd taken with William, as I wanted to be aware this time. Scotty sat by my side coaching me while stingily rationing out the puffs of nitrous gas to the end until I snatched the mask out of his hand for one last big breath. Two more pushes and Baby Two was out!

He barely cried when he was born, but not for lack of awareness. I'll never forget the first look he gave me as they placed him naked on my chest. He looked around at me like he was asking, "Who are you? Where am I? What is this place?" He was already processing this world with an innate intelligence and, oh boy, he had a presence about him. I couldn't take my eyes off him. My strong, healthy little baby. To my surprise, he began instantly nuzzling into his tiny hands and then into my breast, unlike with William. I helped him find my nipple and he instantly suckled; I was in love. Wow, what an experience! Never had I been so in love to the truest sense of the word. The instant bonding was so primal. We agreed he would forever be known as Hamish George Watson, my eternal soulmate.

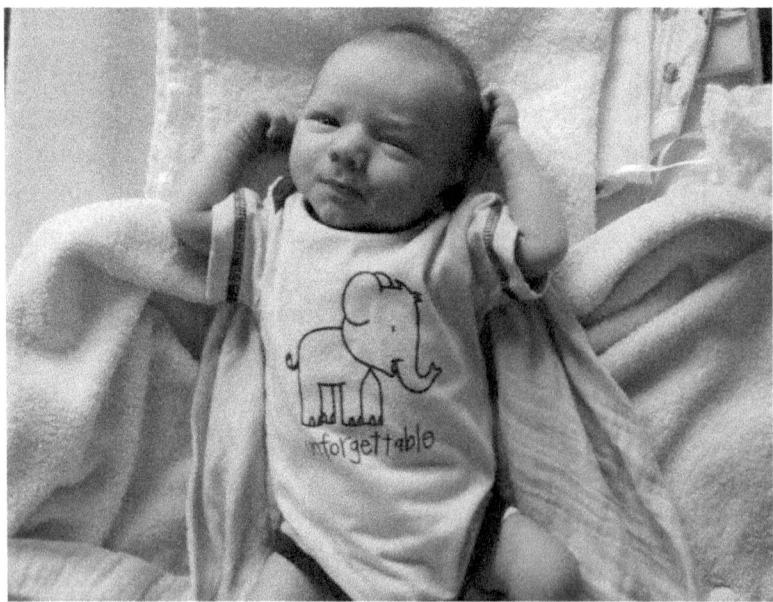

Three-day-old Hamish

We brought Hamish home after just one sleepless night in the hospital. It was Boxing Day, and we were just in time to eat all the food I had prepared with my mum on Christmas Eve.

Our rented home in Sydney was small but comfortable, and Hamish's cradle was in our room beside our bed for the first five weeks of his life. He slept pretty well for a newborn, but, boy, did he make a lot of noises while he slept! Cute little goat noises would emanate from his cradle, not to mention he'd fart and startle himself awake and us, too, for that matter. I wasn't expecting him to be so noisy! I eventually moved him across the hall and into our lounge room so we didn't disturb the sleeping Scotsman when I had to change, nurse, and soothe Hamish in the middle of the night. He didn't have his own room like William, as we planned to move into a bigger home in a few months.

I was fascinated and so relieved to see Hamish was making eye contact and mirroring our faces within hours after his birth. He tracked objects with his eyes around the room. Everyone said he was perfectly typical, though he did have a slight turn in his eye from time to time. I had help from William's physiotherapist later to help correct it. Some days it was worse than others, but everything else was going so well. He was making that cute new baby cooing noise and attempting to reach for toys hanging over his cradle. When we poked out our tongues he'd try to poke his out too. William never did any of that. I tried not to compare everything he did to whether William did this or that but I couldn't help myself. Why was it so hard for me to accept he was perfectly normal?

At around seven weeks old, I took Hamish to the doctor for his vaccinations. She agreed that he was very normal, a strong, healthy baby boy. He still had a slight turn in his eye, which we would, pardon the pun, keep an eye on, but otherwise he was perfect.

After the appointment later that afternoon, I was breastfeeding Hamish when all of a sudden he went limp in my arms. Then he turned blue. I yelled out, "Hamish! Hamish, wake up!" while frantically rubbing him. He gave a jolt and took a deep breath, opened his eyes and started crying. We both did! It was like he had passed out, fainted, or had some kind of turn. It scared the life out of me! I rang the doctor and told her what had happened.

"Does he have a fever?"

"No," I said. I'd already checked.

"Keep an eye on him and call back if he gets worse."

Of course, my immediate thought was he had a reaction to the vaccinations, as William seemed to have stronger reactions to them than most kids. I was scared to speak out, though, since there was enough conflicting information in the news about vaccines and I didn't want to look like I had become paranoid. But, I was paranoid, and with good reason. I couldn't help thinking, what if Hamish had been in his cradle when he passed out? He could have died if I wasn't there to wake him! At night my anxiety haunted me. I had flashbacks of the litter of fading puppies I bred and thought, oh God, not you, too, my beautiful boy! I became hypervigilant whenever Hamish slept and would check on him constantly.

A few days after that incident with Hamish I arranged for a family photo shoot with the same photographer we used for William's early photos. My anxiety started to rush back in when I started noticing similar traits in the photos, although I wasn't sure if they were brotherly traits or if they were an unknown condition's traits.

I sensed something was different with Hamish over the coming weeks as his eye contact started to change. I noticed he wasn't following us around the room, looking into our eyes, or mirroring our movements as often as he did. And his developmental milestones had begun to slow; he was no longer seeking or reaching for toys with curiosity like he had a few weeks earlier.

Hamish was three months old when we began the process of moving interstate. Sydney was expensive and would be even more so if I had to go back to work full time to afford our rent and outsource the boys' care. Plus we had no family in the state we lived in. Scotty's were in Scotland, of course, and mine were closer to Melbourne. I encouraged my husband to move us back to Melbourne to be closer to my family so I could have some support with the kids while he was at work. The only friendly outside support I got was our next-door neighbour, Noeline, and her husband. She was amazing. They were like William's third set of grandparents. She'd come in and sit with William for an hour so I could go shopping or go for a walk or just do something that got me out of the house. But while she was lovely, she was only one elderly lady. I needed more help, physically and emotionally, with two boys, one with high needs. I needed my family.

So we purchased a new home in Bendigo, Victoria, a regional town that had nice affordable family homes and great services, including a highly regarded school for children with special needs for William once he turned five. We knew it was a good place to raise our new family, albeit a lot colder than Sydney in the winter months. This was much to the disappointment of Scotty, who moved to Sydney for the beaches and warmer weather only to end up in one of the coldest states in Australia.

I didn't want to get too panicked about Hamish, so I remained focused on the big move down south. We bought a beautiful, big, ex-display home with wide hallways and plenty of space for William's walkers and future wheelchair. It was a very exciting time. This was our dream home and we were so looking forward to moving into our first family home all together. I dreamed of decorating ours and the boys' bedrooms, buying furniture, and planning for the future. Scotty's work had agreed to let him work from home, as they empathised with William's care needs and our need to relocate for family. We drove down to Melbourne in two cars. Hamish at four months old, travelling in the baby car capsule in my car, and William almost three years old driving with Dad in his car with our little mini fox terrier, Gypsy. While it was a huge process to move, everything went to plan and we settled in.

Previous to our move, I had scheduled an appointment with William to meet his new neurologist down in Melbourne, which was a ninety-minute drive from our new home. We went to this appointment as a family. After discussing our concerns about William the neurologist said, "And what about Hamish? I can see he has slight strabismus, or misaligned eyes."

"Yeah, I was wondering should we patch his eyes?" I asked anxiously.

The doctor pursed his lips in thought. "Not just yet, sometimes they grow out of it and a patch can change how the right and left side of the brain develops. Do you have any other concerns?"

Of course I did. "We can see some similar behaviours and traits to William coming through in Hamish, but I'm not sure if they're brotherly or the same underlying condition."

Unfortunately, his response startled me. "I agree. Let's make another appointment for Hamish, and we'll run some tests for him today while you're all here." The neurologist then ordered a series of genetic and metabolic tests for both boys.

We finished William's appointment and went straight downstairs to pathology, where they took several samples of blood from Hamish. After waiting an hour, we also managed to capture a urine sample before we began our journey back to our new home, somewhat shocked but relieved that we were now in the good hands of specialists who were determined to help us find a diagnosis for our boys.

About a week later, and much to our surprise, the neurologist rang to give us the results. I put my phone on speaker phone so Scotty could hear too. "Hamish's Bratton-Marshall urine test has come back from the laboratory in Queensland. He's tested positive for an extremely rare metabolic disease called Adenylosuccinate Lyase Deficiency, otherwise known as Adsl Deficiency. There's currently only about forty reported cases in the world and there's little known about the disease, except that it causes various degrees of physical and intellectual disabilities, as well as seizures. I'd like to get William tested ASAP, too, as it's a high probability that with their similar traits they have the same condition."

"What treatment is there?" I asked, stunned.

"Unfortunately, there's currently no treatments or cures for this disease," the doctor said softly.

"What about the prognosis?" Scotty asked, getting to the point.

"It's variable from patient to patient. Some have died in early infancy and others in later years," he said, trying to be reassuring.

"And what about the seizures?" I chipped in. "Our boys don't have seizures," I said, somehow not wanting it to be true.

William and Hamish in 2011

There was a small pause. "The boys don't have seizures yet, but there's a high probability they will get them, as this disease causes neurotoxins to build up in the body, which is what causes certain kinds of seizures. We will help you and the boys manage them when and if that happens."

*That is where you are wrong!* I thought, in full denial. *That won't be happening to our boys! Our boys aren't going to have seizures!* William, now three years old, was rarely ever sick. But behind that same thought I remembered a couple of moments when William had seemed to just drift off, staring up at the lights, and I reflected back to the moment when Hamish passed out in my arms and went blue. Oh shit, my mind whirled, maybe those seizures have already started!

Both Scotty and I were in shock, and although I had a hundred and one questions for the neurologist, I just wanted to get off the call and talk it through with Scotty. We finished off with the doctor by booking our next follow-up appointment, now for both of our boys, which would also determine the results of William's pathology test. Then I set about researching everything there was to know about Adsl Deficiency.

*Chapter 8*

# THE DIAGNOSIS OF A RARE PARENT

ADENYLOSUCCINATE LYASE DEFICIENCY (ADSL)—
*Adenylosuccinate Lyase Deficiency is a disease of purine metabolism which affects patients both biochemically and behaviourally. The symptoms are variable and include psychomotor retardation, autistic features, hypotonia, and seizures.*

Also known as:

- Adenylosuccinase Deficiency
- Adenylosuccinate Deficiency
- Adsl Deficiency

In 2010, these were the first words I read about the disease both my boys were diagnosed with. Not from anything as simple and common as the *Encyclopedia Britannica* or Wikipedia, but a full-on medical journal abstract.

The title of the only research paper I found was pretty spot on: "Adenylosuccinate lyase deficiency." You know it's not good when they name the paper off the disease itself, like it's just gotten discovered. The study was published in an academic journal titled *Molecular Genetics and Metabolism* in 2006 by E. K. Spiegel, Roberta Colman, and David Patterson. The study had collected the little that was known from the forty cases reported globally by 2006. There was a "deficiency ratio" with corresponding symptoms done up in a neat little black-and-white table.

I remember feeling completely out of my depth trying to make sense of all this new information: The report read, "Adsl catalyzes two steps in the de novo purine pathway which consists of 13 metabolic steps in the conversion of ribose 5-phosphate into AMP or GMP. These two steps are the conversion of [the world's longest word] succinylaminoimidazolecarboxamide ribonnucleotide (SAICAr) into… blah blah blah…" What the?! What language was this? What world was I in? I didn't understand any of this medical jargon!

I studied all I could to understand the disease but, hey, I was more interested in horses, singing, and boys in high school and I barely passed year eleven. That's as far as I got before entering the job world and never looking back. Scotty was slightly more worldly than I, but even he could barely make heads or tails of the scientific lingo. It was all completely foreign, like talking in another language, and his eyes would eventually glaze over.

I quickly learned the basics through a lot of trips to the dictionary, enough to explain the disease to anyone daring enough to ask. For that knowledge, I have the deepest respect for molecular geneticists and neurologists.

I also had the deepest respect for our new metabolic team, who tried to put everything in language we could understand. They'd been doing their research, too, and knew way more than us about how to interpret those studies. Here's what they told us on the twentieth of January, 2011:

Dear Natalie and Scotty,

Your neurologist has requested some metabolic investigations because both William and Hamish have significant developmental problems, strabismus and cortical visual impairment. Results of the testing showed that both children have a metabolic condition called Adenylosuccinate Lyase (Adsl) deficiency.

Adenylosuccinate lyase is an enzyme, a special form of protein that converts one chemical into another. In particular, adenylosuccinate lyase converts SAICAribotide and adenylosuccinate (S-AMP) into AICAR and adenosine monophosphate (AMP) respectively. These two chemical reactions are important because they are involved in the production of purine nucleotides which play important roles in many bodily functions. If the adenylosuccinate lyase enzyme is deficient, it results in the accumulation of SAICAr and succinyladenosine.

This is the reason why our laboratory was able to detect these chemicals in the urine samples of William and Hamish. These chemicals are supposed to be undetectable in the urine.

Most of the reported children with Adenylosuccinate lyase deficiency presented with severe psychomotor retardation, seizures and autistic features. In some, growth and muscle problems were also observed.

None of the symptoms were new to what I was already noticing in my children. I mean, let's get real, William was almost four years old at this stage and wasn't walking, nor had he spoken any words. His developmental age was confirmed to be that of a nine-month-old. And Hamish's development went from normal to almost completely halted at six months old.

> However, there is a spectrum or variability in the severity and onset of these symptoms. The onset of symptoms could be in the neonatal period, early or late childhood and severity could range from severe (most often the case) to mild-moderate.
>
> Both William and Hamish have significant developmental problems. William also has some repetitive behaviour. However, both have no overt seizures at this stage. It would be important to monitor their clinical progress with time. This will help determine where they are in terms of the spectrum. (The SAICAr ratio determines the severity and often prognosis.)

The doctors wouldn't say it outright, but I knew what my own reading had found in the journal study. Sick to my stomach, I'd felt my deepest horror when I read, "The prognosis of individuals with Adenylosuccinate Lyase Deficiency is generally unpredictable and grim. Most individuals die in their early infancy or during childhood." You know it's also bad when normally neutral scientists use the word "grim" in an academic paper.

> The exact mechanism of why affected children present with the above problems is not clearly certain. Some proposed reasons include toxic effects of the accumulating metabolites (SAICAr and succinyl adenosine) to the body, particularly the brain, and the lack of purine nucleotides and disruption of other cellular functions such as energy production. Further research is needed for a better understanding.
>
> Currently, there is no available cure for Adenylosuccinate lyase deficiency. There have been trials trying to decrease the accumulating toxic metabolites or increase the production of the purine nucleotides. However, these trials have not been proven to be effective. There are many supportive measures, however, that would still help William and Hamish. I am glad that an early intervention program is in place for them. Should they develop seizures, there are anticonvulsants that could help control these.

I knew we were in the deep end and for now just treading water. Having the diagnosis somehow gave me an excuse to accept the fact that my boys would never "grow out of this" and that we better embrace our new normal as a family, as these boys are indeed very special.

> Adenylosuccinate Lyase Deficiency [, or Adsl Deficiency for short,] is inherited in an autosomal recessive manner. Each one of us has two copies of the Adsl gene that carry the "recipe" of how the enzyme is going to be made. If we have one copy of the Adsl gene that has a change ("mutation") in it, the other copy can make up for the faulty copy. This person is known as a carrier for the condition and has no problems. However, if there are two faulty copies of the gene, that is, if there are mutations in each of the two copies of the Adsl gene then Adenylosuccinate Lyase Deficiency results and this is what happened to William and Hamish.

> It is likely that the both of you are carriers for this condition. It is very important to remember that it is nobody's fault that both children have this condition. Everyone is a carrier for about five faulty genes. It is only if you are both carriers for the same faulty gene that a condition will result. When we have children, we get half our genetic makeup from the father and half from the mother. Therefore with every pregnancy you have a 1 in 4 or 25 percent chance of having a child affected with Adenylosuccinate Lyase [D]eficiency [or Adsl Deficiency when shortened]. Likewise, there is a 3 in 4, or 75 percent chance that the child will not be affected. You have agreed to pursue the mutation testing for William. I will send the sample to another laboratory in Queensland once the DNA sample is ready.

I mean, what were the odds of this ever happening? A boy from Glasgow, Scotland, moves to Sydney, Australia, and meets a girl from Melbourne through friends of friends, they fall in love, get married, and unbeknownst to them they are both carriers of an extremely rare metabolic disease. They decide to have children, both of which are born with the rare genetic disease in a one-in-four chance when they lucked out with both recessive genes. The total odds were one in four million of all these stars aligning.

When they were diagnosed, our boys had boosted the reported cases in the world to about forty-five. At the time this book was written, there were an estimated one hundred reported cases in the world. I'm not sure how many of these children are still living.

Were there any red flags that indicated that this journey may be fraught with heartache, or was there such a sole purpose that kept all that camouflaged for us to have this experience? Were we completely blindsided to the odds of being dealt such a shit hand that would totally rob our boys of the life we had dreamed of for them? I even went so far as to wonder if my negative thoughts had somehow manifested the disease.

> The diagnosis is very upsetting for the family. I will request our social worker to call you. It will be very important for you to have all the support services.
>
> Sincerely,
>
> Your Metabolic Team

The meaning of the doctors' words were clear. *Congratulations, you are now a rare mother!* I thought in a somewhat-strange kind of way (if you don't laugh, you'll cry, right?). But seriously, what are the odds of that?! Was this now my claim to fame, to be a parent of two extremely rare children?

It seemed Scotty, after getting the general idea and diagnosis, was ready to move on to how we would live with it. It would take me a little longer to accept that new normal.

I contacted one of the researchers of that first academic paper I found in *Molecular Genetics and Metabolism*. "What can I do?" I asked him. "Is there anything I can do?"

"You can just love them," he told me gently.

"I'm going to do that," I replied. "I'm going to do more than that. I'm going to do whatever I can." And I did.

We got all that information, and on one hand it did make sense. On the other hand, it made no freaking sense. I felt overwhelmed with the giant puzzle presented to me. I could see its outline now, but not how all the bits in the middle fit together. My journey as a newly anointed rare mother was to make sense of it all.

Determined to learn as much as I could about the disease, apart from what the doctors knew (which was little), I kept searching. The research might have been my way to cope and feel like I had some control over what was happening. Knowledge is power, and all of that. I wanted to know how everything worked and why. I wanted to know what makes sense. Maybe understanding the disease in more detail, knowing where it came from and how it worked, would also help me accept it as part of our lives. There was also a part of me that thought I could help. As an adult, I was into diet and nutrition, so held the ethos of "food is medicine" and quickly realised what foods would make their symptoms worse. I explored the benefits of various essential oils and other natural remedies also. If there was so little known about Adsl Deficiency, maybe there was a treatment out there the doctors had missed waiting right under our noses, or at least small ways that the disease symptoms could be lessened. So I set about doing what I could.

I helped make our space accessible.

While our new home was all on one level and had nice wide hallways for wheelchairs, the bathrooms needed modifications so they were more accessible.

We put in a nine-by-four-meter swimming pool to create our own resort-style living. During the summer months taking the boys to another pool would have been near impossible, so it was money well spent. Even on rough days the boys loved to float around with floaties on their arms and a pool noodle under their arms.

I'll never forget the day we spent the afternoon watching the movie *Finding Nemo* and then took the boys outside for a swim. No sooner had we set Hamish up in his floaties and got him in the water, than he literally put his whole face into the water and looked under the water like he was looking for fish. He didn't breathe in or swallow any water, as you'd expect. He just dipped his head forward and looked around underwater while his body floated above him supported by the floatation devices. He was three years old and looked to still have the primitive reflex known as the "bradycardic response," the natural reflex to hold the breath underwater common to many mammals, including human newborns. When a baby is submerged in water, the natural survival reflex is to hold their breath and open their eyes. (It's the same reaction you can provoke by blowing into your baby's face.)

We set up William's bedroom as a sensory room, with a bubbling water fountain that would change colours. It was a long cylinder, probably about fifty centimetres square, and the bubbles would go up to the top and the coloured lights would cycle through it. We set up multicoloured fairy lights above his bed that changed colours as well because he was awake a lot at night. When William woke up, I'd turn the lights on after I checked on him. When the lights were off he had glow stickers on his ceiling, so he was never alone in the dark.

I sought out the best nutrition and supplements.

I learned that gout was another purine-related condition—where the body struggles to break down purines properly. That made sense to me, as the boys would sometimes have swollen joints—hands, elbows, ankles—signs of inflammation. Maybe there was a connection. I began researching gout management, wondering if some of those strategies could help. I learned that purines are found in high levels in foods like red meat, organ meats, shellfish, anchovies, sardines, and even in some plant-based foods like asparagus, spinach, mushrooms, and legumes. Alcohol and sugary drinks, especially those containing fructose, also increase uric acid levels. With that in mind, I leaned into an antihistamine-style diet to reduce inflammatory triggers and steered clear of these high-purine foods.

Around the same time, the ketogenic diet was emerging as a promising way to manage seizures—high in healthy fats and protein, extremely low in sugar and carbs. I adopted a simple, clean approach to their nutrition. They loved protein smoothies, so I made them daily with minimal carbs and no added sugar.

Each morning, I gave them vitamins to support key areas—magnesium for muscle function, and others tailored to their needs. Since Adsl Deficiency affects the nervous system's ability to self-regulate, I also turned to complementary therapies. Chiropractic care, aromatherapy, and daily massage became part of our routine. I'd use pure essential oils in a sweet almond base—frankincense for grounding, sweet orange to ease anxiety, lavender to relax and soothe muscles. The boys especially loved their nightly foot massages. It was our way of bringing calm and connection before bed in order for us all to get a good night's sleep.

I got assistance. There's no shame in asking for help to improve quality of life, both for you and your children. Australia had both governmental and philanthropic assistance available for special needs families, and I sought out what I could.

Since Australia has government-assisted Medicare, the boys' healthcare was mostly covered. We'd pay for medications and had a prescription benefit scheme, or PBS, partially funded by the government. Seizure medications were usually partially covered, but specialty drugs and medical equipment above the base models cost a lot more, which meant applying for funding grants through philanthropic organisations. For a wheelchair better than the base model, our occupational therapist would have to write a grant request to justify why William needed a $17,000 wheelchair versus a $6,000 wheelchair.

The frustrating reality is that we don't get to set the prices for the specialised equipment our children need to have a better quality of life—others do, and they profit, often at our expense or the government's. That means we constantly have to fight to justify the funding we're asking for. It's an exhausting and often overwhelming process. Sometimes, it feels like the system is designed to wear you down, hoping you'll give up. But to get what your child needs, you have to become the squeaky wheel—you have to advocate loudly and persistently.

It's not just about buying the most expensive gear; it's the *level of support* that makes it costly. For William, that meant custom wheelchairs with head support, side support, and specialised cushions to prevent pressure sores on his tailbone. Each item required layers of paperwork and justification. We even had to apply for funding to build a ramp to access the backyard so he could enjoy the swing and trees like any child should. We pulled up almost-new carpet to install tiles in the hallway, making it easier to move wheelchairs and shower chairs between rooms. These may seem like small things—but they make a world of difference in creating a life that's not just manageable, but meaningful.

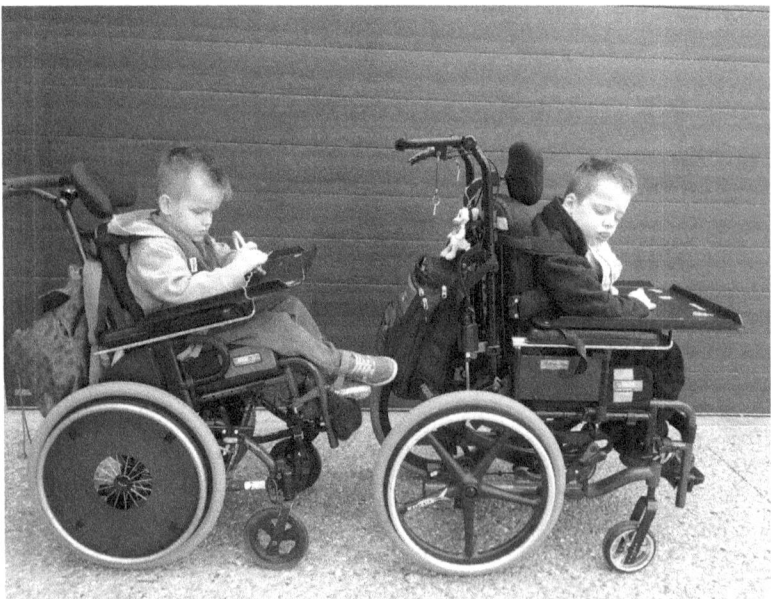

Will and Hamish in their wheelchairs

Assistance also comes in human form. The boys' physiotherapist, OT, and speech therapist in Bendigo were some of the most amazing, dedicated therapists I've had the pleasure to work with. Every week we'd look forward to their home visits. As much as I could, I'd make sure the team stayed consistent because there is nothing worse than having to explain yourself to a new therapist. Don't get me wrong, they're all fantastic and come from a beautiful place and I love the work that they do, but it can be taxing to explain your story to yet another professional and get them up to speed. If I knew them well, I'd also divulge my fears about the boys' progress to the physios and the OTs, who were the most equipped to understand. They weren't my therapists (that would come later) but they listened to me and sympathised all the same which is what I needed.

Both boys had varied degrees of CVI, so we went back to the toys on a black background I'd done with William as a baby. The bright colours were used to gain their attention. But really, they didn't care about toys. They seemed to love for us to be present and interact with them by helping them move, listening to us sing, and engaging through reading books. I requested respite services through our community health team and I managed to find a lovely lady through Anglicare. She provided me with two hours of respite every Wednesday. While I snuck out and did our grocery shopping, she'd sit and sing songs to the boys and play her guitar in their own private concert, or read their favourite books. I often ordered home delivery groceries but also found it a nice excuse to get out of the house and do the big weekly shop while she was there. I'd get home and unpack all the shopping and start preparing the boys' dinner. She'd often stay and help me feed the boys before she'd go home, or give an impromptu guitar lesson. I never properly learned a musical instrument myself, but I did practise at it with her while the boys raptly sat and watched.

I placed a Job Ad for Carers at the local university for students in the Allied Health field, specifically the university students who needed to gain some practical experience, and had four students apply to be volunteers to help assist with my boys' therapies. They were all lovely people, so energetic and enthusiastic to work with the boys' physiotherapist and learn more to help the boys. I could afford myself a sigh of relief whenever they were around and I could run errands or do chores. One particular student named Karlie was studying to be a speech pathologist and the boys took a real shine to her. We all did. She continued to work for our family, caring for the boys each Sunday morning when my husband and I would head out for our long runs or whenever we needed a babysitter, for the next five years.

Along with my sister Catherine, my mum was helpful, too, as she would often come up to our home at short notice if I needed to go with one of the boys to emergency, or just to help with meal time or mind the boys so I could have some time out for myself.

It wasn't until William was five and Hamish was three that I was ready to let anyone have the boys overnight. As a parent, I didn't think I needed respite because selflessness sort of goes with the territory of having young children, right? I wanted them with me all the time because I was so attached to them and protective. The seizures and their care needs meant I couldn't trust just anyone to watch them. The worry was incessant. Are they comfortable? Did they do their therapy exercises? Have they moved their bodies? Eaten enough? Had a bowel movement? Been changed? Not to mention how many times I would get up through the night to check on them just in case they had a seizure.

But as they became older, towards the ages when they would normally become more independent, going off to day care and school, I was able to walk away a little, although I remained on high alert and ready to race back to them at a moment's notice.

Very Special Kids House (VSK) is a charitable hospice in Melbourne established by Sister Margaret Noone that takes care of children with life-limiting diseases and conditions that have been referred by a paediatrician from the Royal Children's Hospital. Being a hospice it has a half hospital, half home-away-from-home feel about it as they care for very sick children, often in various stages of palliative care. So they have specialist equipment, including hospital beds and oxygen and monitors supplied to the rooms as needed. A doctor will attend every day and nurses do most of the daily care. There was a parent accommodation in another building next door.

We got a referral through our paediatrician and became regular guests of Very Special Kids for three weeks every year. There was a three-month waitlist for a spot, so we'd have to plan in advance for a holiday. Sometimes there'd be an emergency cancellation and you'd get a spot sooner which I didn't like to think about too much since a cancellation most likely meant another family was having a rough time. Being that we had two children we were often given first dibs, as the respite wasn't so much for the children as their parents. When we arrived, the boys would wait with me while I completed several admission forms for each child. Their medication charts had already been completed by our GP a few days before our booking date. Therapy and dietary instructions also needed to be provided in the handover. It usually took me about an hour to complete the handover and then the boys would be whisked off to begin an activity or to start a meal and I would be free to relax in the parent accommodation where I could get a decent night's sleep, often for the first time in months. Eventually, Scotty and I got bold enough to take a holiday a little farther away.

The hospice staff just knew what to do when it came to seizures and other symptoms. We didn't have to be called every time something happened. They could manage them at the respite house like we'd manage them at home. It was a great gift to know someone competent and compassionate was taking care of our boys so we had a brief time to turn our minds to other things and take a step back from being on high alert. They were like part of our family in the end. The staff came to the boys' funerals—different people each time, because we'd been going there for ten years. I'm still part of the VSK bereavement group and donate money and items on occasion to help keep this special place going. We meet once a year for their annual Walk to Remember, where we all walk around local parklands and meet for activities on the grounds of the beautiful property, have afternoon tea, and take a moment to reflect on our children's lives, meeting up with people that were part of our lives for three weeks out of the year. VSK is the first of its kind for Australia and Victoria's only children's hospice. It's a shame there are not more places like this, doing the good work that keeps so many parents and caregivers able to manage when the load is almost unbearable.

While carers helped with the day-to-day job of maintaining the boys' health, we also enrolled the boys in school to get them as much mental and social interaction as possible. Both boys went to a special development school in Bendigo. Each student had to have a certain IQ to be accepted. William and Hamish were in a high needs room, where there was basically one-to-one or one-to-two teacher assistants per child in this room. The curriculum was learning daily tasks, fine and gross motor skills, communication devices, and art. There was a swimming component, and the boys would have hydrotherapy sessions. My boys were lucky to get into a program where that was offered twice a week. There was a trampoline. William loved to bounce on the trampoline most of the day when he was well. They'd eat lunch. I'd send them to school with healthy lunches: a salad with protein, walnuts, granola with yogurt and fresh berries. The school used to praise me for the meals I sent in, and I'd pride myself on their nutrition habits. I was lucky because they'd eat anything.

I also grew my own knowledge and contacts. I connected with other parents of Adsl kids. When I first connected with an Adsl Deficiency family around the time of the boys' diagnosis, their little boy was around the same age as Hamish. When that little boy passed, I grieved for him, even though we'd never met and he lived in another country. I felt for his mum. The personal stories of Adsl angels—children who passed from the disease—touched me so deeply that I made it my personal mission to find the other forty families diagnosed with the disease and become an advocate for anyone touched by it. I wanted to give them all a place to meet, share their stories. I felt we had to do whatever we could to get the word out, get these babies tested, get the families some information and support, and get awareness going to promote more research. So in July 2014, I founded the first Adsl Deficiency research and awareness public Facebook page and created a private Facebook group for families to connect personally: "Adsl Deficiency Research and Awareness" and "Our Journeys with Adsl Deficiency."

Me and our boys at VSK March 2015

I created a detailed survey for the families to complete so that we could collect common behaviour and symptom patterns. This citizen research would in turn help inform another academic study, in which the information I shared provided researchers in Rome a further understanding of the disease and how it worked. I even co-authored a scientific research paper with these scientists in Rome along with two other rare mothers of children with Adsl Deficiency. The paper is titled "Clinical and molecular characterization of patients with adenylosuccinate lyase." In early 2025, I also published an ebook titled *Adsl Deficiency Simplified*. Not bad for someone who could barely understand the jargon before. Sadly, with all the work I was doing to help support global researchers, my boys were never actually part of any research project in Australia because no one here was interested in researching a rare disease that couldn't muster up much funding. Rare diseases often get shorted because they are rare, delaying understanding of and treatments for them.

The diagnosis *was* a positive turning point in one respect: We knew what we were up against. We knew now how things might play out in the future and were prepared. Prior to the diagnosis, we were all living day by day, constantly wondering and worrying about the cause of everything. Could it be treated? Could it be stopped? Could it be fixed? Whereas once we got the diagnosis, we knew this disease couldn't be treated, couldn't be stopped, couldn't be fixed.

Mentally, I knew this. Emotionally, I was still in denial that our boys would follow the same fate as so many others. With a diagnosis, I knew we'd be looking after our boys the best we could for the rest of their lives, but I still held onto that kernel of hope that we'd avoid the worst of it. In comparing notes with other families of children with Adsl Deficiency, I'd been hopeful that my boys hadn't developed seizures at the very young ages of other children.

I thought it would be different. That our family would be different. Before the diagnosis, when William was a baby I didn't know any better, so I could still hope we'd get through it. After the diagnosis, I had the truth, but thought like any parent that we'd beat the odds. In my heart of hearts, I didn't believe I'd lose both my boys, especially Hamish, who looked and acted so normal for the first three months of his life. The diagnosis started a period of anticipatory grief, in which a person anticipates a future loss, but while there is a type of mourning there, because you are still in it and living through it, the grief doesn't hit home. Not really. You're in a kind of stasis, waiting for grief instead of feeling it. It takes the actual, full loss to set the real grief process in motion.

I know now that all I needed to do was to retrain my brain to focus on what we can do to give them and us the best life possible. We'd become the parents, not of children who would get through hurdles to become normal, but of children who would forever be rare and special. Who would need us for the rest of their lives. Who would love them, just as they were.

The only way I can think to describe raising a rare child is a prose poem I read by Emily Perl Kingsley, written in 1987, called "Welcome to Holland."* Since I started this chapter quoting science, it feels appropriate that at its end, marking the end of my innocence, if you will, that I quote poetry, for when science fails us, the only thing we have left is art.

With permission from the author, here is that poem in its entirety.

> *I am often asked to describe the experience of raising a*
>   *child with a disability—to try to help people who*
>   *have not shared that unique experience to understand*
>   *it, to imagine how it would feel. It's like this......*
> *When you're going to have a baby, it's like planning a fabulous*
>   *vacation trip—to Italy. You buy a bunch of guide books*
>   *and make your wonderful plans. The Coliseum. The*
>   *Michelangelo David. The gondolas in Venice. You may learn*
>   *some handy phrases in Italian. It's all very exciting.*
> *After months of eager anticipation, the day finally arrives. You pack*
>   *your bags and off you go. Several hours later, the plane lands.*
>   *The flight attendant comes in and says, "Welcome to Holland."*
> *"Holland?!?" you say. "What do you mean Holland?? I*
>   *signed up for Italy! I'm supposed to be in Italy. All*
>   *my life I've dreamed of going to Italy"*
> *But there's been a change in the flight plan. They've*
>   *landed in Holland and there you must stay.*
> *The important thing is that they haven't taken you to*

---

\* © 1987 by Emily Perl Kingsley
All rights reserved
Reprinted by permission of the author

*a horrible, disgusting, filthy place, full of pestilence, famine and disease. It's just a different place.*

*So you must go out and buy new guide books. And you must learn a whole new language. And you will meet a whole new group of people you would never have met.*

*It's just a different place. It's slower-paced than Italy, less flashy than Italy. But after you've been there for a while and you catch your breath, you look around.... and you begin to notice that Holland has windmills....and Holland has tulips. Holland even has Rembrandts.*

*But everyone you know is busy coming and going from Italy... and they're all bragging about what a wonderful time they had there. And for the rest of your life, you will say "Yes, that's where I was supposed to go. That's what I had planned."*

*And the pain of that will never, ever, ever, ever go away... because the loss of that dream is a very very significant loss.*

*But... if you spend your life mourning the fact that you didn't get to Italy, you may never be free to enjoy the very special, the very lovely things ... about Holland.*

*Chapter 9*

# STATUS EPILEPTICUS

THE FIRST TIME I REALISED WILLIAM WAS SEIZING, I CAME into his room to check on him and found him lying in a pool of his own saliva on his bed, unable to close his mouth. He was still actively seizing. He was about four years old and one year out from his diagnosis. He'd just started kindergarten.

It was a few weeks after his four-year-old vaccinations. He had a massive inflammatory response on his right thigh at the sight of his MMR vaccination and subsequently became very unwell, with fevers and uncharacteristic irritability that lasted for a few days afterwards. It took a little over a week for the swelling to finally subside. For a couple of weeks afterwards he wasn't himself; he was quite lethargic and struggled with his balance and visual focus more than usual. Something was different about him.

This wasn't the first time one of my boys seemed to have an

extreme reaction to a vaccine and it wouldn't be the last. I ended up asking the doctors to space out the boys' vaccines. The doctors agreed with me, and while my boys got all their shots, and didn't have to worry about other diseases on top of their genetic one, they got them one at a time with a lot of lag time in between. It seemed to help but I began to wonder if Adsl Deficiency, being a metabolic issue that affected the body's ability to process neurotoxins, belonged in the family of rare conditions that vaccines make worse, and so should have a contraindication.

Meanwhile, four-year-old William was taking a lot of rousing to wake up in the morning and when he did wake he was very groggy. I began noticing his pillow and his pyjama tops were wet with saliva. At the time I guess I was hoping it was just him sucking his finger as he slept. Then early one morning I went in to check on him and he was limp but breathing very loudly with his head and left cheek lying in a pool of frothy saliva. I have no idea how long he had been there in that state but I assumed it had been at least three hours since the last time I checked on him. "William? William! Wake up!" I called, touching his unresponsive body. Immediately I thought, *Oh my God, he's had a seizure!* I sat there with him as he slowly started to wake, all dazed and confused.

After this experience, one of the doctors suggested that maybe we use a seizure detection mat that fitted over his bed and that had embedded sensors that would sound an alarm on a portable pager that we could have by our own bed. But the problem with this was that William also had repetitive behaviours, like his hand shaking, that he'd do when he woke up at night. As soon as he shook his hand, the bloody alarm on the mat would go off. Scotty and I would jump bolt upright in bed and race to his room to check on him to see him kneeling on his bed, bouncing up and down in complete darkness and surprised and happy to see us. The pager was loud enough to wake Hamish up as well, who at only two years old needed soothing also to go back to sleep. Then of course we had a hard time trying to go back to sleep. We'd just drift off and the pager would sound again. We tried to adjust the mat's settings to match the severity of William's tremors but after a few sleepless nights the mat was rendered completely useless for monitoring anything. We got rid of the seizure mat.

To replace it, I put a video monitor in William's bedroom, like ones you use with babies. Intuitively, I'd open my eyes in the middle of the night to check the monitor and I could see him moving strangely in the video. "William's having a seizure!" I'd yell to Scotty, throwing back the covers and running down the hall to his bedroom where we'd find him unconscious and seizing on his back with his arms flailing in the air, saliva frothing out of his mouth. It was a horrifying sight, especially since we were still new to seizures, but by this point I could control my panic to keep him comfortable and safe. He was small enough to manoeuvre into a recovery side position while he was still seizing, on his side so he wouldn't swallow or bite his tongue. We'd surrounded him with pillows to help support his arms as they jerked around. And we'd stay by him, repeating "It's okay" in gentle, soothing voices. A few minutes would pass and the seizure would stop and he'd drift off to sleep and stay asleep for hours.

There was no end to the worry after that. At three years old, babies start growing out of the stage where you follow them around closely, waiting for them to get a fever or put something in their mouths or try to climb something they shouldn't. At four or five, parents can trust they can take their eyes off their kids for a moment and take a breath without something dire happening. With my boys, there was no end in sight to their 24/7 care. It's not like they're going off and playing with friends at the end of the school day, they're with me a hundred percent of the time and they need a hundred percent care. Just like a mother of a young baby, they were completely dependent on me and would most likely be for the rest of their lives.

Not only did they need help with all their daily needs, they needed constant surveillance, as now that the seizures had started, they were unpredictable. You couldn't turn your back on William for a minute. If he wasn't in his wheelchair properly, he could be slumped over and his air supply cut off in moments, and it's then I or whoever was watching him would have to be prepared to get him out of his chair and use CPR to resuscitate him.

About two years after they started, the seizures took hold of William and didn't let go. William's seizures became longer. He'd seize for three to five minutes. And they became more frequent. They'd cluster. He'd have three separate seizures, one right after the other. Thankfully, he managed to breathe normally through his seizures, so as scary as they looked I didn't worry as much about them threatening his life.

Hamish started having seizures around four years old as well. Like his brother, they became more consistent with monthly clusters when he was around six years old. His seizures were different in that they were shorter, lasting only one to three minutes, but his airways were often compromised, causing him to hold his breath and turn blue, which meant his seizures were more dangerous. This terrified his caretakers, who would almost immediately step in to apply CPR. Thankfully, in a brief moment of relief, I learned I didn't have to necessarily do CPR. Like I did with Hamish as a baby, I could rub him frantically or tap his back while he was on his side in a recovery position and he'd come to and start breathing again.

Why do some medications work for some and not for others? I learned that there are different types of seizures which are generally caused by something interrupting the brain's normal electrical functions. They don't all manifest like the whole body shaking you see in the movies, or what are commonly associated with epilepsy. Epileptic seizures will come up on electroencephalogram scans (EEG) that look at brain activity and often are used to diagnose common seizure disorders. And non-epileptic seizures are often not detected via EEG. There's a difference between epileptic seizures and non-epileptic seizures.

Understanding the difference between epileptic and non-epileptic seizures can be really helpful when deciphering a treatment path. Epileptic seizures are caused by abnormal electrical activity in the brain. This can happen for various reasons, such as genetic factors, brain injury, or other medical conditions. These seizures can be classified into different types, like tonic-clonic or absence seizures, and they typically respond well to anti-epileptic drugs (AEDs) designed to stabilise that electrical activity.

On the other hand, non-epileptic seizures (often called "psychogenic non-epileptic seizures" or PNES) and febrile seizures, the kind of seizures triggered by a fever in children under five, aren't linked to the same kind of electrical disruption in the brain. Instead, they might be related to psychological factors, including physiological or emotional stress, or trauma. Because of this difference in origin, standard AEDs usually don't help with non-epileptic seizures.

As for why some drugs work and others don't, it comes down to the underlying cause of the seizures. AEDs are designed to target the specific electrical disturbances associated with epilepsy, while non-epileptic seizures may require different treatment approaches, like nutritional therapy and/or stress management techniques.

Both William and Hamish exhibited various types of seizures, ranging from absence seizures—the stop-what-you-are-doing-to-stare-blankly-at-nothing, barely noticeable microseizure—to myoclonic seizures—seizures that cause muscle jerking or twitching—to tonic-clonic seizures, also referred to as grand mal seizures. Both the boys experienced all these types of seizures. The most scary were the tonic-clonic seizures that both boys started having when they were about four. My dog Stevie, a little Boston terrier, could often sense when Hamish was about to have one of these seizures and would start barking to alert me.

Early French doctors didn't name these seizures "grand mal," meaning "great evil" or "great illness," for nothing. The tonic phase comes first: The muscles suddenly stiffen in the throat and vocal chords and as a consequence the person involuntarily calls out, followed by loss of consciousness and a rapid fall to the floor. They may bite their tongue or the inside of their cheeks and drool as the face goes slack. After the tonic comes the clonic, when the person's arms and legs jerk, tightening and releasing the limbs at major joints like the elbows, hips, and knees. The tonic phase can last for a few minutes and if the person is on their back their tongue may obstruct breathing, causing the lips to turn blue. Anything over five minutes, or seizures that occur one after the other in a cluster, usually means calling the paramedics. If the person doesn't regain consciousness in between clustered seizures, they are in a state called "status epilepticus," or continuous seizing, requiring a hospital trip and emergency medication.

There came a time when we questioned all the medications we were giving the boys and to what effect they had because, for the most part, the seizures were still not under control. Both boys took Clobazam, Topriamate, Epilim, Keppra, and Midazolam—even just writing that word triggers me these days. In hospital, out of hospital, with drugs, without drugs, it all seemed to be the same in amount and intensity. In fact, it almost seemed worse with the drugs, maybe because they repressed smaller seizures until a big one was needed to reset, similar to how pressure builds up with a corked tea kettle. We also worried about missing a dose of the medication, or if they had a growth spurt and their dosages needed to be adjusted, as not enough seemed to trigger another weeklong cluster.

We used seizure drugs for a good three or four years before deciding to try it without. What had we to lose? We wanted to know who the boys were when they weren't influenced by the cocktail of drugs they were on that depressed the nervous system and altered mood. We wanted to know, was it the drugs making them sleepy or was it symptoms of the disease? After all, Adsl Deficiency was a metabolic condition that affected the body's energy production. When we tried the boys without seizure drugs—everything was about the same. Except we noticed more personality coming through in between seizure clusters.

We even tried medical cannabis for a few months; however at the time there was a lot of controversy surrounding its efficacy and it hadn't been FDA approved (Australia often follows US drug guidelines) until later, so our doctors didn't support it. This meant we had to go it alone if we wanted to keep using it and get it sourced privately. Then we became ineligible for the clinical trial that later transpired, which is pretty much how early adoption of experimental treatments go.

Then there was the issue no one much thinks about with seizures unless you live with them: How do you handle them if you are driving? As the boys got older they needed more support to get around. William was no longer in a pusher pram; he transitioned into a manual wheelchair that had specialised supports for added comfort and positioning. I had my own support, my sister Catherine. I was lucky enough that she was able to attend most of the boys' appointments with me, as it was a mammoth task to manage, especially as the unpredictable nature of the seizures increased. Having another adult sitting in the back seat of the car next to the boys was especially helpful when we needed to take long road trips, as the person could help entertain and give them their snacks or a drink while I drove. They could also monitor the boys in case a seizure took hold and neck and head supports needed adjustment so their breathing wasn't obstructed. I remember driving with William in the back without this help. I looked in the rear-vision mirror and he was slumped over in his car seat. I almost had a car accident as I panic-manoeuvred across two lanes of traffic to get over to the emergency lane so I could get out and adjust him so he could breathe. That experience scared the living daylights out of me and I swore after that I'd try to always have another person with me when driving if and whenever possible. Eventually Hamish also outgrew the pusher pram and we needed another manual wheelchair for him. We began the process of purchasing a new vehicle to be specifically modified to accommodate both the boys' wheelchairs, seated one behind the other, with a passenger seat to the side so we could all travel together as a family. Our new family vehicle arrived just three weeks before William died, so sadly we never got to travel in it all together as a family.

Everyday was unpredictable. We'd start by going to each boy's bedroom. How'd they wake up? "How are you this morning, mister?" Observing their overall demeanor. Are they smiling? Did they acknowledge us? Did they give us a great big cheesy grin when we said good morning? Or did they look off?

"Hello, mate, you look like you've had a rough night." After enough practise, we'd get a general feel if a seizure was coming, usually by how tired they were. Nine out of ten nights, I'd be up three or four times to check on them, from nine at night to five in the morning when we got up. Then getting ready for school. Then shower first thing after changing their nappies. Put clothes on them in a delicate orchestration of partially holding them and partially leaning them on the bed so they were upright. Put them in their wheelchairs. Take them into the kitchen. Feed them their porridge with yogurt and berries, chia seeds, and LSA for breakfast. Medications, vitamins, and supplements. I'd do one boy and Scotty would do the other.

"William doesn't look like he's going to last too long today," Scotty would say. Sometimes while eating breakfast, one boy or the other would have a microseizure, which looked like a sudden staring off into space. This was an indicator to be on guard.

"Agreed, it looks like he's going to have a seizure," I'd respond.

"What are the chances of him having a seizure on the bus to school?"

"Yeah, I think I'll keep him home a little longer and take him to school later."

If both looked unwell, we'd keep both home. Then, *bam*! One of them would have a seizure. Then it was back to bed to sleep it off, still in his school uniform.

Some days we couldn't predict it. They'd leave the house looking so well and then twenty minutes later the school bus chaperone would call to say one of them is having a seizure. I'd drop everything and race to intercept them somewhere along the school bus route or meet them at school. Quite often, they'd both go to school looking fine and then I'd get a call from the school to say one of them had had a seizure and the ambulance was on the way. In the early days that meant whichever boy had had the seizure would be taken to hospital as an emergency with a teacher as a chaperone and I'd meet them at the hospital. If the school couldn't get a hold of me right away, nine times out of ten they'd call an ambulance, because the seizures would usually cluster, and the school's seizure management plan policy was to call the parents and an ambulance after two seizures in a row. Needless to say, I didn't venture too far away from town unless I had a backup plan for someone to attend to their care needs, usually my sister as Scotty would be working, to pick them up should there be a seizure emergency.

As the boys got older and we became more familiar with their seizures, a routine formed. The school would call to report that either William or Hamish had a seizure. I would meet the ambulance at the school. Anything over five minutes, or seizures that occur one after the other in a cluster, usually means calling paramedics.

The school staff were trained to respond to these emergency situations as were the paramedics and would administer Midazolam, a seizure emergency medicine to stop them, but it wouldn't always work. We had a formal seizure management plan in place with the school and paramedics. The ambulance would wait for me to arrive and recommend a hospital trip, or the ambulance would take the boy to the hospital. If they had too many seizures, it meant a short hospital stay to recover.

They'd check my son over to make sure he was okay. I'd take both boys home and spend the rest of the day at home to recover. If we went to the hospital we would do the same thing in the hospital, except instead of four hours at home in a familiar bed, we'd be in the emergency room while William or Hamish slept after the seizures. Then they'd wake up well enough and we'd take them home. The doctors would run some general tests which never gave us new information. Once we knew this was a real pattern and this was how our life was going to be we chose to care for them at home. So when either boy had a seizure, we'd bring them home to sleep and recover rather than spend a day or two at the hospital. We were all much more comfortable at home.

Seizures are frightening—especially for those watching. The

person experiencing them may or may not be aware it's happening. Many have no memory of the event and often feel tired, irritable, or disoriented afterwards. For our boys, seizures were always followed by deep exhaustion and long naps.

I know the fear seizures bring, especially with a condition like Adsl Deficiency, where a seizure can feel relentless. But in our case, seizures were a symptom of something deeper: a buildup of neurotoxins their bodies couldn't eliminate. These toxins overwhelmed their nervous systems, causing such extreme dysregulation that the body would resort to seizing in a desperate attempt to restore balance.

It's unsettling to witness, and even to say this, but could seizures be the body's way of resetting itself? As terrifying as they are, they may not be entirely harmful. I believe they were my boys' bodies doing everything they could to regulate the chaos inside—to shed what couldn't be processed in any other way.

I began to notice a pattern; before the seizures, my boys often looked and acted unwell. They'd become withdrawn, agitated, or overly tired, with little to no eye contact. Then, a cluster of seizures would come—sometimes sending us to hospital, terrified. But afterwards, it was as if the storm had passed. They'd be calmer, brighter, more engaged. They'd make eye contact again. It was like watching the sun come out after a rain.

The boys' periodic seizures almost looked like a natural cycle, an idea which strengthened in me when I noticed William's seizure cycle often started around the twenty-third of each month, typically around the date of the full moon. I found this fascinating, although to emergency services like the police and ambulances and hospital staff this correlation was no surprise. On many occasions they told me they often scheduled heavier emergency staff around the full moons. Observing this pattern for a few years made me very curious to what effect the full moon has on physical bodies. I knew it affected the tides and menstrual cycles, even moods, but to affect something like seizures would be astonishing if true.

The body seems to do all sorts of interesting things when it wants to reset its nerves that we, as protective parents and adults, fear and want to stop. Things we don't have control over. When he was born, I thought the best thing to do was swaddle William up tight. It's what my parenting books told me to do. Supposedly, it's to give the infant comfort and security to help him sleep, and also so he doesn't wake himself (and his exhausted parents) with his twitches. But it turns out there's a physiological reason for those nightly twitches.

When I trained to become a Pilates movement therapist, one of the lessons that related to my own children and so stayed with me came from Joseph Hubertus Pilates's book *Your Health: A Corrective System of Exercising That Revolutionizes the Entire Field of Physical Education*. Originally published in 1934, he emphasised the importance of movement for babies' development and criticised the common practice of swaddling, or, as he put it, "bandaging babies so tightly they can't move." He questioned why any parent would want to bind a baby in that way.

Movement, I've come to learn, helps discharge excess energy from an overstimulated nervous system. Babies absorb a constant stream of sensory information throughout the day, and their bodies release that energy during sleep through twitches, jerks, and flails—an unconscious reset. Even adults twitch through the night, often without realising it. Crying is another natural way the body releases nervous tension. It's why babies often cry when they're overtired or overstimulated. It's not just an emotional reaction, it's physiological. By overstimulated, I mean traumatised—anything that is too much, too soon, or too fast for the nervous system to handle all at once.

As parents, we instinctively meet this need with movement, like rocking, bouncing, or walking in the pram. These rhythmic actions don't just soothe; they help a baby's nervous system co-regulate with ours, teaching them that the world is safe. When a baby's nervous system feels unsettled or unsafe, they often cry as a way of seeking reassurance and connection. That sense of being held and responded to helps build the foundation for emotional resilience and trust in the world, *providing you're doing this energetically as well*, meaning you're not just moving their body, but soothing with your voice, your presence, and your heart. Just like animals, a baby's nervous system is highly attuned to discord.

Even in the womb, movement is a key indicator of well-being. I rarely felt my boys move during pregnancy, and it worried me. Now I understand why. When movement is restricted—even unintentionally, like with tight swaddling—the body loses one of its most natural outlets for tension.

The more I learned about how movement and co-regulation shape our nervous systems from the very beginning, the more I felt called to understand what happens when that regulation breaks down. And how we might begin to restore it.

It wasn't until after William died that I experienced this for myself. In the days that followed his death, I began having tremors in my arms, strange buzzing sensations that would come and go. At first, I thought something was wrong. My doctor ran tests, but they found nothing physically concerning. What I was experiencing, it turns out, was a natural physiological response to grief.

That experience led me to discover TRE (Tension and Trauma Releasing Exercises). TRE teaches a series of simple movements that activate the body's natural tremor mechanism—a gentle, involuntary shaking that helps release stored tension from the muscles and nervous system. It's a kind of movement meditation where you become the observer, following the rhythm and flow of your body's own tremor release response.

In *Shake It Off Naturally: Reduce Stress, Anxiety, and Tension with TRE*, a great book for understanding the body's natural response to stress and trauma, Dr. David Berceli, the founder of TRE, describes watching children in war zones trembling in bomb shelters, while the adults around them remained somewhat frozen. As we grow older, many of us lose touch with these instinctive ways of releasing stress. We're taught to hold it in, stay composed, carry on. But crying, shaking, and trembling are all deeply human, biological responses—not signs of weakness, but signs of our body's attempt to heal. We need movement in stressful situations. It discharges nervous energy that would have otherwise been used to run or fight. Without that release, the energy stays locked in the body.

I remember many times having all that emotional energy trapped inside me, like the day William was taken away by the Men in Black. I wanted to scream. I wanted to chase after them. But I didn't. I kept it all bottled up inside. And the same was true for so many moments that followed—moments that shook me to my core but left no space to release what I was feeling. My body trembled for days after William died, releasing what I couldn't speak. And no wonder!

When we suppress these responses, the energy doesn't disappear. It stays stored in the body. Over time, that unreleased stress can contribute to emotional and physical illness. But when we create space for the body to express—through running, crying, laughing, shaking, or even singing—we open a pathway for release and healing.

This is why understanding the nervous system became so important to me, especially after years of witnessing my boys' seizures. I began to wonder: Were these seizures their bodies' way of trying to reset? Could those intense, involuntary movements be an attempt to discharge what their systems couldn't otherwise process?

When I watched Hamish's rigid and still body become fully mobilised during a seizure, I began to see it through a different lens. What if this was his body trying to release the tension, pain, and stress of living with a chronic condition—not just a disease, but a dis-ease? The body has its own language. It expresses what we cannot, metabolising pain, pressure, and even toxins in its own way.

TRE gave me that new lens, not just for understanding trauma, but for seeing my sons' experiences with more compassion, more curiosity, and a deeper respect for the wisdom of their bodies. I couldn't take their suffering away, but I could honour what their bodies were trying to do: survive, adapt, and let go constantly.

But the potential physiological or energetic causes of the boys' seizures did not change the reality that they were happening. And as their full-time caregiver, it was mostly up to me to manage those moments—to hold them through it, to stay calm, and to find my own ways to keep going too.

I had spent so many moments holding everything in—my fear, my grief, my rage—simply because I had to because there was no one else to lean on. The weight of caregiving had pressed against my skin, filling me with more than I knew how to carry. And then there were the mornings that reminded me just how much I was holding.

I particularly remember one morning, while Scotty was away for business. I woke up at 4:00 a.m. with the sudden urge to check on the boys. Trusting my mother's instinct, I walked into William's bedroom and he was quietly having a seizure, shaking in silence in his bed. I was comforting him as he came out of the seizure, and then he became very distressed with what appeared to be one of his legs cramping so he was screaming in pain, and then I heard a short sharp yell from Hamish in the other room. Bloody hell, he was having a seizure, too! (This was in the early days when Hamish had barely had any obvious seizures.) I stood in the hallway in between their two rooms in a state of panic, unsure of what to do and ready to cry out in pain for them myself. Fark!!! Is this our life now? I took three deep breaths and managed to stop myself from screaming. What was the point? No one will come save us. It was all up to me. All I could do was take turns and comfort both the boys. After Hamish stopped seizing I carried him into William's bed and laid him down next to William while he slept and recovered. Then I laid down between them as I continued to gently massage and release William's cramped calf muscle. After what felt like an eternity, his calf muscle released and we all fell back to sleep for another hour.

The day before I had scheduled my sister to arrive at 6:00 a.m. to mind the boys so I could go for my morning run. When she arrived I was still in my pyjamas, tired and lacking any motivation, torn between my duties as a mum and going for my run. I knew that if I didn't go, I'd miss out for the rest of the day. I did my run. I knew the boys' seizure episodes were becoming more and more unpredictable and my running wouldn't change that. I also knew what the consequences could be if I didn't honour my own self-care.

*Chapter 10*

# RUNNING FOR MY LIFE

"HOW DO YOU DO IT?" I'VE LOST COUNT OF HOW MANY TIMES over the years I've been the recipient of this comment. My short answer is often, "It's do or die." Parents really don't have a choice; it starts and ends with you.

It didn't hit home for me until William was seven and Hamish was coming in strong behind him with his own challenges related to Adsl Deficiency, how important our roles really were. That's when the seizures started to come on and turned what had been a workable life to hell. I started to have a different kind of stress as their needs became so many and so pressing: What would happen if Scotty and I died? Who was going to look after our boys? What was that going to look like? Those questions used to scare the bejesus out of me. It didn't help that a friend, who also had a child with special needs, once said to me, "They're wonderful and cute when they are babies, but when they grow up that's when the real hard work starts. Carers are harder to come by when you have adults with special needs." This conversation haunted me for years and would literally trigger mild panic attacks. We knew Adsl Deficiency was life-limiting but not by how long; there was always the possibility of our kids outliving us as adults. I would ruminate on this scenario constantly. What were the chances of me dying and the boys living? I hated the thought of Scotty having to care for both boys alone.

In 2012, about six months after the boys' diagnoses, I began having suicidal thoughts. My self-loathing was at an all-time high and my spirit was at an all-time low. My postpartum depression had morphed into clinical depression, exacerbated by the effects of prolonged sleep deprivation and the overwhelm of the boys' prognosis.

At first, the thoughts would just drop in every now and then, every other day or so. Slowly, over the course of about a month, I found myself ruminating more and more, contemplating not only my own suicide but taking my children's lives too. The negative thoughts multiplied in strength the more sleep deprived I was. I couldn't escape these thoughts or see a path that inspired living. I remember about day three of Scotty travelling for work, when I felt more alone than ever, I found myself totally preoccupied with justifying my thoughts of suicide. Without any kind of reciprocity, I wondered what the point of it all was. I entertained myself with daydreams in which the boys and I would die painlessly and peacefully. I hated violence, I was terrified of guns and blood and I didn't want to make a horrific mess for any family or friends to find, I just wanted it to be peaceful and with love. I thought maybe I could drug myself and the boys, and we'd all die quietly in our sleep…

Now, I know that as a parent it goes against every cell in your body to hurt your children, as you innately want to protect and do what's best for them, but when suicidal ideation takes hold, the brain twists itself into ways of thinking that are no longer recognizable as reasonable or normal. I felt our existence was a punishment to others and our exit would end that suffering—end our suffering. In a way, I *was* protecting and doing what was best for my sons by killing us all. I guess, in its own way, as a parent it was a twisted form of protection as I was terrified of what was to come—all the unknowns of the disease, the unclear prognosis, how long they would live, how they might die on their own terms—the suspense was agonising. I loved a challenge but I felt living this life was going to be hands-down cruel. It was all too much to process and so hard to fathom. I thought the only way out was to check out and start again.

*But, what if it all went wrong and your murders-suicide plan failed and one of you didn't die? You don't want your boys to die without you and you don't want your boys to live without you, either. You love them. If you die without them, they won't understand why or where you've gone. Can you imagine someone else raising them?*

Well, I'll be dead, so what would it matter what I thought? I told this other voice in my head.

*What about all the people you love who know and love your boys? How would this traumatic event impact them? Picture all of their faces individually as if they were just told the news. How brutally cruel this plan would be to them, especially Scotty! He would be absolutely devastated that you were gone.*

Scotty will be better off without me.

*What about your children? You're not being rational, Natalie, you love your children! William's not even four years old and Hamish is only eighteen months! They are totally innocent to all of these morbid, self-destructive thoughts!*

Maybe I can be a little self-destructive sometimes.

*You say you don't want to hurt anyone? You're thinking about killing yourself and your children, for fuck's sake! Get help! You need to get help! Now!*

These panicked shouts from what was left of my rational, higher self ultimately saved me. This wasn't the real me, daydreaming of my suicide, this was another side, my fear side, my shadow side, trying to convince me I couldn't cope. I was being selfish and naive for not wanting to or knowing how to alter my views, turning from thoughts on what the disease took away from me to how my life could be enriched by the challenges that I faced by being my boys' mother. In the end, I didn't want to hurt others, and that overrode the creeping depression and suicidal ideation. I realised I needed to find something that could pull myself up out of my own mental mess.

I don't think I realised how much stress and sleep deprivation can affect your mental health. I wanted the people I loved to be proud of me, instead of hurting them and leaving them with the trauma of me taking the easy way out. I knew if I could get myself and the boys the help that we needed then we could all have an amazing life. I needed help, home help, additional support to assist in our children's therapies. I needed to feel heard, and like I wasn't trapped by my caregiving tasks anymore. I needed to find a purpose for myself outside being a caregiver. What I really wanted was to not only stay alive but to thrive in view of our circumstances.

So I finally spoke to someone, first my eldest sister. I told her how miserable I was. Thankfully, she followed textbook suicide prevention recommendations and asked straight out, "Nat, are you having suicidal thoughts?"

"Yes," I reluctantly confessed.

She talked me through that for a while and then told me that I should go see my doctor. The next day I took myself to the doctor who promptly tested my thyroid and a few days later I was diagnosed with the thyroid disease Hashimoto's thyroiditis, which for the record can leave a person feeling extremely lethargic and depressed; coupled with what I had going on in my life, the condition left me susceptible to physical and emotional overwhelm.

Scotty had his career and his way of managing his stress levels better than me. Every day he'd go for a run to clear his head. I realised that I needed to find a passion and purpose outside of being a mum and housewife. I knew something had to die and I would choose to kill my negative, self-limiting beliefs instead of myself. I also realised that I'd gotten to this state, in part, because I'd spent all my time caring for my boys and left no time to care for myself.

My mantra for the next few months became: "I choose to save myself!" My doctor prescribed some antidepressants and within a week of taking them I started to feel a little better. By the third week, I started feeling inspired. I began by creating my own vision board in my walk-in pantry. Every day, I took time out for myself for a personal goal: researching information about diets and nutritional supplements to improve our overall physical and mental health, reading and listening to inspiring podcasts and self-help audio books while hanging out washing, cleaning house, or going for long walks through the bush. Within three months, I stopped taking the antidepressants entirely. Still juggling our life together and somewhat sleep deprived, I began to visualise a positive future for my family that embraced all of our adversity and led me to accept that we were in Holland instead of Italy and that right here, right now, we were all okay.

One book that helped me reframe our future was Carol Dweck's *Mindset*. It explores how to switch a mindset from being fixed, meaning unable to think it can change, to that of growth, being open to learning from mistakes and working at something until it's mastered. I knew I had to develop a growth mindset that would let me grow in the face of our adversity, keeping focus on what I could control and letting go of what I couldn't. I knew that if I was to be the best version of myself—if I was to kill my old self, metaphorically this time, and transform—I needed to strengthen my mental and emotional resilience.

I tried to eat healthy and although I had lost ten kilos after Hamish was born I still needed to lose another fifteen to be anywhere near my healthier goal weight. My sister Catherine had her own fitness goals, so we made a pledge to each other that we would train for and complete our first half-marathons together. Over the next twelve weeks, Scotty and I worked as a team caring for the boys. Some mornings he'd mind the boys while I ran and vice versa and then, while he was away for work, my sister would come at 6:00 a.m. and mind the boys so I could go for my morning run. We also had paid carers come and mind the boys on Sunday mornings for several hours so Scotty and I could do our individual long runs.

So, I found my passion for feeling good, and my way back to running again, something I'd loved to do before my pregnancies and the boys filled my time. The further I ran the more I believed in myself and the more positive I felt for the future. Running was my new all-natural antidepressant. Sadness, loss, grief, disappointment, guilt, shame, feelings of not being enough—all disappeared when I chose to go for a run. Each session left me feeling proud that I had achieved something greater than I had yesterday, and that sense of accomplishment made me move through my depression on a daily basis, like a horse galloping through an open field. I loved the dopamine high during my morning run and all the feel-good endorphins that would last for hours afterwards.

Six weeks later my sister and I ran our first half-marathon, the Gold Coast Half-Marathon. I remember it being quite warm at 7:30 in the morning and at about the sixteen-kilometre mark I was busting to go to the toilet but they were still another kilometre away. I thought I'd make it no problem but I underestimated my eighteen-month postpartum pelvic floor. When I finally reached the toilets there was a queue of six people waiting and by the time it was down to two people I couldn't hold it any longer. Yep, I wet my pants. I was so embarrassed but no one else seemed to care. I shuffled my wet self over to the drink fountain and washed my legs down with water outside the toilets. I was saturated all over with water and hoped no one could tell whether or not I'd wet myself or whether I just ran under the sprinkler. But wet pants and all, I finished the half-marathon in two hours and forty-five minutes. My training goal was for two hours and fifteen minutes. So while I was happy that I finished, I wasn't happy with my time, especially since Catherine, who was fifteen years older than me, was waiting at the finish line for over half an hour. But that's life, eh? Sometimes you train for glory…then remember your pelvic *flaw*. We look back and laugh about it now. It's a great memory and I'm so proud that we did it together.

Me and sister Catherine 2010

I struggled a bit after this accomplishment. I now had what runners call post-marathon depression. My old self-sabotaging thoughts beat me up for not meeting my initial time goal. I didn't think, jeez, I'd just run my first half-marathon! I'll do better next time! I wasn't in that growth mindset yet. Then the limiting mindset would try to sabotage my attempts of self-care by suggesting that I shouldn't be going out for a run when I had all my parental responsibilities. "Running shouldn't be your priority," it scolded. "You're going to miss out on some special moment with your boys!" I had to fight through the classic mummy guilt to regrasp my newfound confidence and personhood, and what better way to do that than with other mums who love to run too.

Shortly after this first half-marathon, I met Michelle, who would become one of my greatest friends. Her daughter attended the same kindergarten William attended and we served on the Kinder Committee together. One day we got chatting and discovered that our husbands had been running with each other for the past few months in a men's group and we joked about their running bromance. Well, why couldn't we form our own sisterhood? So my "sole sister" and I joined a local women's run group called the Gazelles. I'd laugh at calling myself a Gazelle as I felt I was anything but a gazelle, but we would meet each week for a social run and then join our husbands at the local runners' cross-country club.

Nearly all of Scotty and my social activities soon revolved around running. We'd plan the run event we wanted to run, train for it, and then make it our weekend away. We'd take turns to have a weekend away from our parenting duties as individual respite. One weekend I joined the Gazelles at a girls-only run camp they had organised. It was held at a twenty-room lodge in Daylesford, Victoria. It had an indoor pool and beautiful gardens, an ideal setting for wedding receptions. I think there were about sixteen Gazelles who attended, some of us newbies and many others who had been running for years. I got to room with my sole sister and another Gazelle for the weekend, making the event feel even more like a girls' slumber party. Of course we did a lot of running, but mixed it in around events similar to what you'd see on *The Amazing Race* or the Olympics, albeit if the Olympics were on a much smaller and more casual scale. This group of women became a real source of fun and joy for me and I became as obsessed with all things running as they were. In fact, the run camp was held in the final weeks of my training for my second half-marathon, the Run Melbourne Half-Marathon.

I decided to participate in a fun activity structured like a mini Olympics team event. Each team needed a representative for each leg of the race: an egg and spoon sprint, a sack race, tug-of-war, and rhythmic gymnastics. My team nominated me as the rhythmic gymnast. I was handed two twirling ribbons and a pair of hot pink leotards which I pulled on over my activewear, and within an instant I was transformed into…something like a gymnast. My competitor from the other team and I had to prepare and complete a rhythmic dance routine. Talk about hilarious! Two middle-aged women dancing around the room twirling ribbons in our ill-fitting neon leotards, challenging each other with crazy dance moves while a crowd of onlooking Gazelles clapped and yelled with encouragement. The moves became more and more challenging to win points over our opponent. My competitor did some funky moves and the other Gazelles roared with laughter and cheered us on. *Wow*, I thought, *that was pretty cool! How do I beat that move?* I was exhausted yet determined for our team to win so I threw my legs in the air over my head, and did a cartwheel!

A cartwheel! What the hell was I thinking? I hadn't done a cartwheel sober since I was fourteen years old! I felt a tweak in my hamstring. Everyone laughed and cheered at my dance floor antics, and caught up in all the excitement I did another cartwheel.

The upside? My team won the mini Olympics with my additional cartwheel points. The downside? I had done myself a nasty hamstring injury. I was pretty sure I had torn it as the pain was radiating, and by radiating I mean throbbing, right up into my right sitz bone. I could barely walk or sit down. For the rest of the day I felt pretty sheepish and sorry for myself. We continued to have a great weekend even though I sat on the sidelines resting my sore, sorry ass. I was in good company with this amazing group of women who all had their own running war stories and various anecdotes and remedies to share that night as we sat by an open fire drinking copious amounts of champagne.

Two days later I managed to see a physiotherapist who ordered me to rest for the following week to reduce the pain and inflammation before he'd give me the all clear to run the half-marathon in just over a week's time. Ten days later, I managed to finish the half-marathon although my hamstrings and calves took a severe beating. So I finished another event injured and sorry for myself, yet this time the low coming out of it didn't last as long as the first time. I was determined to heal my torn hamstring and do it all again to improve my pace and finish my next half-marathon in under two hours and fifteen minutes, over twenty minutes faster than my last run, shaving one minute per kilometre off my pace. Running for me was never about speed so much as doing better for myself, to get faster and or go further.

After my second half-marathon I went back to my physiotherapist who was a keen runner himself. He told me I'd greatly benefit from a Pilates-based strength and condition program. He referred me to a colleague of his who taught clinical Pilates. Meanwhile my sister Catherine had also entered me into a "random act of kindness competition" to win six free Pilates classes. You just had to nominate someone who could benefit from self-care through Pilates. Yes, that would definitely be me! Catherine and my mum had been doing Pilates for the past few years and raved about it. They had been telling me to give it a go for years but up until that point I had never had the support to help mind the boys to allow myself that layer of self-care. I won the free classes and I discovered for myself all the goodness they'd raved about.

This random act of kindness would change my life. I began practising Vinyasa yoga and clinical Pilates four times per week while William was at school and my mum and sister helped watch Hamish when he wasn't at day care. I was hooked quickly on this new passion—movement was my therapy. It helped pull me through the tough days.

For the next five years, Pilates and running with the Gazelles became my respite, a vital life force for my whole family's mental health, the boys benefiting from a happier, healthier parent. My girls' weekends away for various running events and run camps are still highlights in my life.

I continued training and ran my first full marathon, the whole 42.2 kilometres of it, while I trained for my first *ultra* marathon in Tarawera, New Zealand, in tandem with Scotty, who was training for his next 100-kilometre ultra marathon in Sydney's Blue Mountains. My ultra marathon was sixty kilometres of trails through beautiful redwood forests in Rotorua. On my first attempt I didn't finish. It was cancelled due to horrendous weather conditions. Scotty had entered the one hundred kilometre event which the weather shortened to an eighty-kilometre course. He managed to finish before the weather forced the organisers to stop the event. Although I was disappointed with not being able to finish my event, I was determined to go back the following year. In 2015, I completed all sixty kilometres. I was so proud of myself! It was hard to believe that only a few years earlier, I thought my only option for a better life was to kill myself. Running helped me prove the limiting voice in my head wrong, time and time again!

Me finishing Tarawera, New Zealand, ultra marathon

Knowing what I know now about movement, it's no surprise that I beat my carer exhaustion and released stress from my body with running and exercise, but that's how I restored myself and gave myself respite. And respite, as a parent who does not get a break from the intense caregiving Adsl Deficiency requires, is not just a "break." I couldn't just take breaks. I had to do something that renewed—renewed my energy, my purpose, my passion, my spirit. Only then, when I was emotionally and physically recharged, did I show up better for my boys.

As carers, we often let ourselves down. We think we're not the ones who need help, or care. Our needs are minor compared to our loved ones, who have much bigger challenges. We're so busy caring for our children we don't care for ourselves. But we're not machines. We think, we feel, we dream, we get sick, we get tired. And when the needs are intensive and you're filling them all day, every day for years, physical, mental, and emotional exhaustion is inevitable. So who cares for the carers?

In Australia, over 2.65 million unpaid carers are giving their all, many experiencing chronic stress, financial strain, and deep social isolation according to "Caring for Others and Yourself," the Australian *2021 Carer Wellbeing Survey*. In fact, carers are more than twice as likely to face mental health challenges, and 56 percent feel socially disconnected. That's why organisations like Carers Australia and The Carers Foundation are so vital—advocating for support, funding, and resources while also creating dedicated spaces where carers can rest, learn, and heal.

As it stands, carers mostly need to do their own self-care, and that includes hobbies and interests outside of the home and those we care for. Not every parent carer is going to take up running—but finding something that lights you up, something that moves *you*, is so important.

Running truly did save me. It gave me strength when I felt depleted, and clarity after long, sleepless nights filled with seizures and worry. It became a reset button—lifting my mood, restoring my confidence, and reminding me that I was capable of more than just surviving. One of my favourite quotes by Joseph Pilates is, "It's the mind itself which shapes the body." If you can see the change you want to become—and believe in it—you can move towards it. That idea doesn't apply just to fitness; it touches every part of us—physical, emotional, and mental.

But when we lose sight of that vision, when life wears us down or demands too much, something in us begins to fray. There's a disconnect, a kind of inner dissonance, between the life we're living and the one we dreamed of. That's when self-care becomes not just important—but essential.

I began to understand—self-care wasn't just about caring for the physical body, but also nurturing the mind and heart of what matters. Especially in the world of special needs parenting, self-care isn't all bubble baths and scented candles. It's knowing yourself well enough to recognise when something's out of alignment—when your energy dips, your patience thins, or your emotions start to overwhelm you. It's a daily practice of tuning in, of checking the emotional dashboard. Sometimes it looks like movement; other times, like stillness. Often, it means sitting with discomfort, facing hard truths, and showing yourself the same kindness you'd offer your child. It's re-parenting yourself with grace. Self-care, I've since learned, is less about what you do and more about how you listen—and how gently you respond.

That mindset—of pacing myself, listening inwards, and honouring where I was—became my foundation. I wasn't just training my body to go further; I was strengthening my belief that I could handle whatever came next. I stopped measuring my worth against others. It didn't matter how fast I moved—it mattered that I kept showing up, one step at a time.

This marathon mindset, paired with a growing sense of self-trust, gave me the confidence to stop just surviving and start dreaming again. It dared me to follow what lit me up, to take my passion seriously, and to believe that my own well-being mattered too. That shift—subtle at first—would go on to shape some of the boldest steps I would take in the years ahead.

Chapter 11

# THE COST OF CARING

IN 2015, HAMISH NEEDED A PSYCH EVALUATION TO QUALIFY him for the same special developmental school William was attending. The therapist who conducted the session for Hamish also did a quick check-in with me, as therapists do.

"How's family life?" he tossed off.

"Pretty shit at the moment," I said honestly. "I've just driven for two hours on my own to this appointment." Hamish growled loudly, obviously mirroring my mood as I tried to be heard over him.

"Why did you travel alone?" he asked, curious about my abruptness.

"Because William stayed home with his aunty today, he's had lots of seizures this week." I then continued to whinge about the traffic getting there, and that Scotty was interstate for work. At the end of my rant, I said, "I'm sorry, that was out of line. I'm just tired and speaking my thoughts."

The therapist's mouth quirked in recognition tinted with sadness. "That's par for the course in special needs families, I'm afraid. The women go crazy and the men get going."

*How rude!* I thought. Out loud I said, "It's not that bad really."

"Hmm," the therapist said, pursing his lips in a telling pause. "Make sure you and your husband both get respite together."

His words would prove prophetic.

When I was young, I had ambitions. I wanted to be a vet. A singer-songwriter. A teacher. Most of all, I wanted the financial comfort I lacked. As a young manager, I thrived on challenges. The moment someone said, "That can't be done," I'd jump in with a grin—"Oh, a challenge? Sounds like fun! Sign me up!" I took on every opportunity, rarely took sick days, and poured myself into special projects that excited me and led to promotions. No matter what, I got the job done. That's why I moved to Sydney and met Scotty. I had a desire to be financially independent. Some might call it a strong work ethic, but looking back, I wonder if I was more of a people pleaser than I realised.

I was back to part-time work after William was born. Because my job was part-time, I saw my husband's job as more important. He was the breadwinner and so needed a safe and secure career to support us all. He had some flexibility after we moved to work from home, but he did have to travel interstate and internationally for various projects and work meetings each month or so. I made sure that he didn't have to give up leave to care for the boys. I'd be the primary caretaker of our sons, the role we agreed upon when we decided to start a family. But as the boys got older and the seizures started I could barely maintain even my small job. I often felt like everyone was watching, waiting for me to stuff it all up when I could no longer handle the role. I worried that I would never regain financial independence again. One of my most cherished roles was being sacrificed for others.

Life, as I have come to learn, sometimes feels like a stage, and parents of children with rare diseases and special needs play a multitude of roles—each one representing a different facet of our identities and journeys. The images of these roles are not unlike archetypes in a tarot or oracle card deck.

I'm the Parent. As a parent, I embrace the concept of teamwork. My partner and I constantly engage in discussions about how best to manage our children's lives. It's like a beautifully choreographed dance; we're in sync, agreeing on strategies, therapies, and daily routines. Every decision, big or small, carries weight. From planning doctor visits to deciding on the right therapies, our role as parents is to work in unison. We have our disagreements, of course, but at the end of the day, the well-being of our children is what binds us together. It's a partnership, a commitment to our children's needs, and a promise to navigate the complexities of their lives side by side.

I'm the Carer. From the pragmatic therapist mindful of body mechanics and regular movement exercises that will help meet the boys' developmental milestones to the empathetic personal carer managing daily schedules, appointments, seizures, medications, feeding, bathing, and toileting to ensure the best level of comfort and quality of life for her patients.

I'm the Mother. This is the nurturing side of me. In this role, I embody femininity, warmth, and affection. I'm the soother, the calm within the storm. My touch can be a source of comfort and my words and songs a source of reassurance. I strive to be tactile and present, to give my children the love they need to feel safe and secure. I remember the gentle way I would stroke their hair as they fell asleep, whispering sweet nothings or singing quiet pop ballads and lullabies to calm their fears. In these tender moments, I feel my strength as a mother radiate, reminding me that love is a powerful healer. I had the hardest time when I put my Mother's hat back on after being the pragmatic Carer. All those feelings would come rushing in and if I wasn't so responsible I'd have fallen to my knees.

I'm the Provider. The pressure to keep a job with steady income as the sole income producer knowing we'll sink as a family if there's no money coming in. Paying the mortgage and all the bills and what's left over to provide for a quality of life that keeps everyone happy now and into the future. Scotty filled this role more than adequately but I loved doing my small part.

I'm the Advocate. I'd not just care for the boys in the moment, but also advocate for them in the future. Emotion is present but it's hot. I'm bringing that brave Mama Bear energy, going in full charge to make sure my sons get the therapies and treatments they need. I learn to wield knowledge as a weapon, equipping myself with information to ensure my children are not left behind. I work with specialists to obtain funding for wheelchairs, standing frames, commodes, special beds, bathroom modifications, and day-to-day personal care assistance, not to mention negotiating the NDIA planning, reports and bureaucratic red tape. I ensure others respect my children's human rights to receive the care and support they deserve. In this role, I am not just a voice; I am a force to be reckoned with, pushing boundaries and breaking down barriers for my children. This role requires tenacity and relentless determination.

I'm the Warrior. Similar to the Advocate but different, this role embodies masculine energy—a fierce protector, the one who stands on the front lines and takes hits for my family. It's not just about physical battles; it's emotional and psychological warfare too. I witness pain, loss, and struggles that no parent should have to endure, yet I stand tall, fighting for my children's rights and their futures. There's a kind of strength that comes from this role, a resilience that enables me to navigate challenges head-on. Even when my spirit feels battered, I summon the courage to continue, all in the name of love for my children.

Finally, I'm the Lover. This is the part of my being that craves connection and intimacy with my partner. Our relationship requires nurturing, understanding, and love. Love is a powerful force. It reminds me to turn to my partner for support, to share those quiet moments, and to allow vulnerability to flow. In the chaos of life, it's the little acts of love—a gentle touch, a shared glance, or a laugh that brings us back to one another, which in turn activates our pheromones and the physical desire for each other. This role is often the most challenging to fill when my own cup is empty.

Playing different roles (sometimes simultaneously)—the Parent, the Carer, the Mother, the Provider, the Advocate, the Warrior, and the Lover—is no small feat. While exhaustion often threatens to overwhelm me, I find strength and purpose in this journey. Each role is distinct and demanding in its own way, but they are all intertwined, creating a kind of tapestry that shapes the archetype of the parent of children with special needs.

The exhaustion that comes with this multifaceted existence can be overwhelming. I loved caring for my children, but Scotty and I were increasingly feeling exhausted, defeated, hopeless, and helpless. There was no end in sight to the intense caregiving, advocacy, and financial needs our boys required. In fact, as the seizures grew worse and the boys grew bigger, these only increased.

Sleep deprivation was the first resentment that began to erode our marriage. As any parent will know, sleepless nights are an expectation when raising children and if you've agreed who's going to be the main income provider then it's important that their quality of sleep is somewhat protected. In our situation, I saw it as my role to be the one on night duties so that Scotty could wake fresh because he had to be focused and sharp for his work.

We would often take turns wearing earplugs to get a decent uninterrupted sleep, so neither of us would disturb each other. However, I found that I would wear the earplugs but I couldn't switch off my motherly sensors. It's an inherent thing mothers seem to have. It would be my night off and I'd still lay there at 3:00 a.m., thoughts racing with worry and anxiety about our children's life and what I could do to help them fight this disease.

We eventually began sleeping in separate beds because I realised I slept better on my own. You see, I would finally come back to bed after attending to the boys through the night, I'd finally fall back to sleep exhausted, start snoring, which of course would wake my husband, and he'd say, "Nat, you're snoring" and wake me again. After six years of juggling this routine, I began sleeping in the room that was closer to the boys.

I bought a new bedroom suite and mattress that suited my back better and claimed the former guest room as my own sleep sanctuary. I did it all up in white: a white captain's bed with bookshelves as the headboard and drawers underneath; two white bedside tables, even though I'd be using only one; a chest of drawers; and white bedspread and linens. I actually began to prefer sleeping on my own, the sacrifice of intimacy less of a problem than I'd thought it would be. I enjoyed journaling into the middle of the night after being woken up to attend to the boys, something I couldn't do with Scotty because the bedside lamp would disturb him. Or I'd wake up early, check on the boys, get my running gear on and sneak out the front door sometimes before Scotty had even woken up. We were looking after ourselves, living under the same roof, but not really living together. We gave each other space; all our unity and care went to looking after the boys.

The rift between us grew by inches. As the boys became older and their health less predictable, I'd often leave one child at home with Dad while I took the other out with me to avoid unexpected emergencies when we were out. "It's easier to just leave one or both here with me and you go alone," Scotty took to saying. While this sounded practical in terms of care, it frustrated me in terms of relationship. I resented my husband for not making the effort to come with me. I wanted us all to go out together. I wanted to attend activities together. I wanted to be a family unit. Luckily, I had my own family in my sister and mum and other carers to help support me and take the boys out as a family. But the times we went out as a whole family—father, mother, and two brothers—became a rarity, almost as rare as Adsl Deficiency. I began feeling I was doing this all alone.

To my mind, nothing much changed in terms of Scotty's schedule after the boys were born but mine was now full to bursting with caretaking, therapy sessions, and doctors' appointments. While I scrambled to adjust my life and ambitions for the boys, it seemed to me like nothing had changed for him. He had a good secure job that provided paid leave and long service leave and superannuation. He didn't need to take days off work to look after the boys as that was my job. Sometimes he'd travel for work overseas. To be fair, I was proud of him for his success and honoured to support him, as he loved his job and was the sole provider for our young family. But as I became more subsumed under the boys' needs, more transformed and fragmented by my new roles, I couldn't help but be somewhat resentful of Scotty getting to keep some of his old life and the roles within it.

I faced a dilemma. I wanted to regain my own financial independence. If I ever wanted to earn any kind of substantial income outside of a weekly housekeeping allowance, I would have to start a new career. I'd given up on my own retail career ambitions by this stage and had used up all my employer leave entitlements. And while I was part time, I would barely receive any employer superannuation contributions payments, so my own retirement had grown at a snail's pace for the last nine years. To add insult to injury, I was barely able to sustain my part-time job, as I'd often have to cancel my shift at the last minute due to the boys' unpredictable health. Eventually, I had to give up that job altogether.

I often felt torn with my conflicting priorities. I don't know how mums with careers can do it. It all felt so unfair. What I did, all those roles I played, should have been worth more. No one with the power to make my work more validated or appreciated seemed willing or able to see what I was doing. In-home, all-day carers are a rarity compared to the rest of the population. Our work is done in private and we often do it alone. It's easy to ignore, and not see the effort and skill it requires.

William was in school, Hamish had started creche, and I had a bit more time during the day to myself. One of our Health Science university student carers was in her third year of study and in her mid-forties. She'd gone back to school to study to be an occupational therapist. One day we got talking about running and Pilates and she told me how she taught a couple of Pilates mat classes each week to supplement her income while studying at the university. She planted the seed in my mind to go back to school and study for a new career.

Initially, I was thinking of studying physiotherapy in order to help our boys. However, I wasn't sure I could handle three to four years' more of study. I decided to test the waters anyway with a shorter twelve-month course and I enrolled in the Allied Health assistant course at our local TAFE. I figured I'd have a qualification sooner and be able to start to use the knowledge to help not only my children but also others out in the community, as I knew there was a shortage of these therapy assistants. These days, Allied Health assistants are similar to what they are now calling "behaviour coaches" and work with clients under the direction of an Allied Health professional, such as an occupational therapist, speech therapist, physiotherapist, psychologist, social worker, or dietitian, aiding and assisting with clients' goal-based daily and weekly therapies by scheduling appointments, writing reports for equipment funding, and encouraging patients to complete specific treatment plans for injury, illness, or disability-related physical issues.

A year later, I remember driving home from one of my Pilates sessions thinking how good I felt after running twenty-four kilometres, the furthest I'd ever run, the day before as I trained for my first full marathon. I knew my success had a lot to thank for the time and energy I put into my recovery days, when I did gentle movement sessions of Pilates or yoga. It was then I had my light bulb moment: I had a passion for this transforming the mind and body stuff. I decided I wanted to do this for the rest of my life, not just for me, but for others.

I made some inquiries and enrolled in a diploma of Pilates movement therapy program at a Pilates college in Melbourne. For one weekend a month for the next twelve months, I'd stay in Melbourne to do my training. My ambition was modest. I wanted to start a small business working from home teaching private clients Pilates, something I knew I could do around caring for the boys. Running and Pilates had awakened me to the potential and contributions I could still make as me, Natalie, not Mum, not Carer, not any of the other roles I filled. I worried what I'd do in the future without those roles. Anticipating William's death drove home the reality that they were finite, and having something I was passionate about was important to me. However, this idea was met with some resistance from Scotty.

"Why do you need something else to focus on? Our boys should be your only priority," he responded, dismayed, when I told him what I wanted to do. His unsupportive words surprised me and played on my guilt, but my dream had taken firm hold already.

The resentment in me grew. Who did he think he was? He could do the things he wanted to do but I couldn't? Hang on a second! It was fine for him to want to coach and control, and help me get physically and mentally better, but I couldn't do what I ultimately loved and what could help others? I wasn't even working a part-time job at this point due to the boys' care needs, so if I wasn't able to leave the house to work, the least I could do was study for a useful qualification and start a small business that I could operate from home while caring for the boys. Pre-COVID-19 it was a rarity to work from home for an employer. My husband did and I thought it could be a perfect situation if we both had jobs we could do from home.

I felt the guilt and shame but enrolled anyway, and for the next eighteen months I felt he begrudgingly supported me while I studied, but it seemed the wedge between us grew wider.

The cost of caring is not only a financial burden, it demands payment from every role played in a special needs family. Scotty's and my personal goals became just that, personal, and we stopped dreaming about our future together. We no longer had the energy or desire to maintain a caring relationship outside our sons. We had become so protected by our Warrior's emotional armour that we hid what was deep inside of us, dismissing our grief and anxiety as a couple and as individuals. Without us really noticing it, our Lover roles became smaller and smaller parts of our lives until there was hardly anything left.

I let my husband, my best friend, down, and for that I am deeply sorry. I didn't know how to process what he was going through and I guess I lacked the communication skills to work through all of that with him on a deeper level. Perhaps I lacked the empathy to understand because I had been trying so hard to save myself for so long. No matter the root cause, we drifted apart while still working as a team to care for our children. We became emotionally detached from each other. Our house became a hospital of shifts, on and off, as we shared the caring roles but no longer parented together.

Looking back on those years, there is no doubt in my mind that we cared for our boys the best that we could, but we let each other down as Lovers by not taking the time to acknowledge the difference of the roles we played and what was needed from each other to sustain a healthy marriage. I suggested we have couple's therapy but therapy wasn't Scotty's thing. It was probably too little, too late anyway. The horse had already bolted out the gate. And I mean that literally.

*Chapter 12*

# THE HORSE WHO BOLTED

THEY SAY HORSES MIRROR OUR EMOTIONS—THEY FEEL WHAT we feel, often before we're even aware of it ourselves. I'd heard that before but I don't think I truly understood it until I met Scoobie. At first, I thought I was just getting a horse, fulfilling a long-held dream. But horses don't just carry us—they reflect us. And Scoobie, in his own way, started showing me parts of myself I hadn't yet faced.

Sometimes I wonder if all my relationships, both with animals and people, have always been a substitute for not allowing myself to have horses in my life. My family knew how much I'd loved horses, no matter how I denied it. My sister Linda thought it would be a beautiful gesture to give me one for my forty-seventh birthday. I'm sure Linda probably thought I'd decline her generous offer and for a moment I thought no…I shouldn't…I've got enough on my plate. Besides, how would I convince Scotty it was a great idea? We were from opposite sides of the fence on this dream too.

My running partner and sister, Catherine, had property on an acreage in Bendigo, within a short fifteen-minute walk from our house, where I could keep it. The prospect of getting a free horse with free board within walking distance from my house was too tempting to pass up. For me, horses had helped heal a lot of my grief from my parents' separation, and I wanted to share the power of connection with a big, beautiful, powerful animal with my boys. So I put all my negative reasoning aside and decided to accept my sister's offer of Scoobie, a handsome liver chestnut Welsh-Morgan cross. He was midsize at fourteen-two hands so would be a good size for my 165-centimetre height. I was so excited! I'd secretly say to William and Hamish, "We're getting a horse, boys!"

I'd been so excited at the chance to have a horse, and maybe because of our growing rift, I decided to hold off telling Scotty about my horse plans until a few days before Scoobie arrived. Scotty did not like my decision, to say the least. He was against the commitment and money a horse took, as well as the risk. "What if something happened to you?" he said bluntly. "What if that horse puts you in a wheelchair? Do you expect me to push the three of you around in wheelchairs? You're being selfish, Nat," he said, sounding scared. I knew I was taking a risk, but I could just as easily get in a car accident tomorrow. As a married couple and co-parents, I knew I should have consulted with him for a number of reasons, but I also knew he would have said no and I still would have gone ahead with it.

His automatic rejection felt like a slap in the face. I thought he was saying, in essence, "Why can't you let go of that dream, Nat?" It felt like, in being against the horse, Scotty was also against me. Against the only personal desire and happiness I'd allowed myself after a decade of caring for others. It seemed like anything I wanted was a guilty pleasure that I should be ashamed of. I couldn't understand why he couldn't find joy in something that brought me joy. It was at this point I became not only resentful, but defiant. And I realised that I was trying to regain some of my own control.

I wrote Scotty a five-page letter expressing my feelings and left it on his bedside table. In retrospect, it wasn't the brightest decision on my part to communicate something so important and emotional in a lengthy letter. I chalk it up to another symptom of our divide in that I didn't feel I could talk to my husband face-to-face. Predictably, Scotty did not take it well. The next day, he basically informed me that we'd each do our own thing and our only common goal would be caring for the boys.

"I feel like you're leaving me for a horse," Scotty complained in a rare acknowledgment of my new extracurricular activity. I was doing leg stretches on the lounge room floor in my riding gear, about to go down to my sister's place to play with Scoobie. Scotty rarely spoke to me when I was preparing for a ride, he just sped on by, hardly looking at me. The running we'd both loved—he'd started me on that path—and we'd had no problem talking over and swapping time for that activity. With the horse, though, I was on my own, and he couldn't understand why it was worth the risk.

I didn't intend to replace Scotty with a horse. I certainly seemed to care about my own wants more than his, though. By this point there was no emotional understanding or reciprocity at all between us as husband and wife, so I guess I tried to get my emotional validation from an animal instead.

William met Scoobie when I first got him in May. I'd ride him in the indoor arena at the Agistment Centre. I didn't expect the boys would ever ride Scoobie but I wanted the boys to experience his magnificent presence, to pat his hair and breathe in the smell of horse and hay. The horse was an activity that the boys and I could tend to together. Scoobie was a healthy, well-trained, and friendly horse. I hoped with a little work he would be safe enough for me to ride with my boys as I did with my sisters when I was child.

Sadly, I had Scoobie for only eight weeks before William passed away. Three of those weeks, I hardly saw the horse because I was caring for William in his final moments. It was an ill-fated time for me to get a horse, like the universe was doing all it could to laugh at me. I felt guilty for snatching the opportunity to have a horse and fulfill my childhood dream. I thought it would be a beautiful thing, to share the beauty and majesty of a horse with my children. William's death burst that dream also, replacing any moment of joy with deep sadness.

A few days after William's funeral, I took some time out to visit Scoobie at the Agistment Centre. Being around horses had soothed me before and I thought it could soothe me now. But I hadn't ridden Scoobie in weeks and our relationship was still new. He spooked at something he imagined in the corner of the arena—it could have been anything, a shadow, a sound, a bloody dust mite, who knows! Maybe because I felt guilty after my arguments with Scotty for being so selfish, or maybe because my grief for William and my failing marriage preoccupied my mind, but I wasn't prepared for Scoobie's sudden spook. He darted to the side and I lost my balance, partially coming off him. My lopsided body triggered a bigger fear reaction in him and he took off, bolting across the large indoor arena at full gallop with me grappling to regain control of the reins while I struggled not to fall off, which certainly could have led to the severe injury Scotty had feared. I managed to slow him down by having him do circles that gradually got smaller and smaller, finally coming to a full halt with him panting and snorting like a wild brumby. "Bloody hell, you stupid horse, you could have killed me!" I got off him as quickly as I could, shaking and almost crying. People came over to me saying, "Jeezus! Are you okay? You did well to stay on him, good job!" I knew at that moment any trust between Scoobie and me had been broken and we needed to do some work to repair it. Until then, I didn't think I could ever ride him again.

I had another horse friend come and ride him to see if the problem was me or him. "Yeah," she agreed, "he keeps spooking at something in the corner at the other end of the arena." We tried to work him out of it by taking him through the corner multiple times in an attempt to desensitise him to his fear in a kind of horsey exposure therapy, a common way of managing equine anxiety over places and items, but I think we ended up making the problem worse. He became more fearful of the corner and its imagined monster rather than less. I think now he'd probably hurt himself shying the first time, and associated the corner with his pain and wanted to avoid it so it couldn't hurt him again.

A friend of mine, a riding instructor in the equine therapy industry who works alongside counselors and their clients, once told me that good therapy horses will wait for someone who's experiencing big emotions. Meaning, if someone drifts off into their grief, cries, loses their balance, the horse will stop and be still, plant themselves into the ground like they are that person's only mooring in a stormy sea and gently, patiently wait for the person to recover themselves. "But some horses end up being too needy," she said. "They can't deal with someone else's trauma. If you don't put their needs before your own, they'll run or bite or kick. Those horses don't last long in therapy programs."

Looking back, Scoobie became a distraction for me after the loss of William. I went from caring for my dying son to a horse who was afraid. I wanted to have a relationship with this horse, form a bond like I'd seen other women do with their horses, but we started off on the wrong hoof, and I'd have to backtrack. I thought I needed to sort Scoobie out, but what I really needed to do was to sort myself out.

Three months after William passed I attended a weekend clinic with Sandi Simons who was greatly influenced by the acclaimed American horse trainer John Lyons. Sandi had developed her own brand of horsemanship called Cowgirl Dressage, focused on women who wanted to regain confidence with their horses and in life overall. There were eight of us at this particular Creating Confidence Clinic for Women, all from various backgrounds. Most had their own horses. I almost didn't attend because at the time I didn't have a horse float to transport Scoobie and I was terrified to float him alone. Luckily my friend Jan offered to come pick up Scoobie with her horse float and bring him back to her property where she was hosting the clinic for the next couple of days. The next morning we started the clinic in the barn with an informal meet-and-greet over coffee while our horses ate their breakfasts in the adjoining stable as we got to know these beautiful women. After our human introduction we saddled our horses and met in the arena to begin learning groundwork skills to create more confidence in the saddle.

In many ways, groundwork with horses is about understanding their nervous system—learning their triggers, their sensitivities, and how they respond to different stimuli like sound, movement, and touch. Just like humans, many horses carry unresolved trauma, often the result of past experiences with people. They're frequently taught to suppress their fear responses during training but those reactions don't disappear—they lie dormant, only to surface when something unexpected reactivates that fear. Or they have an inexperienced rider who can't contain the horse's nervous energy. In those moments, you don't want to be on their back as a horse can revert to its instinct as a prey animal, reacting suddenly and sometimes violently in an attempt to protect itself. As a horsewoman, safety becomes a priority—not just for yourself, but for the horse too. It's about building trust, learning to understand their story, and stepping into the kind of leadership that helps both horse and human feel more grounded, connected, and safe together.

On the second day, we began again with groundwork, gradually building trust and communication, before progressing to liberty work in the round pen. Liberty work takes place in a spacious ninety-foot pen, where the horse is completely free—no halter, no lead, no tack. It's just you and the horse, communicating through subtle shifts in body language and positioning. You ask for transitions—walk, trot, canter, a change of direction, and halt—without ever laying a hand on them. When done well, this practice creates a deep, intuitive bond. The horse chooses to stay with you, not because it has to, but because it wants to. That's the beauty of liberty: working together in freedom, in sync, with mutual respect and understanding at the heart of the partnership.

We entered the round pen together; I unclipped his headstall and let him free to show me the horse he really was. Of course he took off with a buck as if to give me the bird. And galloped around the outskirts of the round pen as fast as he could as if to say, "Eff you! I'm free! You can't catch me!"

It was obvious to the other attendees and fence-sitters that I was a people pleaser by the way I politely asked Scoobie to change direction. Scoobie, of course, ignored me. Then I tried again, this time getting in his way to block him and redirect him. He almost bowled me over as he rushed past me to escape the pressure I was putting him under to respond to my subtle cues. It was clear he had no respect for me or my requests. I had to earn that.

When I initially entered the round pen, I had a false confidence that my horse could see right through. He literally walked all over me. Sandi could see I was struggling to stand my ground so she offered to support me from inside the round pen. Standing with me in the centre of the pen, she held my hand and guided me through the process of reclaiming my authority with my horse. I felt her energy shift as she commanded the centre of the arena, still holding my hand. I became her shadow in tow as she redirected Scoobie with her physical cues around the round pen. "Hold on, girl," she said, reassuring me. "We need to ask—like our life depends on it!" Scoobie pushed against Sandi's boundaries at first, testing her resolve like many horses—and people—do. But when he realised she wasn't going to take no for an answer, he began to soften. With less pressure, he responded willingly, transforming into a big, gentle presence—attuned and respectful, honouring her every request. She then left the round pen for me to practise what I had just been taught with Scoobie alone. Our relationship had completely transformed.

Behaviour is communication—and animals, especially horses and dogs, are incredibly attuned to the nonverbal messages we send. Horses, in particular, respond not just to what we *do*, but to how we *feel*. Our body language, posture, breath, and even the rhythm of our heartbeat all play a role in how they interpret our intent. Energy becomes a language of its own—when we raise it, we might ask the horse to move with more urgency; when we soften it, we signal calm, inviting them to slow down or come closer.

As prey animals, horses are naturally sensitive to pressure and instinctively seek to avoid it. This makes pressure—and more importantly, the *release* of it—a powerful tool for communication. Whether asking for a change in direction or pace, we use varying degrees of energetic and physical cues to make our request clear. But the real connection happens when our internal state matches our external cues—when our mind, body, and heart are in coherence. Horses can sense that alignment, and they respond to it with trust. Sometimes, if they're distracted or push boundaries, we may need to be firmer—but true leadership doesn't come from force; it comes from clarity, consistency, and connection.

This clinic was a game changer for me personally, and what I didn't anticipate was the emotional therapy that went along with this kind of approach to training. "Your horsemanship skills are a mirror of your overall relationship skills. How is what's happening with you in the arena reflected in your daily life?" Sandi asked me later that day. Her questioning was profound and it pulled me up sharply.

Had I been communicating with Scoobie the same way I had with Scotty—unclearly, passively, and without holding my ground? Avoiding conflict instead of addressing it head-on? I hadn't asked firmly for what I needed from either of them. I'd walk away when things got hard, instead of standing my ground and communicating with clarity. But a horse feels safest when their person leads with confidence and conviction—when they know you can hold the line and protect them if needed. I wasn't doing that in my relationship. I hadn't owned my voice or honoured my boundaries.

I continued to work at repairing my relationship with Scoobie. I'd been scared to put Scoobie in a horse float. It isn't uncommon for horses to have problems going into the cramped, dark interior of a float, and the risk of a horse tripping and falling into or out of the float when loading or unloading is one of the most nerve-racking and dangerous moments for horse owners. It takes pract ise for horses to become comfortable and safe at manoeuvring their big bodies in small spaces, but done the right way they gain confidence and trust you more for it. This skill is also essential. A horse must be able to get in and out of a float if they need to be taken to an event, the vet, or if ever there was a bush fire emergency and we had to evacuate.

For the next six months, I worked with Scoobie doing groundwork and liberty and our relationship improved dramatically. I'd just have to whistle and he'd come galloping up from the bottom of the paddock, do a loop around me, and stand at my side like a dog and let me put on his headstall. I could then send Scoobie up to and into the horse float—not even leading him up to it, just pointing, and signal to him to wait before asking him to back out. I'd pat him and send him away again, galloping down across the paddock, his tail high and waving like a flag. We were attuned. I wished I learned these clear, concise communication skills earlier; it could have saved my marriage.

By the time I came to that revelation, it was too late. Scotty and I officially separated during that year, not long after William passed. The paperwork was signed, though we stayed under the same roof until I could find a place that would work for Hamish. Though the divorce wouldn't become final for two more years, we were now financially independent of each other. I bought my own small place and started teaching Pilates for a few hours a week. Along with Scotty's child support payments and a part-time job working as a weekend duty manager at a local hardware store on alternating weekends when Hamish went to visit his dad, I made ends meet. On one hand, I was excited to be starting a new chapter of my life on my own and I loved my freedom. I thought it would be easier to manage Hamish's care on my own without needing to consider and cater to a third person's physical and emotional needs. On the other hand, it was freaking terrifying and I felt like I was free-falling without a parachute. The reality of it all kicked in, and for the first time I began to feel the anxieties of being a single mum with all my emotional and financial support gone. I had to learn a new way to cope with Hamish's and my new life all alone.

At the heart of it all Scotty and I were, and still are, two good-hearted people. Who could have ever thought at that birthday party in Sydney that this would become our life? Again, what were the chances?

Nine months after I moved out with Hamish, I rehomed Scoobie.

We can't expect to ride through this life in perfect balance—perfect alignment. Maybe it's in the contrast—of our desires, our values, and of our vision for this life, that we learn the most about ourselves. It's not always easy to see it at the time, but the difference can be the mirror that shows us the edges of who we are and where we need to grow.

I wish someone had actually given me proper counselling when Scotty and I became unbalanced. I wish I hadn't been so quick to take offense, and bolt when I encountered values and a vision for the future different from my own. I wish I had known the things I do now, was the person I am now, before we split. Then again, would I be this person if we hadn't?

My ex-husband soon found a new life partner. We remained friends and continued the small niceties like wishing each other happy birthday, remembering our boys' special days, Mother's Day, Father's Day, and Christmas. We agreed we would always maintain an open line of communication for the love and care of our boys.

I was deep in grief when Scoobie bolted on me. His finely tuned nervous system picked up on what I couldn't admit—I wasn't grounded. I was masking pain with false confidence, and he sensed the disconnect. Horses rely on congruence; when our inner state doesn't match our outward signals, they feel unsafe. Scoobie didn't bolt out of disobedience—he bolted because he was scared and didn't understand this new energy. And in my human relationship, I had done the same. I wasn't fully present, and I suspect neither was Scotty. In our own ways we both ran. We bolted on each other.

This loss was another weight I carried quietly inside and no sooner had I begun to embrace the potential of my newfound independence, than the disease began to take hold of Hamish, embedding itself in ways we had never expected or experienced before. It was a cruel turning point—one that would teach us all the true meaning of resilience.

*Chapter 13*

# CAPTAIN RESILIENCE

HAMISH ALMOST DIED AND CAME BACK SO MANY TIMES I started calling him Captain Resilience. He just didn't want to quit. Resilience, I came to learn, isn't just about enduring—it's about rising after the fall, finding light in the darkest places, and bouncing back time and time again.

A few weeks before Christmas 2017 and his seventh birthday, one year after William passed, Hamish became progressively unwell. He started having more cluster seizures than usual and he'd barely have any wakeful moments. After a few days of this, Scotty and I decided to admit him into hospital so he could be monitored and the doctors could insert a nasogastric tube through his nose to his stomach so he could get nourishment and hydration, as he was barely conscious long enough to take a sip of water or eat any food.

He was in hospital for three days and continued to seize about every hour despite the emergency doses of medications to stop them. My sister Catherine came up to the hospital to sit with Hamish so I could go to my own appointments. While I was gone, Hamish began seizing again and this time he turned blue. The alarms went off on his monitors signaling he had completely stopped breathing. It was a code blue/resus. A nurse climbed onto his hospital bed and began CPR as more nurses and doctors rushed into the room. All the while Catherine looked at the havoc, thinking, "Not on my watch, Hamish! You're not going to die on my watch!" After what felt like an eternity, Hamish regained his stats and started breathing on his own again. I came back into the ward with coffee and lunch to find Scotty, Catherine, and the doctors all in discussion about the event. Hamish's seizures were getting closer together as he began to transition into status epilepticus, the state that doesn't respond to additional doses of emergency seizure medication.

The doctors asked Scotty and I to meet with them in a separate room to discuss what the next step would be in order to stop the seizures. It involved sedating Hamish so deeply that they would have to intubate him which means putting a breathing tube down his throat and into his lungs and hooking him up to a ventilator machine that would breathe for him so he could stay alive. Essentially, he would be put into an induced coma on life support to stop his seizing so that his exhausted brain and body could rest. If we agreed to this he would need to be flown to the Royal Children's Hospital (RCH) in Melbourne where he could be cared for in the paediatric intensive care unit (PICU) in a bigger regional hospital. We agreed. Scotty would travel with Hamish in the plane to the hospital. Once they had made all the ambulance and flight arrangements, they proceeded to deepen Hamish's sedation while the resus team stood by, ready to insert the tube down his throat, and Scotty standing by one side of Hamish to reassure him, in case Hamish was still aware and fearful in his unconscious state. I was at the end of the bed with Hamish's paediatrician watching the team take over his care. Tube in place, we watched the ventilator take over his breathing. They waited for him to become stable before the ambulance arrived to shuttle him to the waiting plane.

Standing there in this between space, before Hamish was whisked away to Melbourne, I was aware of the massive overhead lights in the hospital room, so bright and white, and the machines' constant beeping, keeping me on high alert, straining to hear a pause and bracing for another alarm. I remember with William, I'd asked the nurses to explain the oxygen and pulse rate stats on the machines so I could understand their readings better, so I wouldn't panic with every beep. It wasn't a peaceful place. There was an ever-present tension in the air, as if the whole building and everyone in it was focused on keeping the body going at all costs. I thought it could be a terrifying place for anyone to die.

I raced home to pack Scotty, my soon-to-be ex-husband and current housemate, and me some clothes in an overnight bag. Then I took the ninety-minute-long drive down to meet him and Hamish in the PICU at the Royal Children's Hospital. Somehow, we all arrived at the hospital at the same time that evening. That first night, we took turns sleeping in the armchairs by Hamish's side. (Why are hospital chairs so uncomfortable?) The PICU room was dark late at night, in stark contrast to the brightness of the hospital room we'd just left. More settled. Just the murmuring of the ventilator and rhythmic beeps on the stat machine. I felt like I slept with one eye open, anxiously alert to the slightest sound or signal from the PICU nurse perched at her station monitoring Hamish's life support. By the next morning, the hospital was able to allocate parent accommodation for us in the hospital, and my stress level came down a notch.

Over the next few days Hamish remained on his life support, sustained IV fluids. However, he began developing a fever and when the nurse suctioned his throat to help clear his airway, I saw a particle of rust-coloured phlegm go through the suction tube. "What was that?" I asked pointedly, fear surging through me. "I think he's got an infection."

I'd seen this with William twice before, though much worse. The last time I'd seen the ominous-coloured phlegm was a few days before he died. "Please, take a sample of that phlegm and test him for an infection," I pleaded. They assured me he was already on a course of IV antibiotics and that it would take at least twenty-four hours to get the results of the phlegm. "Please run the test anyway." Those twenty-four hours were the longest of my life. Hamish was on day five of life support and was producing a lot more of that rusty phlegm, and I was helpless to do anything about it.

Finally, the test results came back. To our horror he'd tested positive for a Golden Staph infection in his lungs. Immediately, the doctors switched over his antibiotics to one that would fight this resistant bacteria and we waited another anxious few days before he was given the all clear to come off life support.

His first attempt to come off the machines failed. Another code blue and back on life support. So we waited another couple of days before weaning him from the machines again, to see if he could breathe unsupported. The failure introduced another stressor, since too much intubation can create scar tissue in the esophagus, which can lead to other respiratory problems. He had success in coming off the machines the second time around.

In all, the seizure episode had put Hamish in the hospital for three weeks. Nine of those days he spent on life support. This was the start of the more severe stage of Adsl Deficiency. We now had to have a larger conversation around Hamish's complex care plan. How long before we administered emergency seizure medication at home, at school, and at the hospital when he went into status epilepticus? What did his care needs look like at home after he was released from the hospital? And probably the hardest consideration, did we want to resuscitate Hamish at all? After that stint in the hospital, Scotty and I concluded we didn't want to be in a hospital whenever possible. We'd keep Hamish at home.

Six months after this event, Hamish was now nine years old and we had moved into our new home closer to town. It was smaller but less upkeep and we had settled in. I had just ducked into the supermarket to pick up a few groceries and bumped into a girlfriend I hadn't seen in a while. She began telling me about this new man she was dating. "We met on Tinder, I think he's the one!" I was genuinely happy for her as she positively glowed. "You should get out there, too, girl," she encouraged.

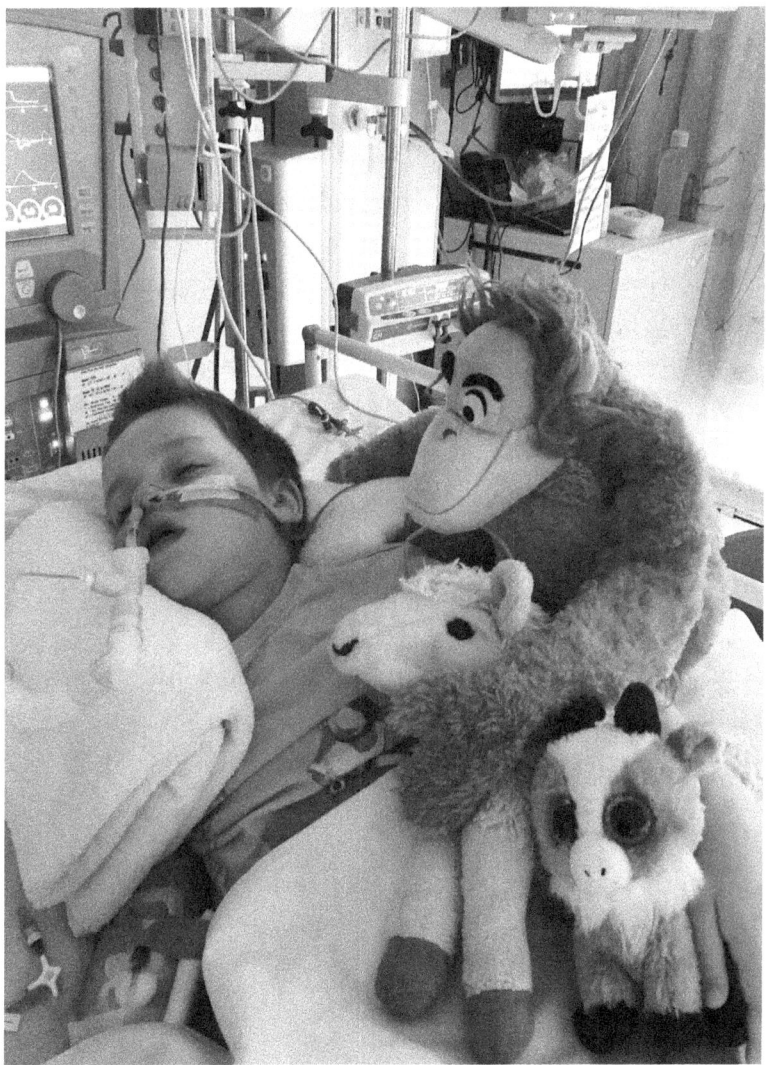

Hamish in paediatric intensive care unit 2017

"Oh no, I'm not ready for that," I replied. I didn't have the heart to burst her bubble about Hamish's recent stint in hospital. But I couldn't get her new happiness out of my head.

A few months later I started dating online, which I found to be soul destroying. With every swipe I felt more and more disappointed with life and any future love prospects I could find through an app. Sure, I had some fun times and met some interesting men, but it wore thin after a while. I couldn't help but feel that every time I told them about my life they'd run a mile. This really messed with my head as I couldn't help but think, who would want me? I have a shitload of baggage and the enormous responsibility of being a parent carer for my severely disabled son who could die in three or twenty years. Who's going to want to embrace that uncertainty and emotional roller coaster with me? No wonder they'd run a mile! I guess, in a sense, I was trying to run too. I was now love shy.

I felt a sense of shame and desperation with "needing" to find a new man to complete my life. Of course, I created a romantic ideal of this new man and all the attributes he would need to fill in order to win his way into my and Hamish's hearts. I held firm hope that a man would suddenly appear like a knight in shining armour, sweep me off my feet, and all our problems would miraculously disappear. He'd be kindhearted, emotionally sound, physically attractive, and would openly embrace and accept Hamish—coincidentally, the same values I'd expect of my future horses! And of course love horses and dogs. He'd feel comfortable enough in my son's presence to openly include him in our day-to-day activities and in our plans for the future. This was, of course, a key reason for my marriage breakdown, going out alone with my children. I hated someone being left behind.

At first, I wasn't sure why that meant so much to me but reflection showed me that family and community is one of my strongest values. My parents divorced when I was five years old and that whole family feeling was something I rarely got as a child. My immediate family has seven people and I have only a few memories of us all together in one place. We had become so dysfunctional that we couldn't attend a social gathering without it ending in some kind of disagreement with my mum or older siblings.

Having a healthy family unit is really important to me. A supportive partner says, "I'm proud to stand with you. You are my people. I've got your back. I enjoy your company. With you, I am safe to be me, without judgment or discrimination." It's strength, it's security, it's community, it's love. It's everything that makes me feel whole.

I was lucky enough to meet such a guy through more realistic and perhaps more serendipitous terms at the local gym. Andrew and I became good friends and after a few months began dating. We have been in each other's lives ever since but not without our share of new emotional challenges. He's kind of like that patient therapy horse that waits for me to come back to myself whenever I shy away or bolt.

When Andrew met Hamish for the first time, I couldn't help but feel torn between the two of them—my new man, the guy I wanted to impress, and the love of my life, Hamish. Would they accept each other? I would turn myself inside out as I played the everything's-alright-I'm-an-independent-woman-looking-after-her-disabled-son-and-life-is-good act, when in fact I was frickin' devastated that this was our life now. Of course Hamish could sense that discord. For a while, I thought I had made the biggest mistake of my life by leaving the security of my marriage. But then I'd remember the reasons why the relationship disintegrated and try to not beat myself up over it as Scotty also played his part in its demise.

Together, Andrew and I began to work through our emotional baggage from our previous relationships. That activity wasn't without its challenges. He began to see all my insecurities. Eventually, he was honest and brave enough to admit he wasn't sure if he could cope with being Hamish's stepdad. This conversation stirred up all my old doubts, which led to a new level of vulnerability. The relationship still moved forward, but at somewhat of a distance, sometimes together and sometimes apart, with no firm commitment from either of us. It felt more like friends with benefits, but of course I wanted more. Maybe we were both a little love shy.

I wondered if it was harder for men to step into the parenting role with a special needs child than it was for a woman, who may be more naturally attuned to that nurturing role. It was a really awkward space to be in and discuss with my new potential partner. I knew he carefully reserved his own opinion when Scotty and I made decisions around Hamish's care needs. I suspect he didn't want to add fuel to my anxieties or reignite sensitive issues. When tensions were high he respectfully kept his distance.

The next time we thought we'd lose Hamish was in 2019 when he was ten years old.

Then again in 2020.

Home again, Hamish developed a new mysterious symptom. We thought he was in severe pain but we couldn't work out where the pain was coming from. It was the most distressed I had ever seen Hamish and there was no way he could tell the doctors where he hurt when they examined him. We'd move his arms, move his legs, poke and prod, and he wouldn't do anything. For three weeks, every now and then, he'd scream like something was broken inside him.

Finally, we looked at his teeth and found he had developed an ulcer inside his mouth and lip. I hated brushing his teeth because I knew he hated it and I felt mean when I cleaned them by force. I couldn't use the tricks other parents do to make the process more understandable or interactive so it was a continuous battle of wills. I couldn't explain why he needed to brush his teeth in a way he'd understand. So I stuck to the old face washer over the finger technique and brushed his teeth like he was a baby. These are things I get sad about and what caused me the most guilt as a mum.

Hamish was now off his cocktail of daily seizure medications because they didn't appear to be helping, but the doctors did prescribe a form of morphine for the mysterious pain episodes.

The pain could have had something to do with Hamish's physical growth, which may or may not have been affected by the Adsl Deficiency. Hamish would be sitting in his big comfy chair watching John Mayer live in concert but his body was rigid. He was getting taller, his limbs longer, but the bigger he got the more his joints stiffened, almost like they were locked and hard to bend; it appeared he was developing contractures. I could see and feel his pain and was always looking for the magic solution that would reduce his suffering and give him a happy distraction.

Animals were always part of my life and I thought it would be good for the boys to have their companionship. After William died and I moved out with Hamish, we lost our old dog Gypsy. She was sixteen years old. So we got Stevie, a Boston terrier. I had visions of them forming a close boy-and-dog friendship, but Stevie seemed to be a little scared of Hamish, or maybe it was indifference since Hamish didn't engage her. He didn't call her over, or pet her, or feed her like she was used to from children of that size and age. Briefly, I looked after another little Boston terrier named Candy for a while and she was all over Hamish, licking his face and hands constantly while wriggling her whole body in excitement. It was clear that they had formed a connection. Unfortunately, we had to give Candy back to her breeder. I continued to encourage Stevie to make friends with Hamish. I'd bait her with food so she'd jump up on his bed, attempting to get her to sleep with him. I wanted him to have that companion dog.

Stevie remained somewhat aloof with Hamish, however, preferring to sleep on the couch when I didn't let her sleep in my bed. There was an interesting wrinkle to her relationship with Hamish. She was particularly attuned to Hamish's physical state and ever watchful. She took to barking just before Hamish had a seizure. Hamish would be in his chair off to the side of where I was sitting and Stevie would be in my lap or laying next to me asleep. Suddenly, she'd raise her head like she'd heard something that I didn't. "What is it, Stevie?" I'd ask her. And Stevie would just start barking like she sensed an intruder, but not in any particular direction. She could sense something was up, as if the energy in the room had changed. I'd look over to Hamish in his chair beside me and in that instant, his arms and legs began to reach out and suddenly stiffen, then clench back into his body as he'd call out and start to violently jerk into a full-blown seizure. Pretty soon Stevie learned that Hamish was associated with that pre-seizure vibe she was sensing and became very good at alerting me by barking in his direction.

To boost Hamish's mood, and my own, I'd often put on some fun, upbeat dance music and I'd help Hamish out of his chair and support his body. He could bear weight through his legs and his core was strong, but his rigidity meant he needed help to move his arms to the beat of the music. This was our puppet dance; he'd smile and laugh as we'd dance together.

Hamish also had a standing frame which was fully adjustable from seated to standing that he would use at school on a daily basis. Some days he liked being in the stander and others not so much and he'd protest our puppet master requests. I think he just wanted to be left alone to rest and daydream of a better life.

To keep him engaged, I encouraged any passion he seemed to express. Hamish continued to be interested in water and loved watching dolphins and whales on the TV screen. He loved the whale songs the most. I put on documentaries of whales singing and he'd sit, enraptured, wriggling his chair back and forth when the whales swam past the screen. A few months before William died, Hamish got his wish granted by the Make-A-Wish Foundation to swim with dolphins at Sea World on the Gold Coast. So Hamish, Mum, Catherine, and I all went to Queensland. It was Hamish's first time on a plane and he slept the whole way there and back. He wasn't feeling very well in the morning as he had a couple of seizures through the night. My other sisters and nephews and nieces who lived in Queensland met us at Sea World and we had a lovely day together and Hamish got to swim with the dolphins—okay, we sat with the dolphins. Hamish was still excited to be that close. I think he'd recognised the dolphins from the videos we watched. He loved going into the underwater glass domes where the sea life swam all around him while he was in his wheelchair. He gasped with excitement as the seals swam past us. It was so rewarding as a parent to witness this reaction from him. More often than not, he processed this life internally but this experience brought out another side of him.

Hamish's Make-A-Wish swim with dolphins

I wanted to give him more experiences like this. In addition to the videos of whales, I'd also play videos of horses. It may have been a bit selfish of me to want to insert my own daydreams into Hamish's mix, but I still had the hope that I could share my passion with my son. So I'd put on videos of horses running down a beach, kicking up sand and water with their hooves, and children riding horses bareback through a flower-filled meadow. Sometimes one of those dark doubts touched me, and I wondered if he understood that he'd never get to ride like the children in the videos, and if I was rubbing salt into a wound.

I was determined to let Hamish have the experience of sitting on a horse's back. My friend Jan, who had hosted the horsemanship clinics with Sandi, offered to let Hamish hang out with her gelding, Shadow. He was the complete opposite of Scoobie in terms of temperament. He was well-adjusted, well-trained, well-mannered, and respectful of people's space, though he had a bit of a pony in him that gave him enough cheek to keep things interesting. He knew how to spook in place, so if he did get scared he planted his feet and stood still.

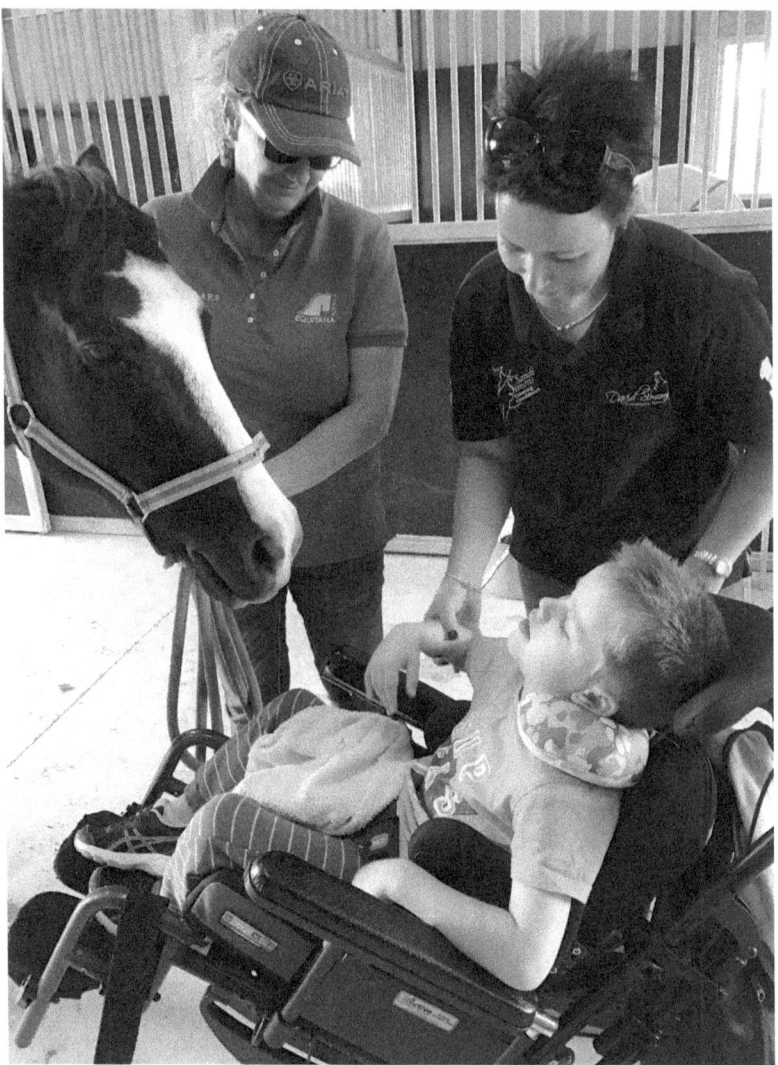

Hamish and Shadow

I walked into the cool, shaded shed at Jan's place where Shadow was kept, pushing Hamish in his wheelchair. This was the moment, as many horses are fearful of the weird contraption of a wheelchair and the humans occupying them who do unusual things. Shadow just looked at Hamish like he was anyone else and accepted him into his little space.

Once, I'd taken William to an expensive therapeutic riding facility, but I found the whole experience to be too forceful and all about William's physical body learning to ride, not about his spirit or his connection to the horse as a fellow being. I felt they were way too quick at lifting Will up and plonking him up on the horse's back and taking him for a ride around the yard. William cried the whole time. It was distressing to watch from the fence line as I wasn't even allowed in the arena to soothe him. I wanted Hamish's horse experience to be about the essence of the horse, all that spiritual and physical energy coming through both horse and human.

I remember the first time Hamish met a horse on my sister's property in Queensland. We were sitting in the grass watching the horses over the fence graze in their paddock. A big black gelding came up to Hamish and put his nose in Hamish's face. For someone visually impaired the sudden appearance of a big dark shadow carrying big energy in your line of sight can be a bit of a fright at first. But then Hamish became fascinated. He kept rocking forward on the grass trying to nudge himself closer to the fence and the horse. I could see the pull these animals had for him.

Watching Hamish with Shadow, I briefly saw the boy I would have loved him to be, a boy who got to make choices about his experiences and what he did with his body. A boy who could ride a horse if he wanted to or just stand by one and breathe. A boy who was free and not held captive by a body that held him back from his fullest potential and expression of self.

We whiled away the afternoon hours in Shadow's stall as both horse and boy stood side by side, Shadow tipping his head to gently breathe on Hamish's hair and face. Horses often do this with each other. They go up to a herd friend or family member and greet them by breathing into the other's nostrils, sharing their inner scent. "This is how I'm doing today," they say. "This is who I am. My soul to your soul. Your soul to mine." Shadow accepted Hamish for who he was and what he could do. Hamish didn't have to ride him, or act like other humans, he only had to be himself.

Hamish on Shadow

Shadow was calm enough that we were able to drape Hamish over Shadow's back, so Hamish could feel that big heart beating next to his. That went well, so we eased Hamish into a sitting position astride Shadow with Jan holding his lead and me ready to snatch Hamish off if needed. Hamish had enough core strength to sit up on Shadow, a bit rigid, but he sat up. It took a lot of energy out of him but he seemed willing to try. I was so proud of him. Happy for him. He was sitting up on a horse, doing something a lot of other kids would have loved to do but wouldn't get the chance to do. Those other kids may have done everything else, talked, walked, run, but there's not many who get the opportunity to sit on a horse. It was a special moment for me.

I bought a standing-support harness which was a body harness that Hamish could wear, and it could attach to a harness I would wear, similar in function to a tandem skydiver harness. It would enable Hamish to stand assisted for more extended periods of time with me supporting the weight of his body and arms so he had more freedom to pat and feel the horse. Then I started putting together a plan to get Hamish up on a horse more comfortably and safely. With his OT, I brainstormed how to use a sling to lift him up onto Shadow's back. The goal was to one day set up a hoist in Jan's barn to help lift Hamish into Shadow's saddle. I'd already be on the horse and Hamish would ride double in front of me, first being led by Jan and another support person to the other side of Shadow. Ultimately, I wanted to ride Shadow with Hamish on the beach. It was a dream of mine to one day ride a horse on the beach. Shadow was a likely candidate, since he was so even-tempered and already used to the beach. We'd make a documentary video of our journey together from wheelchair to saddle. It was a beautiful dream, but Hamish's condition grew worse and then COVID-19 halted all our plans, so it became another dream I had to let go.

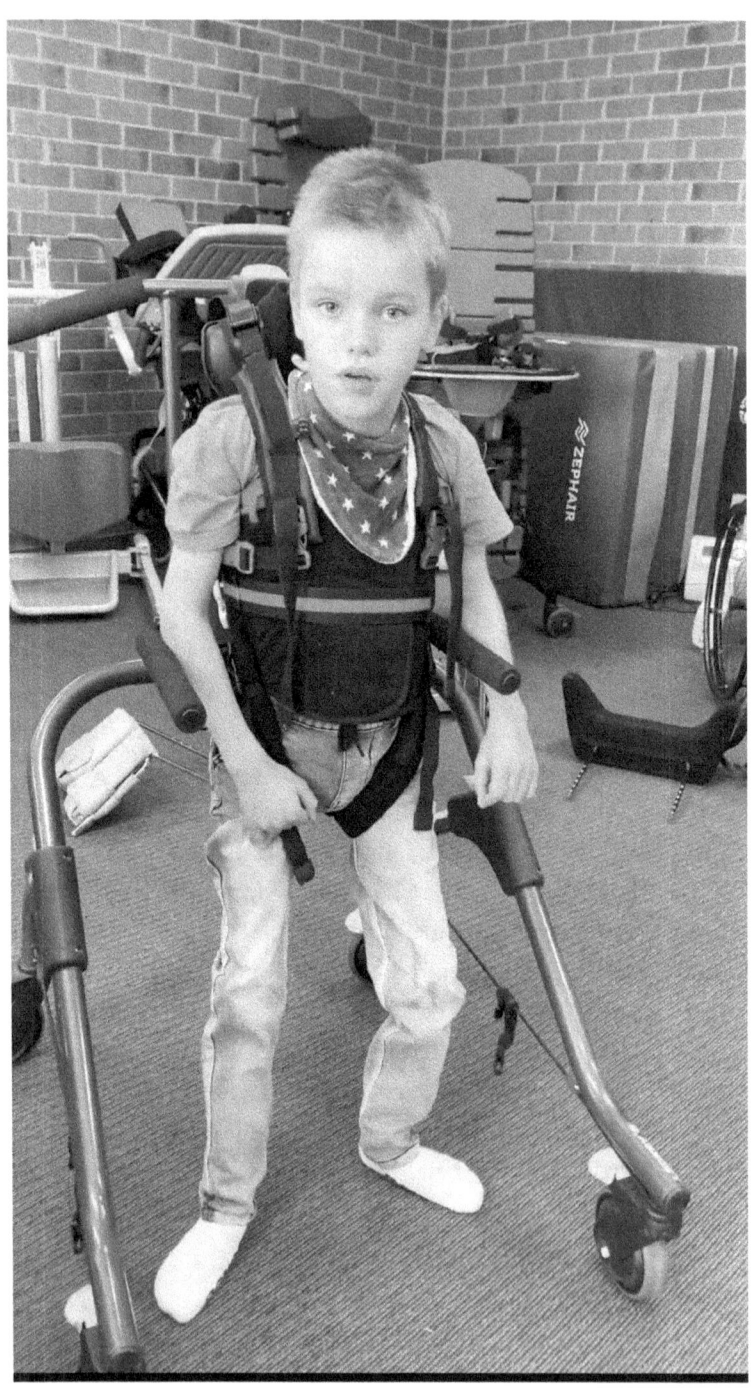
Hamish in his standing harness

In my new townhouse, Hamish's echolalia and vocalisation became an obsessive behaviour. He sounded like a chain saw and some days he'd be growling constantly for several hours and even through the night. (I was surprised he never lost his voice—at times, selfishly, somewhat disappointed too.) He also had the repetitive behaviour of rubbing his heels together and if he wasn't wearing his protective shoes or socks he caused his own friction blisters, and even then he wouldn't stop though they had to be painful. He was most in danger of hurting himself at the respite house, or with other carers, who sometimes didn't notice or were not aware of this behaviour and its consequences. Since he couldn't talk he was telling us with his body that he was extremely distressed.

I tried everything to distract him. Scotty and I even spoke to doctors about the possibility of humanely removing or altering his voice box as his near-constant vocalising was unbearable to others and limited his social activities within our community, but we were told it wasn't an ethical option and quite possibly against his human rights. I did understand this; deep down I knew Hamish was entitled to have his voice however it manifested and that he didn't know fully how his behaviours affected the people around him, but we were at our wits' end. I didn't know how torturous an unending noise could be until I had to live with it for weeks. Sedation was an option but I didn't want to do that either. So we worked hard to find a solution to relieve Hamish's stress and tension, hoping that would calm his storm.

In 2021, I discovered neurofeedback while studying to be a TRE provider to complement my Pilates teaching. One of the four books recommended in my TRE training was *The Body Keeps the Score* by Bessel van der Kolk. In this book, van der Kolk offers a new paradigm for effectively treating traumatic stress through regulation of the nervous system by syncing the body and mind while using sport, drama, yoga, mindfulness, meditation, and something called "neurofeedback." Curious, I did my own investigations and discovered a system called NeurOptimal® neurofeedback which is a form of brain training that uses a brain feedback system. Brain wave activity is recognised via an EEG, and the software processes your brain's signals in real time, detecting moments of "instability." When it identifies these fluctuations, the music or movie playing briefly pauses—which is what is called the feedback. Research has shown that it can help restore a disorganised brain and optimise executive functioning to improve overall performance, health, and wellness.

However it worked, neurofeedback seemed to help relieve Hamish's agitation, vocalisation, and repetitive behaviours significantly and gave us a reprieve for the next eighteen months. He became more settled and engaged with his immediate surroundings. I ended up purchasing the system myself and I, too, benefited from using the system a few times a week along with Hamish. But of course this wasn't a cure-all and sadly this inspiring reprieve wasn't to last.

COVID-19 was roaring to the forefront in 2021 and added another concern on top of everything else. Previous to this time I had never neglected Hamish's care or needs, but here, at this time and in this space, I struggled to find the balance I needed to cope. COVID-19 lockdowns were hard for everyone, and in particular it was difficult for Hamish, as his daily routines and activities had all been reduced. While I believe I never neglected his physical care, I do feel ashamed that my own emotional struggles and despondency made me less attentive to his emotional needs. The neurofeedback helped on a few levels but I think Hamish still missed his brother and the buzz of our old home and family unit. In the quiet isolation of the pandemic, so did I. I actually felt that he had begun to resent me. He appeared to have much more fun at his dad's place with him and his new partner, hooning around the neighbourhood in his sporty bike trailer. Or was that all in my head? At those moments, I felt extremely guilty and sorry that Hamish had to endure the family split.

I watched Hamish become sadder and sadder until I swear he, too, had developed depression. My guilt kicked in and then the shame. I had underestimated Hamish. I figured what he did not know wouldn't hurt him and I assumed that he didn't care to know or understand about our new life without his dad or his brother. Three years had passed since William had died, two years since we moved, and I had never really had those discussions with Hamish. I thought, as long as he was physically comfortable, everything would be okay. But his body became more and more rigid, and he was easily fatigued and more withdrawn. The seizures were regular and constant now, and Hamish would sleep for several hours a day, napping on and off in his wheelchair or in his big comfy lounge chair. I often wondered where he would drift off to while he napped and I hoped it was some other wonderful place.

One morning, I went into Hamish's room and he was lying in bed with his head turned away from me, looking out his window. He barely looked at me when I spoke to him. It was like he was ignoring me, so I asked, "What would you like to do today, Hamish?"

I'm not sure whether it was my experience reading his body language, empathy, or some sort of telepathy on his part, but I was dead sure Hamish replied, "*Nothing, I hate this life.*"

"I know, mate, I'm sorry. This is not how it was meant to be."

He then turned and looked right at me, and I felt him ask, "*William?*" Not in words, like "Where is William?" or "I miss William," but in a kind of transmitted thought. So I laid down on his bed next to him, both of us looking out his bedroom window at the massive neighbouring elm trees that stored their own wisdom about life and death, and I talked to him about William.

We watched the 2020 Pixar movie *Soul*, about a jazz musician who has a passion to play piano. It's what he always wanted to do but he teaches at a high school instead and lets his passion go by the wayside. He trips and falls in a hole in the street and wakes up in a hospital, but only his soul, not his body. He sees his body before he travels up to the afterlife to be processed and, after many misadventures and one stint of accidentally swapping souls with a new cat friend, he's sent back to Earth for a second chance to follow his true passion. The cartoon has a lot of good music, so I thought Hamish would like it, but the subject gave me a way to talk to Hamish about his brother, and even explain his own potential experience, since I had no way of knowing if Hamish's code blues and resuscitation episodes included any out-of-body experiences. Maybe Hamish had caught glimpses of his failing body lying in a hospital bed before getting sucked back into it when it was put on life support.

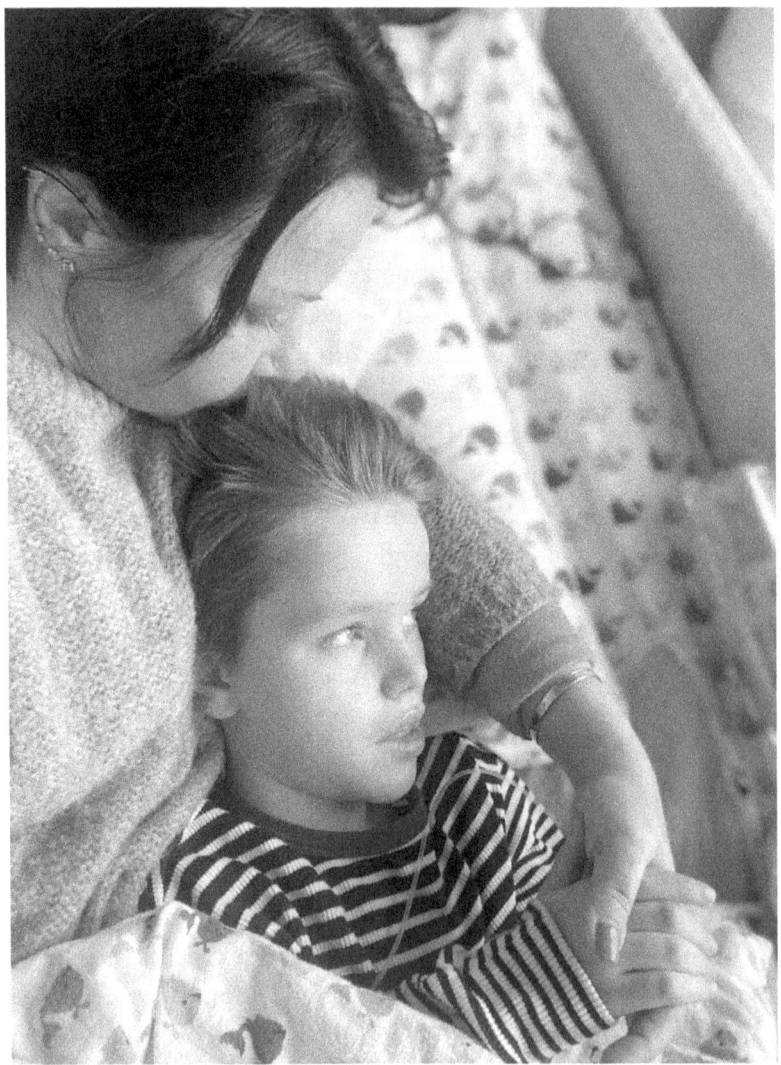

Hamish and me looking out the window

"William went to the same place the musician did. His soul left his tired, sick body and is now somewhere better. Is this where you go, too, when you're in the hospital?" I asked him. "Is this where you go when you fall asleep? You sleep so much lately, Captain Resilience. Is your dreamland so much more fun and exciting than here? Does William ever visit you in your dreams? I only hope, when you sleep, you go somewhere peaceful."

*Chapter 14*

# ART FROM THE HEART OF RESILIENCE

SCOTTY AND I WERE VERY CAUTIOUS ABOUT GIVING HAMISH THE COVID-19 vaccination because of his prior reactions to shots. Consequently, he didn't get his until February of 2022. Predictably, Hamish became quite unwell for several days afterwards. I felt guilty that I might have added more toxins to his body than his metabolic system could process, but with all the trips to hospital and the days missed from school, I reluctantly deemed the cost was worth it so he wouldn't be excluded more than necessary from social activities in the community. I sometimes wonder if that was the straw that broke the camel's back.

Through all of Hamish's hospital stays and near-death experiences, he kept bouncing back. In 2017, 2019, 2020—he'd come back to himself a few days later and be his smiling, happy self.

But a day came when Hamish didn't bounce back. After each set of cluster seizures, he came back changed, a little less than he was. His body became more and more rigid. His quality of life was diminishing, and I suppose for us too. It was like watching my child be tortured on a regular basis by his own body. The gaps between the good days and the bad days were getting smaller and smaller until he was having more bad days than good. That's when we had to start going, okay, we still hold out hope for the best but we have to accept that Hamish is suffering. Every day, more and more, he was losing his smile.

Captain Resilience was gone.

Late July 2022, I finally accepted Hamish wouldn't be able to escape his fate. We made a new complex care plan for Hamish with his doctors and palliative care team, which documented our preferences for Hamish's end-of-life care, including treatment-limiting orders. On paper, legally signed and delivered, Scotty and I would decide on Hamish's behalf if and when we would intervene if Hamish's stats started crashing. Would we try everything possible to keep him alive, like we had been, with an Artificial Nutrition and Hydration (ANH) order, or did we want a Do Not Resuscitate (DNR) or Not For Resuscitation (NFR) order? There is an enormous degree of vulnerability in having this conversation with a sick loved one, let alone the complete strangers within their medical and palliative care teams. It may well be the hardest conversation a human can have, no matter the age of the patient involved, and it's still the hardest chapter of my journey for me to write openly about. Please, bear with me, and I'll try to express it the best I can.

Christmas 2022, five years after his first major hospital stay, Hamish was unwell again. Every time he was unwell and he didn't drink enough, his seizure activity would worsen. For the first time, he developed pressure wounds on his heels. Not blisters from rubbing but an actual pressure wound. He was so rigid his legs would wrap around each other and the weight of his heels would imprint into his own feet and bed. We started using sheepskin padding around and in between his joints for added protection.

Hamish was admitted to hospital on December 29, days after his twelfth birthday and after a few days of cluster seizures. I was worried for him because he wasn't awake long enough between seizures to take in food or fluids, so I called the hospital. Even though it was a short drive, I organised patient transport because he was seizing so much he was in no state to sit upright in his wheelchair. I had no one to chaperone him in the back seat and of course there was no doubt he'd have another seizure.

His doctors ran blood tests and found he was severely dehydrated and needed IV fluids and a nasogastric tube (NGT) for extra hydration and to increase his calorie intake, like he'd gotten during his other long hospital stays. Hamish continued to have seizures but at least he was becoming hydrated and more comfortable. Technically, NGTs are a form of force feeding. A thin tube is inserted up the nose and down the esophagus to the stomach and a slurry of food and nutrients are pumped through it. The IV, an intravenous needle in his arm, would give him fluids and drugs. The nurses at our local hospital did these procedures swiftly and with minimal fuss, as nine times out of ten Hamish was too lethargic to struggle or protest against this uncomfortable procedure. When he was well enough he'd find great pleasure in pulling the NGT out, and I'd revert to using my syringe and straw technique, where I'd fill the largest syringe I could find—we called it the "horse syringe"—with a healthy protein-rich smoothie and add straw-sized flexible tubing on the end just long enough to sit on Hamish's tongue. Then I'd very slowly syringe the fluid into his mouth until he began to suck and swallow. I used this technique on and off for years with the boys and it allowed us to avoid the hospitals during the pandemic lockdowns.

However, NGTs had their drawbacks. I'd been told that overuse would lead to scarring on the esophagus which caused its own problems with respiration and eating. So I discussed with Hamish's care team the option of inserting a Percutaneous Endoscopic Gastrostomy (PEG) feeding tube. The procedure looks like this: A tube is inserted surgically into his stomach through the abdominal wall. The tube is then held in position between a mushroom-shaped retention flange in the stomach and a flat disc (skin flange) on the abdominal wall. This initial gastrostomy will stay in for three to twelve months. You attach a feeding tube to the semipermanent gastric tube to assist in hydration and nutrition, particularly in situations like Hamish's where the patient has been barely conscious for several days and only taken small sips of water. The tube allows you to eat normally when you are well and it helps with administering medications. It could be hooked up to a little portable machine that would automatically drive the fluids, both food and meds, in at a set dosage rate.

Scotty wasn't on board with the idea of PEG feeding. A few weeks after coming home, Hamish began to regress again—this time, by refusing to eat. When I offered him his favourite porridge and smoothie, he turned his head and pursed his lips, silently rejecting what once brought him joy. For Scotty, this moment felt inevitable. He believed we shouldn't bend over backwards to deny what was happening. "What about what Hamish wants?" he asked, his voice filled with sorrow. "Refusing to eat is the only way he has control over his life—and we're taking that away from him." Mealtimes had always been one of Hamish's greatest joys. He never refused food—until now. And that, more than anything, broke our hearts.

"You're giving up on him," I accused. In truth, though, I wasn't just thinking about Hamish's longevity, I was thinking about how hard it would be for me to keep feeding Hamish via the syringes and straws I'd used up till this point. Without the PEG insert into Hamish's stomach my life would be more difficult! I thought…but wait, no, that was wrong. It wasn't me that was suffering the most, it was Hamish! And my insistence on giving him nourishment was keeping his body alive enough to function, but not strong enough to do anything else. I'd turned one of Hamish's few pleasures, eating, into a mechanical function. As parents, I knew we could do a lot medically to keep him here, but now I had to ask myself, when did that end?

It was not long after I'd taken another TRE workshop that I woke up with a horrible thought: It's my fault! I'm the one responsible for my son's continued torture! I was keeping him here like this! But I could stop it. All I had to say was no to the PEG stomach feeding and honour Hamish's right to refuse food when he wanted to and let him take back control of his life the way Scotty had advocated for. Hamish was twelve and a half years old, and though he was behind on his development and there was little way to test him on his level of understanding, he was mature enough to know his brother was gone. He was mature enough to know how all this ended. My job was to love him and keep him comfortable and pain free. Like I had learned from Hamish in those moments dancing with him in his standing frame, I was not his puppet master. So at what point did I stop making him dance? My child had stopped eating, stopped engaging, stopped smiling. Was his body that much more important to me than his spirit? Even as a special needs child, Hamish had the right to make the final choice of when to live or die for himself. I'd spent Hamish's whole life trying to understand what he wanted. The least I could do was ask him.

The bedroom was bathed in a grey early-morning light when I grabbed my journal and began to write. I cleared my mind and opened myself up to our mother-son bond. *What's going on, Hamish? What do you want me to know?* These were the words that came through:

*My body is a torture prison*
*And it's you who keeps me trapped inside*
*I close my mouth, you force feed*
*It is you that keeps me alive.*

*I am bigger than this body imprisoned*
*Can't you see what I'm telling you*
*And yet when I stop breathing, you resuscitate*
*Let me go, you've done all you can do.*

*I don't deny your love and hope for me*
*I know how much you deeply care*

*But your love can no longer soothe the suffering*
*That shows through my rigid body and dissociated stare.*

*Mummy, I am tired of this tortured body*
*With all this energy trapped in inside*
*I am bigger than this body, I am an eternal soul*
*Who will connect again and communicate from the other side.*

What would I want if I were in this situation? I had never thought of care from this perspective before. As a mum, I thought everything I did was out of selfless love—until this very morning. Until these very words from Hamish. The dilemma for palliative care is often that loved ones want to do everything in their medical power to keep their family member alive, despite the consequences of possible continued suffering within the context of a life-limiting prognosis. So much so that the family member will never die naturally or comfortably. Medical science is almost miraculous in what it can do to keep a body alive, but it cares little how someone's mind and spirit feel about that. So what do I do when Nature can no longer make the decisions on life and death? When I'm the one who gets to decide how my loved one should die? When is it about their suffering, instead of mine? I'd fought so long for William and Hamish, it was all I knew as a mum—fight, to make their lives better. But what happens when that life is no longer worth fighting for? When the body is trying to die and I'm not letting it? When is enough, enough?

Early in my research of Adsl Deficiency, I stumbled across an amazing blog that shared a young family's heartbreaking journey. The mother lost her two daughters within eighteen months of each other. It happened in a slow, sad slide. The eldest daughter had been consistently seizing for quite a while, severely enough that medical intervention was required to save her. She was put in a medically induced coma with drugs to stop the seizing and then intubated and put on life support for a few days. In private communication, the mother revealed to me that when her daughter came out of the coma she'd "lost her smile." Every time heavy medical intervention was needed, it seemed the little girl lost another piece of herself. She was more and more damaged emotionally, seemingly more and more depressed. After the first daughter died in hospital, the mother decided she couldn't do it again with her other daughter and chose not to intervene in the same way when the seizures took her.

When I first heard this story, it was hard for me as a parent to understand this mother's decisions. *How could she let her daughter die?* I thought. But when it happened to me, I understood. I hadn't known what seeing my son suffer would do to me until I was in that situation. How much could I tolerate watching my own child's suffering? How many pieces of himself could I watch him lose and still see the unresponsive body in front of me as a benefit to his soul?

When you're outside of that, it is very easy to say, "I can't believe she made that decision! Why didn't she do everything to save her child?" But when you are watching it for so long and you see the changes in your child, because no one else knows them like you do, that's when you start to question yourself. Who am I doing this for? Why am I keeping him here like this? Am I saving him—or saving him for myself? Every time the child comes back from the brink, he is sadder and sadder. He's more and more damaged, if not physically, then emotionally and spiritually. You realise you are not making him better; you are prolonging his suffering. I guess no one understands that until they've lived through it.

I imagined being in my son's shoes—leaving his body and heading towards that bright light that offers relief from suffering and pain and then, *bam!*, sucked back in to go another round of torture.

I saw all of that now, but I knew nothing of the journey's end when I first contacted this family. I saw the description of Adsl Deficiency and all the scientific evidence, the characteristics, the symptoms, the prognosis, plus all the parent testimonials, and I just thought, *It's not going to happen to me. I wouldn't act like that. I wouldn't do that.* I had all my reasons and responses prepared, all my confidence and denial. But in the end, when you experience the severity of the disease, it gets the better of you, no matter how hard we might try to outrun it.

What does it mean to die with dignity? It's hard to talk about death and dying openly and honestly in a society that privileges life above all else. But death, like birth, happens to all of us sooner or later. If we are able to openly discuss what a good birth would look like, then we should be able to discuss what a good death would look like for each of us; then we can save so much suffering, not only for our dying selves but for the loved ones who will witness our passing and may be called upon to make decisions about what that passing will look like.

Once medical interventions take place there is no going back. Who's to say, with each prior intervention, each time we brought him back, we didn't make Hamish's health and quality of life even worse? What if the doctors intervened and needed to intubate and something went wrong? Hamish would die in hospital completely out of his and our control, in chaos and pain. I couldn't bear to watch and take part in the intense drama of trying to save his life again, only to watch him go through yet another round of this disease torture. Wasn't it better to prepare the way for a peaceful, dignified death surrounded by love? To make the choice to die the way he would want to?

I had to acknowledge, after all that I'd seen and felt, that Hamish's behaviour was his way of communicating. I had to see his actions as a choice, albeit he was a child. If he was a frail old man sitting in a chair at a nursing home and refused to eat, would I intervene? "These boys were robbed, Nat," Scotty said to me on more than one occasion. Robbed of the life they should have had. And now I was trying to rob Hamish of his own exit, his death.

For those who study death and grief, dying, like living, is considered a human right. As a society, we don't force people to die, and I came to the conclusion that I didn't want to force anyone to live. There comes a time when we all accept that death is inevitable and we turn from keeping a child's body alive at the expense of their quality of life, to showing the child's spirit respect and mercy. This is the toughest decision for any parent. The decision to let your child go is filled with guilt, shame, and regret on one side of the fence, and courage, vulnerability, and undeniable love on the other. Scotty was ready long before I was to let go. I had to let the sand run through my clasped fingers a little longer.

When I looked at Hamish, I finally got where that other mother was coming from. This is what she felt too. But I don't want any other family to have to understand that feeling until they are ready, when they are also in that place. I don't want to be the one to tell anyone to give up now because it will only be worse later; there is always the possibility that maybe it won't. There have been Adsl Deficiency children who, at the time of writing this book, have survived until forty-one years old. One was twenty-five and worked a job washing buses with the assistance of a carer. I don't want to dash anyone's hopes when they are at the beginning of their Adsl journey. But I had to recognise that all our options were now exhausted. My journey as a parent was at its end. I could now accept that I would always be a mum, even if my boys were not physically with me. It was my turn to let go.

Hamish was dying.

Once I accepted that Hamish was never going to get better, the next question was, how did we want the end to go? We could either make it painful and scary for him, or comfortable and peaceful. We chose peaceful.

The shift in thinking was complete, once it was made. If we couldn't fight for a better life for Hamish, we'd fight for a better death. We became very passionate about not causing Hamish any further stress even at the risk of losing him. Scotty and I agreed we would no longer force-feed, resuscitate, or intubate Hamish. We would take him home and make the switch to palliative care. Nurses would visit twice daily, morning and night, to help us manage Hamish's pain and make sure he wasn't suffering unnecessarily. We'd accept the hardest role, the one we'd already occupied briefly with William, that of a parent saying goodbye to their dying child.

Scotty and I took Hamish to my house to make his final days the best possible.

We put out the call for Hamish's friends and carers to come say goodbye. Friends, carers, teachers, and family members poured into the house, visiting while Hamish was still relatively awake and alert. We used only morphine now, administered by the palliative care nurses, and Hamish could engage a little now that he wasn't in acute pain or on emergency seizure medications with their mood-altering side effects.

Because of William, I knew what was coming. I didn't want people seeing Hamish so close to the end and having that image as the last one they took with them. Seeing Hamish fading and thin was heartbreaking and I feared being judged for our decision not to force-feed him. I feared being overwhelmed by everyone's collective grief. That was hard to deal with. Knowing that other people loved Hamish, too, and our choices would take Hamish away from them.

I had a family contact me to let them into the private Facebook group. Their baby was not even six weeks old, and he was already seizing, already had the diagnosis. But it was the week that Hamish was dying, and I had to put them on hold. I just couldn't go there. "I'll be in touch in a couple of weeks," I said. I didn't want to tell them the reason I couldn't talk to them. I didn't want their first introduction to the group to be alongside Hamish's obituary.

Intense feelings of anticipatory grief filled me. It feels like a kick to the stomach and I now understand why people feel like wailing. Not crying, *wailing*. The sound pushed up from the pit of my stomach, or maybe from deep inside my womb. The feeling filled me with panic and I was scared to let myself go there and feel the depth of my pain. I was scared to let it all come up and out, like an emotional vomit.

I tried to control this intense emotion by being busy. I'd get up and go to the kitchen, open the pantry and grab a handful of nuts. I caught myself. This was the old Natalie, stress eating her cares away. "No, you go back and acknowledge all this pain, stay here with it and feel it! Stop avoiding it!" I told myself. "You aren't expecting visitors. You don't have to prove you can cope to anyone. Put on that I-can-handle-it mask. It's just you and Hamish here. You can let yourself do this."

So I sat back on the couch and let the tears flow. Then the wailing and howling came. "I'm so sorry, my beautiful boy. It was never meant to be like this," I sobbed, rocking my body with my hands on either side of my head, pulling at my hair. It was ugly and real and I'm glad I let myself be completely honest without shame. Afterwards, I felt better, like I had followed a higher process and stayed in the moment, rather than running away from it. I'd then carry on my duties caring for Hamish.

Two days before Hamish died, I woke at 2:00 a.m. to a heavy feeling on my chest, almost like someone was sitting on it. My heart was pounding and a feeling of doom washed over me. At first I thought something was wrong with me. Was I having a frickin' heart attack? Then, panic—oh, shit, has Hamish died? I threw back the bedsheets, leapt out of bed, and raced across the hall into his bedroom.

He looked so peaceful lying there in his bed with his soft music playing and the colour-changing night-light. I gently placed my hand on his chest to see if I could feel his heart beating. I could. It was faint, but there. For a moment, I felt a strange sense of disappointment, as I was certain from what my body felt like when I woke that he had died.

"Hamish, baby, I thought you had died!"

He barely opened his eyes enough to see me but I felt him communicate back to me. *"My soul woke you."*

"What do you need, my beautiful boy?"

*"I want to share a message with my friends. I'll be leaving you soon."*

"What do you want me to do? Do you want me to write for you? Help you create words?"

No response.

"Would you like to make a photo collage with music?" This was my preference.

No response. Then, *"Help me make picture art."*

"Yes, of course!"

Then and there, in the deepest part of the night, when some people think the veils between life and death, the physical and spiritual, are thinnest, I went and grabbed my laptop on charge in the other room. For the next few hours as I sat by his bed, it was like his soul had taken refuge in my heart and I allowed him to use my hands and eyes to create heart-centred art. From far away, a Vincent van Gogh quote came to me: "Paintings have a life of their own that derives from the painter's soul."

"Who do you want to create this piece for?"

"*Dad*," Hamish replied. We named it *In a Galaxy Far Away*.

Hamish's *In a Galaxy Far Away*.

The next piece was called *The Boy in the Moon*, a winter wilderness scene with an image of Hamish's face in the moon.

"*Also for Dad.*"

We went on to create more images using dolphins and whales. Hamish first chose the image for the whale or dolphin and then the colours. In each one of the pictures we decided to put an image of Hamish in the background, so that if you looked carefully you could see Hamish in each one of his pieces of art, like a signature.

It was the most loving experience, to sit there with Hamish for hours as he breathed softly and skirted the edges of consciousness, while his soul transmitted what he wanted me to do beyond his body. I never really questioned what was occurring between us at that moment, I just followed his requests through my heart's intuition, in awe and wonder of our connection. Looking back, I question if I truly channeled my son's soul, if that kind of thing is even possible, but I'm grateful that in that moment at 2:00 a.m., I listened to my heart and honoured what was being asked of me and that I didn't go back to bed, ignoring what was to be his final request of me.

After making the pictures, Hamish continued to sleep while I attended to his care needs, bathing each of his now-bony long limbs with warm soapy water and then drying them with a pre-warmed towel that I had laid over the heater vent. I massaged his body ever so gently so as not to startle him into a seizure before dressing him in clean pyjamas and repositioning him on his pressure-care air mattress; I propped him up with pillows and adjusted his bed so he could look out his window to the wisdom trees beyond as the sun came up and the day and afternoon began. These actions cared for his physical body, but I felt like a piece of his soul was still inside of me. He was so close to dying now and yet here I was, so in love with him, in part because of the act of creation he had shared with me. I felt like I was floating alongside his flailing body.

Scotty spent the rest of the afternoon standing vigil with Hamish. In the many days before, we took turns sleeping vigil next to him on a fold-up mattress on the floor, being the primary carer through the night. When we weren't with Hamish, we stayed in our respective beds, me in my room and Scotty at his house. We'd put aside our personal grievances with the divorce to make Hamish's final days as calm and respectful as possible. Now was not about us.

I sent Scotty an update the next morning, as usual when it was my turn. "He's very peaceful, only a few short seizures through the night. He's very close. This needs to happen today." Which I know may sound horrific to anyone else who thinks I was advocating murder, but what it means in palliative care is that the person has suffered enough. No one wanted to prolong Hamish's slow starvation any more than was necessary. No one wanted to continue to watch him lay in his bed, unmoving, barely breathing. That was not living, it was dying, and there was only one outcome. When the end is near, the nurses can start increasing the doses of morphine to ease pain and the soul letting go. I knew this, and maybe that's what I was asking for from Scotty. We knew he was close and that he could pass today but we agreed that I needed to get out of the house for a while, as I hadn't left in several days. I kissed Hamish goodbye on each of his cheeks.

"Don't worry about me," I whispered. "You're free to go anytime you're ready, my beautiful boy. I'm always here for you."

I told myself, my work here was done. There was nothing more I could do. I left Hamish in the loving care of his father and the palliative care nurses who would soon arrive for their afternoon visit.

This may seem like a strange action to take when my son was on the doorstep of death, but a part of me knew I didn't need to be there for Hamish's passing. I wanted Scotty to be present for that final moment, as he'd not been present when William passed. Scotty had only just left the house to go to the post office and it was as if William followed him out. I knew Scotty had some guilt over that, so I wanted him to be there for Hamish instead of me. I knew it was the right thing for all of us for me to leave and lead the way, so Hamish could follow. I hoped he'd follow me out, as William had done with Scotty.

So I left the house and went for a walk to the park and sat down by the lake, reflecting on our life together, hoping Hamish would pass soon so this indomitable time of dying would be done, yet anxiously waiting for Scotty to call with the final news. I went to visit Andrew and distracted myself on my laptop computer creating a blog post about art therapy, using the images Hamish and I had created together the day before.

I'd been gone for two hours when I received the message from Scotty. Hamish, our beautiful boy, had passed. I marked the time and day: 5:45 p.m., September 3, 2022. Scotty reassured me that there was no need to rush back. He'd been on the phone with the palliative care team as Hamish passed and the doctor was on her way to complete the formalities.

It was hard to believe our vigil was over. Grief, real grief, not the anticipatory kind, crashed into me. I began howling, a primal cry from the depths of my belly like the cry I let out when I gave birth to Hamish twelve years ago. I had come full circle. I cried out all the sorrow I had for this little boy who was robbed of a normal life. I wasn't afraid to go there anymore, even with Andrew nearby. So intense was my pain that I vomited. I had done a lot of crying over my lifetime, but never like this. I cried for Hamish. I cried for William. I cried for Scotty. And I cried for myself. I cried for everything that was and had never been. I cried for all of it.

Andrew held me lovingly and let me cry. He didn't say, "Shhh, it's okay" or tell me to calm down or to stop, the usual things I'd heard before. Andrew held the space for me to completely break down. For the first time, I felt loved and supported in a time of immense grief.

*  *  *

I take my hands off the keyboard and look at what I've just written. The screen is all blurry and I blot my eyes. I'm glad I'm not wearing mascara today.

I sip my coffee. It's cold.

Stevie is in her bed. She looks back at me and then brings me one of her toys and crawls between me and my laptop as if to say, "I'm here for you too."

I think about the songs I sang to my boys when I wanted them to fall asleep. I'd sing the nursery song "Twinkle Twinkle Little Star." I'd sing Cyndi Lauper's "Time After Time." I'd sing the lullaby I made for Hamish:

*Rest your head upon my shoulders,*
*Baby, baby.*
*Sleepyhead, your day is over,*
*Baby, baby.*
*Close your eyes as I sing this lullaby,*
*My baby.*

For a moment I wonder, would they recognise the songs if I sang them now? The melody of the lullaby floats through my mind as I rock from side to side in my chair, as if my boys were in my arms again, peaceful, smiling, knowing.

*Chapter 15*

# BIGGER THAN MY BODY

THOUGH WILLIAM AND HAMISH COULDN'T COMMUNICATE IN full sentences, there was always the question of how much they truly comprehended. Disabilities exist on a wide spectrum, and many people who are nonverbal understand far more than they're able to express. But with both boys, it was hard to tell. They didn't track things with their eyes the way we do, so we were often left guessing whether they were really paying attention—or if they were processing at all. It was a constant puzzle: What's getting through? What isn't?

I have a video of William barking like a dog—that was his go-to sound for a while. Otherwise, it was mostly yells or other nonspecific noises. Occasionally, he'd make subtle gestures if he wanted something. He'd say "eh" and give a little nod for "yes." He could smile, laugh, cry. In the world of special needs, this is considered "nonverbal" or sometimes diagnosed as apraxia of speech—a neurological condition that disrupts the brain's ability to coordinate the motor planning required for speech. In short, they knew what they wanted, but their bodies wouldn't let them say it.

Because neither boy had strong fine motor skills or reliable vision, even signing was a challenge. But we found other ways. With modern technology, communication devices can give a voice to those who don't have one, and we leaned into what we could. The boys learned simple signs and a few visual symbols. They could point to the symbol for "toilet," and when I placed them on it, they understood what that meant. William could give a thumbs-up or clap his hands. Sometimes they'd point in the general direction of an object, and we'd play the guessing game: "This one? Or that one?" They'd nod for "yes."

I often gave them two choices: "This or that?" And if no clear answer came, I'd decide for them. "I know you like this one—let's go with that." We had symbols for mealtime, for bedtime, and could build a basic sense of routine. But the deep conversations I longed for never came. They couldn't ask for what they wanted. I had to guess, improvise, and go with what felt easiest in the moment—for them, and for me.

These small gestures and simple choices became our everyday language—a patchwork of signs, symbols, and intuition. But while they offered some connection, I couldn't stop wondering what more my boys might want to say, if only they had the means. That longing to unlock their voices led me to explore more structured communication systems, hoping that with the right tools, we could move beyond guessing games and into something more empowering.

While the boys were young, I tried my hardest to get everyone on board with an experimental assisted communication system for non-verbal children called the PODD (pragmatic organisation dynamic display) book which helps the user communicate via categories of images, each with an associated word. First, the user is given a wristband that says, "I have something to say." Then, the user is taught to indicate they have something to say by tugging at their wristband. You respond with, "Oh, you have something to say," and then you get the communication book and start the process. It's an intense, committed learning process for everyone—I had to take a two-day course just to learn how it worked—but I thought being heard was a human right and it was so rewarding to see a new user understand the process. A young woman with severe cerebral palsy learned to communicate using her eyes on a transparent screen with a caregiver on the other side who tracked her line of sight and spoke the word of the image she looked at. Her first sentence to the group was: "Learning to communicate has changed my life." She'd go on to tell us about her graduation from university, all thanks to her PODD communication device. Today, the systems are even better, as screens can track line of sight and say the words of the speaker.

Hamish with his PODD book

I laminated fifty pages of images for my PODD book to use with the boys and I worked with them every day. However, my efforts proved to be futile. I couldn't be consistent with it alone and I couldn't convince my husband that it was something our boys would eventually be able to use.

"Just watch the video!" I said to Scotty. "I think we can do this!"

"Nat, I think this is a waste of time. Our boys don't have that ability. And how long is learning all this and doing it going to take?"

He may have been right, as William's poor eyesight and coordination meant he had issues seeing the symbols and pressing the buttons. It was like I was trying to teach our children to speak in Italian and yet everyone else would still speak only in English to them. I even tried to get the boys' special development school on board, but the school principal at the time was happy with the system they currently used and was not prepared to invest any more money, time, or energy into the PODD system.

"See?" Scotty told me triumphantly. "Even the school thinks that the whole system is too hard. It's a really hard thing to expect everyone to communicate with all those kids with a system like that. I'm not surprised the school isn't using it."

As a parent, I lived to hear my children's first words but that was never to be, not even by way of pointing to pictures. I gave up the effort. I couldn't teach a whole language system on my own. However, a couple of years later the school engaged a new principal and started using the PODD system across its classes. The teachers would walk around with a small PODD book hanging from a lanyard like a handbag. The children would go up to the teacher and use the book to communicate what they wanted or needed. They'd tap on the symbol for "I want something," then turn to the pages that showed symbols for categories and select "Food." "Okay, what kind of food?" The teacher would then go to the page that shows all the food symbols and the child would select what they wanted. It was heartwarming to see the children who previously had no real way of communicating their true needs now have a voice and be heard. So although William never experienced its benefits, the system was still useful for Hamish and so many others!

It saddens me to think that there are many generations of children with special needs that never learned how to communicate, never got a chance to speak, because those with louder voices said no, you're not allowed to have a voice, you're not worth putting in the time and effort into allowing you to share your thoughts and feelings. It's assumed because a child can't speak or move their bodies like everyone else, that they don't have the intelligence or the ability to communicate in other ways. But that is increasingly shown to be a false assumption. And while there are varying degrees of intellectual disability that co-occur with various conditions and diseases that could affect communication, you never know until you try. Some children have been locked in. They're learning everything all the time, observing life, and able to comprehend everything said to them; they've just never been able to say anything back.

Children who don't know or can't physically speak the words have to be given a vocabulary, and images are the first and simplest step, or we figure out other creative ways to get around visual and hearing impairments. I didn't want to underestimate their potential. How could you deny someone's chance at a voice? If that young woman's parents had had a limiting mindset she'd never have been exposed to a communication device, and she would have spent the rest of her life unheard, pushed to the side, put on a heap, classified as unhelpable.

Still, believing in their potential and fighting for every opportunity didn't mean it was easy. There were days when the weight of it all felt overwhelming—the therapies, the trial and error, the emotional toll of constantly guessing. Wanting the best for your child and doing what's realistic in the moment are often two different things. Somewhere between hope and exhaustion, we had to find our own version of balance.

I understand now what Scotty was feeling. Amidst everything, sometimes, to keep our sanity, we had to "pick our battles," as he would say. As long as the boys were happy, what did it matter if we made the decisions for them?

One of the most difficult things with our boys' development was that they appeared to have very little motivation to seek and explore objects in their environment. It would take them hours to roll towards something I deliberately placed near them, something I thought they'd find interesting. Could they connect their mind and body to seek and explore? To learn about themselves? To learn about the physical world around them and what they could do in it?

Neither of the boys could follow instructions or make deliberate actions. They never learned to feed themselves, not by hand and definitely not by spoon. Or more to the point, they learned in theory but needed us to do the physical part. I did try to teach them this task for the first two to three years of their lives but I gave up as they had no desire to hold food and their fine motor skills were minimal. We all got frustrated and it was easier to just meet them where they were at and just feed them by spoon. I could see their enjoyment when they ate, and both boys were good eaters. That would have to be enough. I'm sure they were more fascinated by the person trying to teach them than the strange objects and lessons they didn't know they were supposed to learn. I was never sure if their failure to learn was because they didn't understand the instructions or because they couldn't physically do it. I couldn't say, "Touch this," and have them touch something to find out. Sometimes I could say to William, "Keep still," when he flapped his arms and the flapping seemed to slow down.

Auditory stimulation, especially music, always got them excited and they seemed to always look around to find the source of sounds. Their eyes were somewhere else, but it looked like they were listening. I remember Hamish being on the floor in the lounge room amongst a pile of toys. The piano keyboard was the only one he seemed fascinated with, I think because as a switch toy that responded when he pushed a button, it evoked a cause-and-effect response. He began to learn a little about himself and the world around him. If I do this, then this happens. If I press this switch, it says a word for me and I get my mum's attention.

Other than toys that made sounds, though, the boys seemed completely uninterested in reflection. Of any kind. I clearly remember William being on the floor as a young baby and he wasn't the slightest bit curious about looking at himself in the mirror I'd put up next to him. At the age of five he started to get more curious. It wasn't until seven that I remember walking into his room, which had mirrored doors on his wardrobes, and finding him looking at himself. He was kneeling and resting his head against the mirror, gazing into his own eyes, his own face, making his sounds to get a reaction. Was he merely a bird in a cage looking at another bird in the mirror? Or did he know who was looking back at him? Did he recognise his own body? Either way, he was interested and curious, and I glimpsed his humanity.

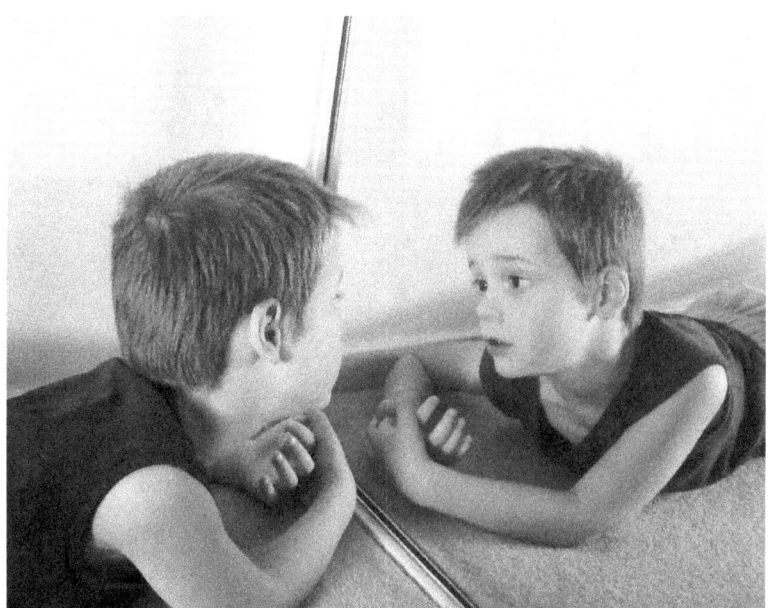

William looking in the mirror

Looking back, I guess I can now see that as they got older we observed a half-physical and half-nonphysical life. My husband and I took care of all their physical needs; we were literally their arms, legs, and voices, and they were totally reliant on us while here on this physical journey. Our job was to love them, keep them comfortable, pain free, and protect them from any undue, prolonged suffering.

That's the physical world, isn't it? The body piece of it all. But there's a whole lot of stuff that goes on that's not physical that can add to someone's life and enrich it, so it can be quite fulfilling. It's almost spiritual, or telepathic. I used to feel that very much with my boys, that sixth sense attuned to their wants and needs, so finely tuned because there were no words. It was similar to how people swear they can communicate with animals, who often neither need nor want words from us. They understand our soul, just standing next to them. An energy, or presence, that is just as solid and real as any words you can see or hear.

William's eyes were captivating. Of course I'd say that, I'm his mum, but before we knew something was different with him, I noticed something unique about his eyes. So much of the talk from his admirers was centred around his eyes. They say, "The eyes are the windows to the soul," so maybe there was a hint as to the message William was to share with us here.

I like to believe that my children were universal, more spiritual than physical, connected to me on a deeper plane that didn't need words. In fact, what if we viewed all our special children with the same belief? That they are souls that came here for this physical experience but were robbed of experiencing the physical part in its entirety. Perhaps they are hybrid—at their essence they are more soul or energy than ego and body. I didn't understand this until after William passed but now that I look back I can see something so much bigger was at play.

It was almost like they were my imaginary friends in physical bodies, in the sense that I'd hold one-sided conversations with them every day, imagining what they were thinking and feeling—expecting them to be thinking and feeling, even if they could not say what those thoughts and feelings were. It was a practice of extreme empathy all the time: What would I feel if I were in that situation? If I were stuck on that bed or in that position or couldn't get that toy or could taste that food? Would I be okay?

They seemed to have a form of empathy too. If I was having a bad day, I could see it reflected in Hamish straightaway. If I was upset, he'd get upset, waving his hands around more frantically or making more noise. If I was good, he was good. But it was also more than that. I'd see my depression or overwhelm reflected back to me, so I'd make a conscious decision to do something about it. Let's sing a favourite song, or go for a walk, or play a game, or watch a show. We'd go do something fun and uplifting.

Those are the things I miss today, when I'm having a flat day and there's no child to make me jog myself out of it. There was no reason to be positive or a reason to turn it around. There was no little person who depended on me to make the world less fearful. So I had to learn how to do it myself, switch on and decide to get off the negativity treadmill.

Hamish could watch music concerts for hours on the TV, sitting on the floor quietly in the lounge room. One day, he and I were enjoying John Mayer live in concert when I noticed Hamish moving his fingers in what seemed a conscious way. It almost looked like he was trying to strum a guitar along with Mayer.

"Mate, do you want the guitar to play with?" I asked him. I still had the guitar I'd gotten when we had the respite lady with her guitar come out to sing for the boys. I knew Hamish heard guitar at his school too. His teacher played it often for the students in his classroom. Not waiting for an answer I knew might never come I got up to get my guitar and gave it to him. He sat on the lounge holding the guitar like a guitarist, which was as much motor function as he could manage, but his hand was doing the fingering on the frets. "Wait, mate, you're right-handed," I realised. I flipped the guitar over to the proper position for a right-handed player and his hand moved even better. He graced me with his best performance of fine motor control I'd yet seen.

I watched Hamish play his guitar along with John Mayer for a good long while. Towards the end, Mayer broke into the wistful lyrics of "Bigger Than My Body." As Hamish mirrored his own duet with Mayer, lost in the music, I saw the man he could have been.

We're more than we give ourselves credit for. My boys were bigger than their bodies in ways I still don't entirely grasp. When alive, their spirits and energy took up space and hugged me just as surely as flesh-and-blood arms. William was nine when he passed away and Hamish was almost thirteen. My boys are not only nonverbal now, they're nonphysical. But ever so often, I feel their presence. The same inexplicable, immaterial energy that I felt from them when they were alive. I cling to the idea that we are all bigger than our bodies, whether those bodies are perfectly able or not.

True connection doesn't always need words. Just like love, it lives in energy, in presence, in the way we sense from the heart. Those who communicate on a different level, be it animals, musicians, or children, show us that deeper understanding isn't always spoken—it's felt. We all long to feel safe, seen, and loved, and sometimes the clearest messages come in the quietest ways. That's part of their legacy: to remind us we're more than our bodies, more than our limits—and to leave us better than they found us.

*Chapter 16*

# REST IN PEACE

IN THE MOMENTS AFTER HAMISH DIED, I EXTRACTED MYSELF from the loving arms of Andrew, put myself back together as much as I could, and he drove me back to my house where Hamish and his dad were waiting. The palliative care team and Hamish's doctor had come and gone, the doctor officially declaring Hamish's time of death. Then Scotty had sat with his boy waiting for me to return home.

I stood at the bedroom doorway. Hamish looked so peaceful, lying there on his bed with his teddy under his arm. Scotty had carefully freshened him up and put him in clean *Star Wars* pyjamas that said, "In A Galaxy Far Far Away." (I noted the PJs because one of Hamish's artworks was titled the same.) Scotty had refilled the diffuser with a calming essential oil blend of lavender, sweet orange, and geranium that wafted through the entire house. He'd gone through my house and found two little silk frangipani flowers and put them in Hamish's hands and placed them on his chest.

I came into the room. Scotty got up from his chair next to Hamish and we gave each other an awkward but heartfelt hug. "I'm sorry our life with these boys wasn't what we expected. We did our best. He's with William now," Scotty said.

Tears welling in my eyes, I responded, "I know, I'm sorry too."

The Men in Black called back and said they could come within the hour. "Will you be ready?" they asked.

"Yes," I said.

The Men in Black arrived when they said they would arrive. I thought I was ready. We'd already done this once before. But I felt a spurt of panic flood my body when they came in my house with the dreadful body bag and I wish now I'd told them to wait, to give me a little longer with Hamish after he had passed and not be in such a hurry to let his body leave the house. There's great spiritual value in sitting with the dead, so that ending is fully taken in.

"Do you want us to take him out?" the Men in Black asked. The idea ratcheted up my panic. My house was small and I had stairs. I couldn't take that rattling contraption being forced awkwardly up the stairs and through my door.

"No," Scotty responded hastily. "He's my boy. I'll carry him out." I could have hugged Scotty again at that moment.

The Men in Black turned to me. "Would you like to come out and say your final goodbyes?"

"No, I'm done," I said, a bit prickly. "I've said my goodbyes already." I couldn't bear to go through the whole process again, watch the van go down the drive and carry Hamish away. For me that was the hardest part.

Scotty carried Hamish's thin, pale frame wrapped in a warm fleece blanket out to the trolley set up in my driveway and laid him to rest. He was the one who watched the van leave.

Meanwhile, I sat on Hamish's bed and sobbed into my tissues, holding the frangipanis in my hands. I hadn't let Hamish go with the flowers, like I hadn't let William go with Tigger. I'd given the Men in Black some of Hamish's other teddies and special things with him in his body bag. Those would go to the crematorium with him. But I kept the flowers Scotty had laid on his chest beside his heart. Two months later, I would attend a metaphysical and emotional kinesiology workshop. In the hands-on portion of the workshop, the facilitators tested my muscle response to a series of questions. The object was to see which ones my muscles responded to, indicating what my body needed in the moment that could inform future healing work. "*Aromatherapy*," my body indicated. Then, out of the sixty oils and various other elements, my body chose two. The first was frankincense, the oil I used most often with Hamish to help ground his limbs, important for a boy always in a wheelchair whose feet barely ever touched the floor. The second oil was frangipani, the silk flowers Hamish held on the day he died and the oil used for grieving in Eastern Asia. I took this as Hamish's subtle message to me from the other side.

Hamish's funeral was like a take-two of William's funeral, but with some notable differences. Grief memories are spotty things. When someone bumps into me out and about and says, "I haven't seen you since Hamish's funeral," I can't remember seeing this person there. What I do remember is this.

At William's funeral, the foyer of the funeral home was hung with the artwork he'd made at school over the years. Everyone was invited to take a favourite piece home after the service, and I still have friends and family report his art is hanging on their fridge. Catherine's husband, John, who's also now deceased, wrote and read the eulogy as neither Scotty nor I could emotionally handle that part. Scotty did a photo slideshow to music he'd made, and William's poem "A Brokenhearted Legacy" was read by the funeral celebrant.

At Hamish's funeral, I had a stack of copies of the heart-centred artwork I'd made with Hamish two days before he died. Hamish had indicated which person got which image, so I gave those individuals their image. Catherine and Carly had helped me roll the extras up like scrolls, tied with ribbon, and everyone was invited to collect a piece of artwork at the end of the service. People would send me photos afterwards of the art displayed in their home, alongside a photo of Hamish and a little candle, their very own sacred space for Hamish.

Hamish's frangipanis

At William's funeral, I hugged family members and friends I hadn't seen in years. The armour was removed and it was comforting, but I felt self-conscious having all these people I effectively didn't know well seeing me so raw. I held Will's Tigger teddy tight to my chest like a child's security blanket—like *my* child's security blanket. Security he would not need again, but that I desperately needed in that moment.

My sister-in-law had given Tigger to William when he was born, before we knew anything was different about him. It was one of his first toys. Later, William loved bouncing along to the song "The Wonderful Thing About Tiggers." Bouncing was his thing. It was fun fun fun! And I think he felt a kinship with the active friend of Pooh's who always leapt before he looked. We had a plastic switch-activated Tigger as well, that would bounce up and down and sing Tigger's song when you pressed its head. William loved music. He loved bouncing. So I guess it was fate he'd gotten the teddy when he was born, and it was fate that Tigger would see off his loving owner.

Tigger would be passed around to all of William's loved ones who would give the teddy a cuddle and a kiss, a proxy for the cuddle and kiss they could no longer give to William. The next morning, we would hold a breakfast for the friends who travelled to the funeral and everyone seemed to have a photo with Tigger. Everyone had a chance to share their grief and heal, if only a little. The images struck me. A wristband made by one of William's friends of white and black plastic alphabet beads spelled out William's name around the teddy's neck, as if in some way a part of William was now part of the teddy. Tigger held a little grey Heffalump in its hands, the Winnie the Pooh version of an elephant, and we were all now holding the Tigger—holding William—in ours. Despite the years that have passed since the funeral, I can't bring myself to wash Tigger. He has William's last kisses, both from him and the people who loved him.

At Hamish's funeral, over two hundred people attended. I wasn't used to crowds, and being surrounded by that many people felt overwhelming. After the memorial, I stood from the pew and followed behind Hamish's coffin as the pallbearers carried him out. When I turned and saw how many people were there—watching, witnessing—I felt completely exposed in my grief. I walked behind Scotty, struggling to hold myself together. At one point, he reached back and gently touched my arm to comfort me. Andrew followed close behind, alongside our family and friends, as we made our way to the waiting white hearse.

One by one, our friends came forward to pay their respects—many of them faces I hadn't seen since William's funeral. Scotty hadn't wanted a large, public service, but people came anyway. Hamish wasn't just ours to grieve. He was known. He was loved. Our community showed up because he had touched their lives too.

One of his teachers, Mel, had written a beautiful poem called "The Blue Eyed Boy." It was read aloud by Donna, one of his devoted school carers, her voice steady but full of feeling. I remember Jan—Shadow's owner—walking up to me after the service, flanked by my other horsey friends Mel, Bec, and Alison. They pulled me into hugs and I could barely speak. "My God, you're here," I whispered through tears. "Of course we're here," they said. "Why wouldn't we be?"

And then there was Linda, standing near the white hearse, her eyes fixed on Hamish's little coffin. She had flown in from Queensland to represent our extended family. When she turned to me, her face was stricken. She wrapped her arms around me and said, "I can't believe this is happening. I'm so sorry."

At William's funeral, we asked our friends and attendees to take one of the hundred red or white balloons decorating the room where the service was held and line up along the private street that wound away from the funeral home. As William's white hearse and coffin passed they released the balloons up into the sky. We followed along behind the hearse. I held William's Tigger up to the car window as if he was saying William's final goodbyes. The whole procession was led by Scotty's bagpiping mate, China, on his bagpipes. A lone piper playing, leading the dead to rest. There wasn't a dry eye to be seen. Why do people cry when they hear bagpipes? Their mournful yet majestic notes can evoke profound feelings of sorrow, reflection, and reverence. The drones are responsible for the characteristic low "humming" sound that emanates from the pipes, a frequency and tone not unlike the human heartbeat that somehow reaches into our bodies and vibrates our inner fibers in a form of trauma release. This is maybe why they became a mainstay of serious occasions: graduations, going off to war, funerals. There is a Scottish folk belief that bagpipes are the only instrument that can be heard in heaven. A piper and the sound of the bagpipes helps to direct departed souls towards heaven's gates. When a piper plays, they walk away, symbolizing the piper leading the departed to the hereafter. The piper will stop short of the gate, through which the living piper cannot pass.

William's coffin

After Hamish's service it rained. We didn't do a balloon and piper processional like we had for William. We kept it more intimate. We put flowers on Hamish's coffin before he went into the hearse, and then everyone huddled around Hamish's hearse to keep out of the weather and share their condolences. As Hamish's hearse drove away a beautiful rainbow spread across the dark part of the sky. No doubt, Hamish felt the collective energy of love and admiration for him and put on this show for all of us. I looked at the rainbow so I couldn't look at the hearse as it left my sight. I did not follow Hamish's coffin to the crematorium. I had told the funeral director I couldn't do that part again.

Years ago, at William's funeral, extended family and friends gathered at the Bridge Hotel down the street while Scotty and I did our final send-off for William at the crematorium. There aren't many depictions of the process of cremation in modern film and media like there is with burying a coffin in a cemetery, and I had little hands-on experience with the process of funerals. I hadn't thought of this detail and was completely underprepared as was my immediate family that attended the crematorium with us.

I remember it like this.

We were led from the foyer of the crematorium into a big, square concrete room. Large open windows gaped out onto the car park in front of the building on the side we entered. They were the only things in the sterile room that didn't make it feel like I was trapped in a box. William's little white coffin sat on top of a large concrete block. Draped over the coffin was William's Sydney Swans scarf, his favourite football team. It resembled some sort of altar. We all stood in a row before the coffin. There were a few brief words and the coffin on the platform started to lower. Something primal rose up within me and I snatched back William's Sydney Swans scarf and wrapped it around the Tigger I held. The rest of the teddies weren't so lucky. We watched as the coffin sank into the floor along with the concrete block, like it was on some massive elevator or very slow trapdoor. A moment of silence followed as the thick floor swallowed William's coffin by centimetres, lowering him into the ground, no, the *furnace chamber* that I now realised was right beneath us and probably the reason for the brutal concrete room we stood in. William was going into the fire right in front of us…no, I couldn't see the fire, of course… or could I? I don't know whether I could see the fire or not. For safety reasons, the funeral staff would wait for us to leave first, wouldn't they? I can't quite remember. It's like my brain protects me from this image. The ground closed over the top of the coffin as it cleared the thickness of the floor. I had time to suck in a breath and a whirring noise started from below us. I don't know if it was the elevator coming to a stop or the actual start of the flames but it was eerie enough that I will always remember that sound. And that was it! We were free to go. We all stood around for a moment awkwardly hugging each other and still quite stunned until Scotty said, "Right, we'll see you back at the pub." We all walked back to our cars to head back to our friends waiting for us at the pub for William's wake.

When it came to Hamish's funeral, I knew I couldn't go back into that concrete box. I just couldn't.

At Hamish's funeral, Scotty read his son's eulogy which was the hardest thing for any man to do in front of many complete strangers. That took some serious brawn. And as the rainbow spread across the sky after the rain, about fifty of us made our way to the pub at the Bridge Hotel near the funeral home for an extended wake. A subdued but loving gathering followed as we caught up with friends and reminisced over a few drinks with people we hadn't seen for a long time, friends and family who had travelled interstate to pay their respects. Scotty's boss, Hamish's school teachers and friends from school, his carers and nurses—I can't thank them enough for their support through our time with William and Hamish as they shared the journey with us. Our boys hadn't just touched our lives as parents, they'd touched everyone they met. In my own grief, I sometimes forgot that others grieved also.

A week after William's funeral, Scotty got the call to come pick up William's urn. He collected William's ashes and brought them back home. We'd yet to choose an urn, so he came back in the equivalent of the funeral home's to-go package: a thirty-by-fifteen-centimetre box. I thought, *That's my baby. That's all of him in there. That's what's left of our life together in this physical world. Did it all even happen? Did it matter?*

For a long time I didn't want to disturb William's ashes, so they remained in the little rectangular box we got from the funeral home. When Hamish passed, it was me going to pick up his ashes. I saw a beautiful silver urn embossed with birds and angels. It was small, a child's urn. I chose a little heart-shaped one as well, in a similar style, silver with a dove. I asked the attendants to put a bit of Hamish's ashes in the heart urn so I'd have him with me always. And I do. I still have this urn. It's small enough to take with me anywhere I go. Particularly in the early going, the first year or so after Hamish passed, it came everywhere with me along with William's Tigger. The main urn stayed at my house with the rest of Hamish in it.

It took me a while to wrap my head around separating Hamish's ashes between households. I was very protective of them, not letting Scotty have half while I kept the other half. Instead, William lived with Scotty in his box and Hamish lived with me. Before Hamish died, Scotty went away on a holiday and I asked to keep William's ashes with me while he was gone so William wouldn't be alone. Little things like that revealed I wasn't ready to let go. I was still hanging on to the last piece of their physical remains.

A couple of years after Hamish passed, Scotty moved to the beach up on the Sunshine Coast, where, as the name suggests, the weather was a lot warmer. Humpback whale mums have their calves in the warmer waters of that coast, making it a popular tourist destination for whale watching. He no longer had to stay near me for the boys so he followed his passion back to the water and warmer weather—what he'd moved to Australia for.

Two years after Hamish died, Scotty sent me a message to tell me he had found the most beautiful spot over on K'gari Island and suggested it would be the perfect place for us to scatter our boys' ashes. Scotty and I organised an excursion to do so, Scotty bringing William and me bringing Hamish. I drove from the airport to meet him at a marina. He'd hired a small tin fishing boat with a canopy and outboard motor. We loaded Hamish and William into the bottom of the boat in a waterproof rucksack Scotty brought along, along with my travel suitcase because I didn't want to tempt car thieves, and set off for the island of K'gari, where the waters are still in small protected coves and we could put the boys out in the water together and watch them drift away. I started to take video on my phone to document our last sentimental adventure with our boys.

Getting to the island, though, was proving to be a chore, especially since it looked like a storm was rolling in. The water was pretty choppy going out. Then it got really choppy. I thought we were going to be tipped out of the boat! Since the boat was for hire, its motor was much less powerful to prevent accidents caused by inexperienced boat-goers, but that meant the little craft struggled to climb up and out of the waves. I knew we were in trouble when I stopped taking video so I could hold on for dear life. I watched my poor little suitcase with my laptop and passport and all my overnight necessities slosh about the bottom of the boat. I had a vision of us capsizing and all my belongings ending up in the water. I was sure, if they were watching us, they'd be laughing at their mum and dad, rocking around in a little metal boat going, "Oh shit, hold on!" as we chugged up another steep wave to come crashing down the other side. I trusted Scotty as a captain—he had his private helicopter pilot's licence—but I didn't trust our roofed fishing tinnie, which bucked like a brumby and had the same attitude.

"Let's turn around!" I yelled, clutching my phone so it wouldn't slip from my hand.

"No, it'll be alright!" he yelled back. "It should get calmer around this point!"

"No, let's just turn around. I don't think we're going to make it back. It's getting worse!" I screamed over the struggling motor and the increasing wind.

"We'll be fine!" he roared back cheerfully. It was the same as when he had taken me up in his helicopter and I screamed the whole time for him to put me down. "We're a thousand feet up," he pointed out. I think I lost a year off my life that day.

If we weren't careful, I'd lose my whole life on this day. Just zip it, Nat, don't distract him! He knows what he's doing, I told myself. Holding my arms across my middle and the totally saturated rain jacket my brother had lent me, we went over another monster wave that slammed us down hard back into our seats.

"Yeah, okay, on second thought," Scotty said, sounding more subdued, "I think we better turn around."

"Thank God!" I muttered, but now we had to make it back to the harbour. Needless to say, we didn't talk the whole way back as we white-knuckled it all the way, me clutching my suitcase between my legs and holding on to my seat and Scotty standing up to see over the bow of the boat and steering us around and over the massive waves.

When we arrived back at the marina we gathered my luggage and the boys out of the boat's soggy bottom and reconnoitered at the boot of his car to towel off and check everything. "That was bloody scary," I pointed out. For once, Scotty agreed with me.

My suitcase was wet on the outside but it was dry on the inside so my laptop was safe. I heaved a sigh of relief. Then we opened the bag with the boys in it. Scotty's "waterproof" bag wasn't so waterproof and a puddle had gathered at the bottom. Hamish was good in his sealed silver urn. William wasn't so lucky. Scotty had moved him from his funeral box to a biodegradable urn, since we'd planned to put the boys in the water, and it had gotten wet and was starting to disintegrate as he lifted the urn out of the puddle, threatening to spill William's ashes all over the boot of his car. We had to get him out of that bag!

Scotty awkwardly scooped up William's soggy container, and the ashes inside started to spill out its widening cracks into Scotty's hands, which overflowed into the back of his car. "Oh, my God!" I said, horrified, and grabbed up Hamish's urn and popped the top so Scotty could pour William's rapidly escaping ashes in with his brother. Then we spent a few minutes scraping up the spilt ashes from the carpeted floor of the boot of the car into the urn as well. Not wanting to look at our hands now covered in our son's ashes, we stared at the lone urn which now contained both Hamish and William, something I never thought I'd do but which seemed weirdly appropriate. Maybe that's what the boys had wanted all along.

"You keep them here with you," I said to Scotty. "One day we'll do this again and we'll do it properly, and hopefully the boys won't try to kill us again."

Scotty's partner had made a picnic lunch to eat out on the boat, so we ate our slightly soggy sandwiches at a picnic table by the water. We spent the rest of the day talking about the last couple of years after losing the boys, what we'd learned since then, and our grief. For the first time, we acknowledged each other's pain and apologised for our own part in all of that. Vulnerability didn't come easily for the brave flying Scotsman, and in our fifteen years together I had never seen him so tender. He was grieving in his own way, which wasn't about me and my grief. When I was dealing with the thick of my own grief, it had been very hard to deal with another person's as well. That's what destroyed our marriage.

I didn't fall in love with him again but my heart opened for forgiveness to enter and we agreed we'd be friends forever. From here, we could only hope for better weather for our next attempt at spreading the boys' ashes out on the waters where the whales lived and had their young. But for now both the boys would reside with Scotty by the water.

I was about to leave and Scotty called me over and gave me a big hug. "You were the best mum those boys could ever have had."

"And you were the best dad."

As of writing this book, that was the last time I saw Scotty.

*Chapter 17*

# WELCOME TO GRIEF

GRIEF DOESN'T COME WITH A MAP, EVEN WHEN YOU THINK you've walked the road before. I thought I knew what to expect after losing William. I thought the years of anticipatory loss, of watching and waiting with Hamish, had prepared me. But grief is never the same twice. It arrives in waves, in whispers, in storms—and it remakes you each time. What I learned is that grief doesn't get easier; it gets deeper. And when Hamish passed, I wasn't just mourning one child, I was finally feeling the weight of losing both.

The depth of grief creates chaos and confusion in the mind as things fall apart and you attempt to realign into the person you'll be after this partial loss of self. When I think of my grief in the worst moments after Hamish's passing there are no cohesive images, only a mess of words: *roar, fragile, wound, tipping point, gut-wrenching, scattered, scrambled, free-falling, empty, bottomless pit.*

In the days following Hamish's funeral, I felt strangely lighter. There was relief woven into the grief—finally, it was over. But that relief was tangled with disbelief. I was most likely in shock, moving through each moment as if suspended between two worlds. The contrast of his life and death played on repeat in my mind. He was free now…and in a way, so was I. But with that freedom came a deep sense of guilt. I felt both unburdened and ashamed. And I absolutely could not deal with other people's grief on top of my own. I didn't have the strength to comfort others or help them process what had happened. I was barely holding myself together.

Why was the grief I felt with Hamish worse than William? They were both my beautiful boys, so why did it hurt so badly now, this second time?

Looking at his baby photos, Hamish was so normal and healthy looking. He'd smile, he'd giggle, he'd laugh. He'd wiggle his head and follow us about the room with his eyes. Hamish was perfect when he was born. I thought, for a brief moment, he'd be William's normal younger brother, he'd be the one to go to school, play sports, graduate, get married, have kids of his own. I truly thought he was going to be our legacy. Until he wasn't.

Hamish was about three and a half years old when I fell pregnant again by accident. I had big stomach cramps that doubled me over and I went to the doctor to figure out what was wrong. "Let's have you take a pregnancy test, just in case." I didn't think for a second I was pregnant, but the test came back positive.

With both my boys' recent diagnoses, knowing it was a rare genetic disease, I was very concerned I'd have another child with Adsl Deficiency. Either that, or as an older mum I was at increased risk of having a baby with another disorder, like cerebral palsy or spina bifida, which also required a lot of care and could be life-limiting. I toyed with the idea for a moment, as I'd always wanted three kids. Do I take the risk or not? But it also wasn't just me. I discussed it with Scotty, who had a stake in the pregnancy too. Do we have another child and take the risks? I thought again how anxious I would be this time, after two babies with the disease, after drinking alcohol all that month, after running long distances, and now knowing it was a roll of the dice no matter what I did. I was certainly not a candidate for a spontaneous pregnancy given our history; I felt I would regret not going to a genetic counselor or a fertility specialist, who, knowing what to look for in the DNA, could carefully select a healthy, non-affected embryo made from my eggs and his sperm and implant it in me through in vitro fertilization. And that would need to be proactively planned, not spontaneous. In the end, we decided the risk was too great, and I terminated the pregnancy at fifteen weeks. It felt like something sacred was taken—a human heartbeat replaced by moral shame. I still bear the weight of that heart-wrenching decision.

I'm both glad and sad with my choice. Glad, because knowing what I know now of the boys' future care, I don't think I'd have been able to stay sane taking care of three kids, especially if they all had Adsl Deficiency. Sad, because sometimes I wish I had another child to hold. I know it's all hypothetical now, as my body is past the point where it can have a baby, but I can't stop wishing I could fill the space left by my boys with another child. Isn't that why a woman's body is designed to have so many children? So she gets lots of chances to be a mum? Once my boys were born, that's all I wanted to be.

When Hamish died it was the end of everything. It wasn't like I could keep his things and hand them down to the next child. I'd either keep his belongings set up like a museum (which I did for some) or give them away (which I did for others). Either way, no child of mine would ever use them again. I had no children left. I was worse off than my boxer dog, who'd lost six pups out of ten. My child mortality rate was 100 percent. You don't expect to lose all your children. And when you do, you need another life to fill that void. I really feel that you do. As painful as it is to no longer feel your child's love, it is even more painful to have no one to give your love to.

With that loss of legacy came a loss of my own future. My own idea of who I was and what my purpose in life was to be. When William passed I continued on with my life. I was busy planning my and

Hamish's new life apart from Scotty. I could do anything. I was an independent woman. I had big plans. When Hamish passed, I didn't just lose someone I loved, I lost a role I loved. No, more than one role. Many of my roles just…went away. There was no one to wake up in the morning, or make breakfast for, or take to school. I wasn't juggling doctors' appointments and funds requests and my own self-care in between. I lost all my superpowers—the Parent, the Carer, the Advocate, the Mother—all were gone. It was the end of everything.

I had lost pieces of myself and struggled to put what was left back together in the semblance of a whole person. Nothing I tried helped me find relief from this new grief of losing my old self. I wanted to simultaneously roar at the world and run away and hide from it. I wanted to die. This wasn't the overwhelm and exhaustion that led to my suicidal thoughts after the boys were diagnosed, it was a complete lack of mooring. I felt like I had lost my anchor in the stormy seas of grief and everything that ever held meaning or purpose had drifted away. An empty pit yawned open inside my stomach and nothing seemed to fill it. Believe me, I tried!

Running had been my saving grace the first time I went through a deep depression, but I'd stopped running seriously after William passed. Running would release my thoughts about William and my throat would tighten up with emotion and I couldn't breathe. Towards the end of one marathon I started having an asthma attack. The feeling of not being able to breathe scared me, and I started to slow down on the amount of running I was doing. Then came the divorce and single motherhood to Hamish, and it became even harder to get out on a regular basis. When Hamish became so unwell in the last year of his life I virtually stopped running altogether. He passed, the grief flatlined me, and I ate it away with food. First healthy food, but it didn't take long before the junk food crept in. I could eat and eat and eat but I couldn't feel full. I put on twenty kilos in a couple of years. I was eating myself to death and didn't care.

I may have been eating a lot, but my bank account was on a diet. After the boys died, all of a sudden I was left with no superannuation, no annual leave, no income coming in for myself. I was in active grief but I had to go back into the workforce. It was a hard pill to swallow. I took charge of what I could. I worked my Pilates business plus another part-time job.

Weighing the heaviest I've been my entire life, I was so damn depressed and miserable about my weight and lack of control that I had stomach surgery to make my stomach smaller. For once, I felt full, and I was able to physically halt my self-destruction with food.

I've come to think the food was only a metaphor. In my grief, my needs couldn't be met, so I tried to meet them with food. I tried to fill the empty space inside me with food, like I'd done as a child. I didn't know it or didn't care at the time, but food was never going to fill the enormous void my boys had left behind. I had to face the true root of my pain and grief: not having something or someone to fill my life with purpose.

To top off the shit cocktail that was my life, I was going through menopause, which is another subject social conversations shy away from. Hormones are big mood regulators for women, and with mine going through their death throes, I was tossed about by my body as well as my emotions. It felt like every cell in my body wanted me dead. Menopause crossed with grief is a bitch. And I never want to meet either of them again!

Before my children were born, I read several books about birthing and becoming a new mother. (*Birthing*—the physiological and emotional process of birthing a new being into this physical reality and attaching their life to yours.) With birth, I studied and prepared myself for what was going to happen in nine months' time. Nearly every mother will openly share their birthing experience and offer advice to make this experience better for others if given the chance. It's an exciting time where you feel like you're winning at life, doing what you are supposed to be doing as part of your family and community. It's perfectly natural for new mothers to think of nothing else but nurturing their new baby.

With death and dying, however, aside from the discussions with palliative care doctors of NFR and developing complex care plans, I didn't know anything. No one happily bequeaths a book titled something like *What to Expect When You're Expecting Someone to Die* to the next generation of mothers. I learned more about death and dying after the fact, through my own search for answers.

*Grieving*—the physiological and emotional process of standing vigil for a loved one who is dying and ushering them out of this physical reality and detaching their life from yours. I recognise now that there's a subtle difference between grief and grieving. Grief is the instant feeling of getting kicked in the gut when the loss of a loved one occurs or when you are triggered by a memory. It's a visceral feeling and an instinctive response. Grieving is the intellectual process of managing old routines and memories and the feelings that go along with them after a loss occurs. This is distinct from mourning, the time just after someone passes where you expect to process and respectfully wallow in your grief and allow yourself to do accepted rituals around it, like funerals. Mourning has a set time, sometimes dictated culturally, like the old Victorians who set aside one year to mourn the death of a child. Grieving, however, is forever. You'll remember, feel, process that feeling, and move forward. Grief is the raw emotion, while grieving pulls you through that emotion to the other side where you can live alongside the grief but not be ruled by it. That's what happens when people get stuck in grief, what Sigmund Freud called "melancholia," when you are on the edge of tears all the time and feel that something is always sitting on your chest. They cannot pull themselves through the emotion and calm back down to a baseline where they can function fully.

Grieving takes time, and that time is different for everyone. It's a relearning process, figuring out how to navigate your life without your loved one. That takes time. When other people get impatient, it is often with the amount of time someone needs to grieve fully. They think the first grief and the immediate mourning afterwards is enough.

Birth is the joyful start of life. Grief is the sorrowful end of it. As such, it holds a stigma. If you talk about death, especially when the subject of that discussion is still alive, you're seen as morbid, or like you're giving up. There is more shame, regret, and alienation as others cease to understand why you are still crying, especially if you are crying about something seen as beneath pity or love, like an animal, or someone who died in a taboo way, like a drug overdose or suicide. It's a conversation many families struggle to discuss openly and honestly.

My Grandma Sharpe's grief over the death of Clive, one of her seven children, back in 1961 when he was nine months old—lost to pyloric stenosis, a condition that was treatable by surgery with a proper diagnosis—haunted her for the rest of her life. As a child, I remembered she'd spend a lot of time in bed. I could tell she was often sad and that she often cried. The loss of her husband years later didn't help. I didn't talk to her much, this being the days of formality between grandchildren and grandparents, and it was polite not to pry, but I knew she wrote. What did she write about, I wonder? What did she think or feel or do? What was the root of the sorrow she never could shake that kept her distant from her loved ones? Why did she keep her grief to herself? My reflection on the computer screen with my little glasses, pale and dim in the morning light, looks like my Grandma Sharpe. I didn't want her fate to be my own. I didn't want my grief to break me.

Grief is deeply isolating. Even when surrounded by people, it can feel like no one truly sees the ache inside. I often find myself holding my grief close, not out of secrecy, but because the distance between me and those I love both physically and emotionally has existed since I was a child. Though I stay in touch with my family, connection is sporadic. My siblings live hours away, and while there are the occasional phone calls answered joyfully with "I was just thinking about you!" that makes me feel remembered, they're fleeting. For the most part, I grieve alone. And at first, I thought I preferred it that way.

Why did I want to be alone in my grief? Why did I not want to be with someone who might support me? Maybe I was afraid if I shared my grief the other person would not be able to hold space for it and I'd be rejected yet again in a time of emotional need. Or maybe I was afraid my grief would trigger theirs, and I'd feel pressured to diminish my own grief so I could help support them with theirs. Would I be able to hold space for someone else's grief when I had so few examples to teach me how?

When William passed, it was our grief, both Scotty's and mine. We shared it equally. Scotty and I were also separated and were cautious about showing vulnerability around each other. We didn't have the capacity to support each other's grief, and my family, while they tried, didn't always know how to respond. My mum, upon William's passing, said to me, "It's for the best!" I wrapped my arms around her shoulders as I clenched my teeth and said, sharply, "Just don't speak," holding her for a moment in time. "Just don't say anything right now."

Sometimes, the best thing to say to someone grieving is "I don't know what to say. I'm just sorry for your loss." Nothing you say is going to change anything. No profound bloody words of wisdom is going to make it all easier. You don't have to deal with the depths of it all. The person just needs to be held and allowed to cry, howl, scream, whatever, to move through the grief. Later, there might be some talking, or writing, or artwork, or therapy. For now, there is only darkness.

There were many losses I had yet to process upon Hamish's passing. My parents' divorce. My separation from my siblings. My relationship with my mother. My beloved pets. The boys' diagnoses. My diagnoses. The loss of my job and purpose outside being a mum. My marriage. My dreams. My very concept of who I was and what I did.

When Hamish died and I no longer had the next dream to distract me, the dam broke and the grief of all these losses flooded out, affecting every aspect of my being, to the point where I almost didn't recognise myself. Or worse still, I did recognise who I was—the woman I feared most, my shadow self, a woman torn from society by grief.

*Chapter 18*

# MY GRIEVING BRAIN, MY HEALING HEART

WHEN YOU ANTICIPATE A LOSS, YOU DON'T WANT TO WASTE A minute, even on the toughest of days—because you know how deeply you'll miss them. You brace yourself for the end, but when it arrives, it's heavier than anything you imagined.

This is partly due to how the brain treats the actual loss. It keeps flipping through old habits and memories, trying to get you to do what it's used to you doing. You start going down that path but soon realise you don't need to do that anymore. That's when the emotion comes. Patterns have to be relearned, new neural pathways made, before the emotions that come on the heels of a routine denied can be tamed. Only once this re-parenting takes place can one fondly remember the loved one with minimal pain, like handling a broken bit of sea glass where the edges have worn off over a long, subtle processing. But when grief is new it is sharp and painful enough to rip at your soul.

Six months after Hamish passed, that relief that I felt shortly after he passed gave way to a deep, hollow ache—grief in its rawest form. I felt exposed, like a nerve without skin, caught in a permanent vulnerability hangover. The pain was no longer internal; it started to show. My posture and expression changed and my weight crept up, and with it, old shame resurfaced. How could I be a role model to my clients when I felt so undone?

My emotional filters dissolved. I found myself oversharing—offloading details of Hamish's palliative journey to clients, acquaintances, anyone who'd listen. It was trauma bleeding into trauma, as if I was more comfortable confiding in strangers than in my own family. Each morning, I'd wake up regretting what I'd said the day before, ashamed that I hadn't kept it contained. Grief, I thought, should be quiet—tidy. It should live in the silent moments before sleep, not spill into work or weigh down conversations. I had managed it after William, hadn't I? So why couldn't I now?

I remember one day Andrew and I went to a local café for brunch. It was a quiet place where we could sit outside in the garden and talk. I was doing all I could to stop the emotion that was building inside of me, trying to eat my breakfast with tears rolling down my face, not listening to a word Andrew was saying as I tried to hold back the floodgates. I thought I was losing control of my mind!

Thankfully, Andrew sensed my sad moment was turning into an anxiety attack. "Do you want to go home?" he asked.

"Yes!" I squeaked.

We got the bill and left in a hurry, half our breakfast still sitting on the table. As soon as I got into the car, I fell apart. The tears came hard and uncontrollably, and by the time we reached my place—just five minutes away—I was a complete wreck. I'd been feeling low for weeks, but this was different. This was a collapse.

"I'm so frickin' scared," I sobbed. "It feels like the end of my life."

I was falling into a dark hole with nothing to anchor me. No spark of inspiration, no reason to pull myself out. I wanted to run away and sleep forever—both all at once. My nervous system was in overdrive. I knew from my TRE training that I was experiencing the fight, flight, freeze—or even fawn—responses all at once. Just like a deer caught in headlights, my body screamed *run!* but I couldn't move. My wheels were spinning, but the handbrake was on.

I was emotionally and physically burnt out. I didn't want to do this life anymore. My body was saying *no*. No more.

"I think I need to go to the hospital and be sedated," I said. Secretly, I thought I also needed to be there on suicide watch. I wanted the pain and torment in my mind to end. Andrew rang my sister to let her know his concerns for me and then he rang the mental health triage hotline for support for both of us. Andrew shared some background history with the mental health nurse and she asked to talk to me. By this stage, I was exhausted from crying and sharing my deepest, darkest fears with Andrew, and drowsily reclined on the couch. I felt like I could faint and yet still sobbed into my tissues.

Andrew handed the phone to me and the MH nurse introduced herself. "How are you feeling now?" she asked. I told her.

"Who are you grieving for?"

"My two sons."

I felt her soften with compassion when she asked, "How old were they?"

"Nine and twelve."

"Are you having thoughts of self-harm or suicide?"

I'd been down this road before and knew to be honest. "Yes. I'm exhausted trying to process all this. I just want the thinking and pain to stop!" I sobbed.

"First," she spoke, firm yet gentle, "I want you to know there is nothing wrong with you. What you are feeling is grief, and it will come and go with varying degrees of intensity indefinitely. It will take time to process so be kind to yourself. It sounds like you have great support there with your friend Andrew. You don't need to come to our triage today." No sooner had our conversation ended than I rolled myself up into a ball and fell asleep on the couch, crumpled and stained tissues still clutched in my hand.

The next day I made an appointment with my doctor to get on some antidepressants. This time I stayed on them for almost twelve months. I was scared of going back to my dark and depressive state and getting taken over by my shadow self. The drugs took three weeks to start working. Funny, I had all my other self-care tools—neurofeedback, TRE, movement therapy, aromatherapy, exercise—but I knew I needed to find something else this time around. But what was it?

Grief tore me from society, just as much as my boys' disease. It isolated me, made me a stranger to myself. I was ashamed that I couldn't handle my grief better—ashamed that I was falling apart. And deep down, I was terrified this would be the thing that finally broke me. I didn't want people to witness that. I had always managed to wear a brave face, but now I couldn't. I felt like people didn't know how to look at me; like I was some kind of car wreck they couldn't help but glance at before quickly looking away, relieved they weren't living my reality.

So I shut down. I stopped checking social media and handed over the Adsl group admin role to the other mums. I ducked into different aisles at the supermarket to avoid familiar faces. I left messages unread, let calls go unanswered. I stopped teaching Pilates; something that once brought me joy and purpose—I now no longer had the energy to hold space for anyone else. Logically, I knew my friends didn't care if I wore makeup or gained weight or showed up tear-streaked. But I couldn't bear to be seen like that—raw, unravelled, and giving life less than the person I wanted to be.

Shame, always hovering on the edges of my psyche, berated me. *"Jeezus, girl, what's wrong with you? You're a frickin' wreck! Why can't you pull yourself together?"* The inner noise was relentless. I knew I had to leave. I needed to step away, to ride out the storm in privacy. I had to accept that my grief was very real and that it's something I couldn't mask or hide from and that the shame I felt needed to be healed alone.

Grief is so fucking exhausting. And after that dark-night-of-the-soul experience, all I wanted to do was sleep, cry, and write. That was all I could manage. And for a while, that had to be enough.

I called my sister Julie and asked if I could come stay for a few weeks. My sister and her husband live in Queensland's Gold Coast hinterland on a beautiful mountainous horse property, a two-hour flight from where I lived. I didn't want any fuss or social events, I just wanted to chill out and reconnect to myself and see if I could find a new reason to live. "Of course!" Julie said. "Stay as long as you like."

So I took six months off work as I temporarily closed my business and sold my car, and escaped to Julie's place in Queensland for four weeks to spend time in nature and with her horses. Each day I'd wake at 5:00 a.m. and journal for an hour and then head out for my morning walk. I'd pass several warmblood mares with their foals grazing in the paddocks. Some would follow me down the fence line as I walked down the long steep driveway. I'd walk for another thirty minutes in the early morning sun to the river, where I'd climb through the fence to access a spot where I could watch the water flowing over the rocks. One morning I even saw a platypus! I'd never seen one in the wild before. After this meditation in nature, I'd walk back up the driveway to the house perched on the side of the mountain to have a coffee with my sister and her husband on the porch. Then they'd go about their work day, leaving me to enjoy the serenity of this beautiful property and all its inhabitants. It was just the place I needed to heal.

On a few occasions, I'd take advantage of the morning sun a little longer and sit cross-legged in the middle of the paddock, where four mares and three foals grazed and played. Each mare took turns to curiously approach me with their foal in tow. They'd sniff at my hair and try to catch my bright, pink-coloured fingernails in their lips as I sat cross-legged in the grass. I'm sure they were trying to figure out who this strange human woman was and why she was sitting in their pasture. Curiosity satisfied, they'd return to grazing the grass around me.

One mare took to standing closer to me than the others. She was a big black mare at sixteen-two hands, with a rich black coat, mane, and tail. The sun had bleached the tips of her mane to light brown and I laughed and took a selfie with her because her mane matched my ombré hair highlights, except mine had been done at my sister's hairdresser a few days earlier. The mare soon followed me around whenever I came into the paddock. It was interesting to watch her boss the others away if they came closer to me than she liked. I laughed as she would stalk over to them, flatten her ears, toss her head, and give them the evil side-eye only a bossy mare can manage. That's all it took to clear the others away. Then she stood with her side to me, a respectable two-horse body length or so away, far enough to not pressure my intimate space, where only family and close friends could go, but close enough for a new friend I'd just met. Then she'd eat around me in a circle, physically holding the space for me.

"There's a mare down there with the same hair as mine!" I reported to Julie.

She laughed when she saw the photo. "That's funny! That's Satori's mum, Jade. You know Satori, my dressage champion?" Her eyes softened a bit. "Yeah, poor Jade. She lost Satori's brother last year shortly after giving birth. He was found dead in the creek at the bottom of the embankment. She must have had him on the hill and his wobbly newborn legs weren't able to stop him from rolling down into the water."

"My God, that's sad," I said, now realising my connection with this mare. Jade had been alone amongst her mare friends with no foal at her side when she came to greet me. She would have lost her foal last spring, around the same time as I'd lost Hamish.

The next morning at five, I started my day journaling as I usually do. I'd started journaling several years earlier but I'd taken it up more recently as a way to help heal myself. The technique I used when I first started to journal was automatic writing, where I'd ask a question, and write the first words that came through my fingers, consciously not altering the words that flowed naturally onto the page.

Journaling allowed me to truly express my feelings and be heard, without needing a trusted therapist nearby. No one had to read what I wrote. I didn't have to go back and reread it. Some people will even burn up or destroy their completed entries, in a final cleansing. Healing came when I used my journaling time to step away from the ego and connect to my authentic self—my higher, inner self—as well as messengers and loved ones who were waiting to communicate through the channel that was me and my pen. Horses had always been a big part of my life. As a young child they were always there, as an older child and teen I wished for more, and as an adult they taught me so much, mostly about myself. And right now, my heart was telling me that this big, grieving mare had something to teach me. These feelings flowed through me and into a poem called "The Path of the Horse," which has been revised several times over the years.

*A long lost love has returned,*
*I am overwhelmed by her beauty.*
*Those big shiny dark eyes,*
*So captivating and so deep.*

*She breathes me in and draws out my soul.*
*She feels my pulse, my heart, my intention.*
*Those big shiny eyes reflect the love for the child I too have lost.*
*She sees my dreams unfulfilled and all hope frozen through fear.*
*She feels my sorrow, yet she welcomes me into her herd.*

*With one deep breath, she soulfully whispers,*
*"I can see the real you and there is nothing you need to hide here."*
*Then right before my eyes, she becomes my mirror, I feel her empathy.*
*I bear witness to her courage and compassion,*
*As she senses my grief and sorrow, she bows her head in sympathy.*

*We stand side by side in our connection,*
*There is no way of escaping her or my pain.*

*I embrace my fear as she begins to remove my*
    *protective armour, layer by layer.*
*With her I cannot deny my truth, she knows I am broken*
*Yet she doesn't judge, because she is the same.*

*Then with a stomp of her hoof she jolts me back to life,*
*I find my strength and courage, my fear begins to be resolved.*
*I feel her energy connect to my heart and with each breath,*
*My tormented mind is released from its negative hold*
*And then, in this moment, a truly innate friendship unfolds.*

*Time and time again, they show us their perfection.*
*For the Path of the Horse is more than they'll ever know.*
*It is here, I am truly one of the herd.*
*It is here, I can feel my heart for the first time in years.*
*And thank God, it is here, I am saved from my slow*
    *suicide, as today I am hopeful of my tomorrow.*

*With such simplified, dignified life reflections,*
*She shows me she is more than just a horse.*
*It is by her side I am brought back to life.*
*The ultimate connection to a higher source*
*I'm coming home with the Path of the Horse.*

We are so much more than this life, and it's our hearts that show us how. Healing starts with self-compassion and recognising the layers of wounds from this incarnation down through to our soul's beginning. I wanted to tap into that ancient wisdom now, and follow the Path of the Horse.

Now, while the Path of the Horse is redemptive, it isn't necessarily easy. The next couple of years ahead of me were a mess of false starts and secret wisdom, complex grief and melancholy. It was quite the journey.

My magical reprieve at my sister's was only the start of my journey.

Coming home and back to the real world of work and relationships, I still felt scrambled and put in immense effort to get my brain to accept I was okay. While I could accept that my boys were no longer here, I was confused as to who I was or where I needed to be in order to find a meaningful life again. The path that I thought I could follow as a disability support worker or therapist, my running, even Pilates, were now all too triggering and I felt useless in the pursuits I had devoted so much of my time, money, and expertise to. Even stalwart Andrew couldn't escape my volatility.

I felt empty. Everything that I once loved and enjoyed I now felt nothing for. I desperately looked for a high. I'd bounce between ideas and activities, chasing a dopamine hit, trying to feel good if only for a moment. I stayed away from drugs, but I excused all other choices and behaviours in this time of mourning as I tried to find that one magic silver bullet that would make all my problems go away. I spent a lot of money searching for something that made me feel better.

I came back from Queensland, split up with Andrew, and did a wellness retreat with friends in Thailand.

I came back, bought a new car, got back with Andrew, and went on a 4x4 off-road fundraising adventure for Variety, the Children's Charity.

I came back, moved in with Andrew, relocated to Melbourne, started a new job, and sold my car as I had a work vehicle, and later travelled to Peru with my brother and his family and hiked the Inca trail and explored Machu Picchu.

I came back and enjoyed a beautiful Christmas with Andrew and his family; I thought the worst of it was over. Until I bolted again.

I wanted to sell my house now and travel for another year, so I spent the next few weeks travelling back and forth from Melbourne to Bendigo, getting my house ready to put on the market. Yeah, yeah, I know! I'd heard the adage, "After a significant loss don't make any big decisions for at least twelve months." My counselor told me, "In your case, make it four years."

Michelle, my sole sister, asked, "Do you really want to live so far away from all your friends?" I should have listened. I'd listed my house for only three weeks when surprise, surprise I had a change of heart and took it off the market. What used to be painful triggers twelve months ago were now calling me back to live in my home again, those triggers transformed into loving memories I could lean into to heal and write this book.

I was torn between starting a new life together with Andrew in Melbourne or completing unfinished business in Bendigo. Or moving to Queensland and starting a new life with the family I have there and with the horses I've always dreamed of. I knew exactly where I needed to be in order to heal but I wrestled with that decision, doubting myself for a while longer before I came to realise exactly where I needed to be to start my new life.

You could say I panicked and bolted several times as I tried to put the pieces of my old and new lives together. I was very aware of the fact that my grief and all my back-and-forth indecisiveness was also affecting another person's life. I felt ashamed, particularly because when Andrew met me I was this single supermum, running her little Pilates studio at the gym and juggling life with Hamish's care needs. I appeared to have all my shit together. Nope, not entirely true! As Hamish's care needs intensified, the pressure I put on myself to keep it together was actually destroying me and I was a prime candidate for compassion fatigue and burnout.

Andrew watched stoic as each wheel slowly fell off this little red wagon. He was passive and subtle in his guidance with me, kind of parenting me, in a way, not wanting to control me so I could learn for myself but also not letting me run myself off a cliff. He'd listen to all my hopes and dreams and then watch, slightly confused and bewildered, when I'd decide otherwise and would suddenly change course yet again. I'm sure a relationship with me at this time would have felt like herding cats. No sooner was I at one place looking settled than I was up and over there. At one point, I wondered if I had ADHD (which I'd like to add is exacerbated by chronic stress).

Lucky for Andrew, I realised that I couldn't make decisions for myself while I was in a relationship, so I asked for some space again. He gave me that space. It wasn't easy to walk away, but I knew I couldn't do what I needed with him standing guard. I needed and wanted to pull myself up out of this on my own.

I have everything inside me to live happily. Yet, I often looked towards others to bring me happiness and joy. It wasn't until I sat in the fire of my grief and grieving that I realised there was nothing I could get from anyone else that I couldn't get from myself.

Living alone in the home I'd shared with Hamish, I allowed myself to truly grieve and find a new level of compassion for myself. I was no longer William and Hamish's parent, but I could be a parent to myself, allow myself the time and space to become fully embodied and honoured. Finally, I gave to myself what I thought I could only get from others: acceptance, validation, approval, reassurance, guidance, appreciation, and love.

*Chapter 19*

# A GRIEVING HEART'S WISDOM

*When there are no words to convey your pain and
sorrow, turn to the language of the body.
Take a moment to feel the fire of grief inside and allow
the body to express itself anyway it desires.
Remove your social composure, allowing grief to move through
your body unrestrained by the controlling ego. Tremor, cry,
write, talk, laugh, sing, dance or run, observe the innate
wisdom of the body as it begins your healing process.
Allowing grief to rise up and offer it a path to exit through
movement, denying any self-destructive urge to use your body
as a storage vessel for all your pain and suffering. Rest assured
that there is a process beyond your mind that will soothe your
body as well as your soul towards its healing transformation.*

It was the first of September, 2024, when I felt it again—that quiet, unmistakable knowing. A solemn heaviness settled in my chest and I couldn't quite place it. Was it the season? A full moon? And then I remembered: It was close to the two-year anniversary of Hamish's passing. That day, I recalled the moment Hamish's soul had stirred something within me. We created art together—something sacred, something lasting. My heart remembered what my mind had momentarily set aside.

When I look back on this journey, I see how many times my body carried what my voice couldn't say. The trembling, the tight chest, the tears that seemed to come from nowhere—even the chemical and neurological imbalances—it wasn't random. It was sacred. The body and heart each hold their own intelligence, and they speak through sensation. Grief is their language, an inner dialogue that leads us back to an eternal knowing. It teaches us compassion by softening what was once armoured, illuminating a deeper connection to life, to love, and to what truly matters. In allowing ourselves to feel grief fully, we awaken the timeless wisdom that lives beyond the intellect—in the sacred, wordless space of the soul. This chapter was born from listening to that inner language, a surrender to what my body already knew and what my heart had never stopped whispering. It was my body's way of remembering what my mind tried to soften.

During that special time in Queensland with my sister, I came across the work of healer and author Carmel Glenane. Her writing spoke of the immortal wisdom of the heart—a concept that resonated in a way I couldn't ignore. She wrote about the heart as a keeper of ancient memories, even memories that may not originate from our own lived experience. I read stories of heart transplant recipients who began having flashbacks or sudden emotional shifts—only to later discover that these feelings, preferences, or dreams mirrored the lives of their donors. It left me wondering: What if the heart truly is the seat of the soul?

In the days before Hamish passed, I had experiences I couldn't explain: moments of knowing, deep emotional shifts, and what felt like spiritual communion. That time reaffirmed for me that the heart is more than an organ. It's an intelligence, a compass, and perhaps even a home for the soul. I've carried that belief with me ever since.

My fascination with the heart deepened. I wondered, was it just a coincidence that I wore a pendant close to my own heart, shaped like a heart and etched with the fingerprints of my boys? My business logo, which I designed several years before this knowledge, is also a heart, intentionally chosen to reflect not just love, but connection, intuition, and memory. Journaling became a lifeline in my grief. Each time I wrote, I was listening inward, tuning in to something deeper than thought. Something older than words. My heart.

Science is beginning to catch up with what many of us who have experienced great love or loss instinctively know: The heart has its own intelligence. The heart-brain connection—often referred to as "heart-brain coherence"—is a measurable state where the rhythms of the heart and the brain come into harmony. This process also engages the vagus nerve, a vital part of the autonomic nervous system, which plays a key role in regulating our emotional state and sense of safety. The heart and vagus nerve work together to help the body return to balance—unless, like I experienced with PTSD, the system becomes stuck in a hypervigilant state. In this state, the body is constantly scanning for danger, and memories can resurface not as distant recollections, but as full-bodied flashbacks. The body relives the trauma as if it's happening again in the present moment—racing heart, shallow breath, tight muscles—making it incredibly difficult to feel safe or grounded. When coherence is achieved through breath work, meditation, or even mindful journaling, it creates a cascade of positive effects in the body: reduced stress hormones, improved emotional regulation, clearer thinking. In grief, where everything can feel fragmented, this connection can be an anchor.

What does it mean to "follow your heart"? We hear the phrase so often it starts to sound like a cliché. But when you've lost what you loved most, and your mind feels shattered by grief, following your heart becomes less of a romantic idea and more of a lifeline. For me, it became a survival tool—because it was the only part of me that still had something to say.

Grief has taught me that healing isn't linear, and it's never tidy. It comes in waves, in layers. Just when you think you've reached the end, another layer emerges. My mum would often say, "Everything will be okay, Nats, if you just stay positive." It used to frustrate me because sometimes I didn't *want* to "be okay." I wanted someone to sit with me in my pain and say, "This is hard. I see you. I'm here." Eventually, I became that person for myself. I learned to validate my own grief, to listen inward when no one else could hear. And it was my heart that helped me do that.

Sharing my story hasn't been easy. Some people in my life questioned why I would write about such personal, painful things. "Why share that?" they asked. But the answer is simple: because it happened. And because sharing is how I affirm my experience—not for pity, but for connection. Just like a child who tells you they're hurt, not to be fixed, but to be affirmed, to be seen. To be heard. To know that what happens to them matters.

My heart—my true compass—keeps asking: How do I make this more than a tragedy? How do I honour my boys by creating something that outlives all of us? I may never have grandchildren, but I will leave behind something that matters. A legacy from the heart. An emotional imprint that might help someone else on the edge of grief find their footing to step down off the ledge and set out on a new journey to find their soul's purpose.

Not everyone grieves the same. We show only what feels safe. Sometimes it's not the fear of being judged, but the fear of being truly seen—and truly loved—that holds us back. I am the latter. Vulnerability feels risky when your heart has already been broken. But healing asks us to soften anyway. Because only when we allow our real selves to be seen, can we begin to feel truly connected.

Finally, I see myself: My grief is messy, my art is raw, and my writing is unfiltered. But it is all mine. It is how I come home to myself.

Writing this book became its own pilgrimage—a form of exposure therapy. Each morning, I returned to the page. I had to revisit my memories not just mentally, but somatically. I relived them viscerally in my body and emotionally in my heart. I dedicated four hours a day to remembering, to feeling, to tracing the shape of my story through words. Before I began, I'd often ask, "What message do I need to share with my readers today?" I'd hook myself up for a neurofeedback session, grab a pen, heart open, and dig up the memories that shaped me—and write them out.

In hindsight, I wish I'd taken a good month off work and all social interactions to live with my story for a while and process what was being unearthed. Writing this book brought on another layer of grief—grief for myself and for all of my past hurts, traumas, and losses. I decided to let myself grieve it all. I had to take all those pieces of my life and acknowledge what happened, how I felt about it then, and how I feel about it now. I sat in the fire of every emotion that surfaced with each chapter. I acknowledged and apologised to myself for all the ways I'd hindered or sabotaged my healing. I cried a lot of tears writing this book. On other days, I would shake—literally—during a TRE session, letting my body release what words couldn't hold.

I gave myself a hug, a moment of self-compassion, and moved through my deep pain. And once the thing is immortalised on paper, I can let it go and say, "What you went through was really tough, Nat. I'm so proud of you for getting through it. It is okay now." I guess I turned myself to ash so I could be reborn. I call this re-parenting myself—like stepping back in time and being the empathetic adult I needed in that moment to soothe my nervous system.

Is all my fear and grief gone? Hell, no. I just don't feed my fear anymore. And I acknowledge my grief with respect when it appears. I don't push it back down in shame. If it comes up in a space that isn't appropriate to fully express it, I tell myself to park it for now and revisit it with compassion later. My grief, while not a welcome friend, has become a polite flatmate. It didn't happen overnight, but it did happen. And it took things getting a little messy before they got clear. I'm pretty confident that after writing this book I'll never go back to my melancholy.

As I deepened my relationship with this heart wisdom, I began to understand more about the heart's energetic field. I first experienced this through kinesiology and muscle testing—techniques that use the body's subtle responses to reveal stored stress or emotional imbalance. I'd ask a question or hold a thought, and my body would answer. Not with words, but through strength or weakness in my muscles. It was like the body had its own language—one I had simply forgotten how to speak.

Later, I began working with a pendulum, tapping into the heart's magnetic field for clarity. At first, I thought, *This is a bit woo-woo*, but the more I practised, the more I realised how ancient and intuitive it really was. Using a pendulum isn't about fortune-telling or superstition—it's a simple, somatic tool for accessing the body's subtle biofeedback. The micro-movements that guide the pendulum are often responses from the subconscious mind or the nervous system—what many refer to as the ideomotor response. This technique, like kinesiology, reflects what the body already knows but the conscious mind might not yet have words for. The pendulum responds to the electromagnetic field that extends from the heart—something both measurable by science and recognised in energy medicine traditions for thousands of years.

The heart has a magnetic field that is over sixty times stronger than that of the brain, radiating several feet beyond the body. This is why we can sometimes *feel* someone enter a room before they speak, or sense when something is off with a loved one. The heart doesn't just pump blood—it communicates through frequency, vibration, and resonance. And when we learn to attune to it, it becomes a powerful guide. The HeartMath Institute suggests that this field not only influences our own physiological state, but may also play a role in energetic communication between people, explaining why we can sometimes sense the emotions or presence of others before a word is spoken.

Animals, especially horses, are deeply attuned to these subtle energy shifts. As prey animals, horses rely on sensing the emotional and energetic states of those around them for safety. As I mentioned before, horses mirror our emotions. They feel what we feel and reflect those feelings back to us. This is what makes them powerful partners in somatic and trauma-informed work.

Perhaps this is also what William meant in his poem when he said, "I am the child who communicates on a different level." That he was also a mirror. William and Hamish seemed to sense what I was feeling before I could name it myself and vice versa. Their presence had that same intuitive quality as a horse's—a quiet knowing that held me, mirrored me, and, in their own way, helped me begin to heal.

Through muscle testing, pendulum work, and breath-led movement, I started to understand what my body needed to heal—physically, emotionally, spiritually. I didn't need to look outside of myself for all the answers. The wisdom was within me, in my heart, waiting to be remembered. What once felt like spiritual guesswork became a conversation between body and soul. It taught me to trust myself again. To honour the nudges, the pulls, the inner noes and yeses. This is what I now mean when I tell myself to *follow your heart*.

It's not fluffy advice. It's an invitation to return to my body's most ancient intelligence—my inner compass—and let it show me the way.

After all the processing, the writing, the tears, and the healing, I found myself in a quieter space, still grieving, but steadier. I realised that grief had softened me, shaped me, and left me changed. Not broken, but transformed. Those long hours spent reflecting, remembering, and releasing had shifted something deep within me. The ache was still there, but it no longer ruled me. It became something I could carry with reverence. I had rewritten my story, not just on the page, but in my own nervous system. And with that came a new perspective—a peace, even amid the sadness. One that's best described by Elisabeth Kübler-Ross and David Kessler in their book *On Grief and Grieving*:

> The reality is you will grieve forever. You will not "get over" the loss of a loved one; you will learn to live with it. You will heal, and you will rebuild yourself around the loss you have suffered. You will be whole again, but you will never be the same. Nor should you be the same, nor would you want to.

So how do I become different? How do I carry this immense pain and shape it into something meaningful? How do I begin again—not in spite of the loss, but in relationship with it?

These were the questions that lingered once the pages were written and the emotional waves settled—for a time. They became the seeds of what came next: a deeper reflection on how we grieve, what we carry, and how we stay connected to what we've lost. Not through forgetting, but through love. Through choosing to remember.

Many cultures have their own rituals, beliefs, and processes for helping support those in mourning, but for us colonials we tend to push it down and expect that our social conditioning will dilute our grief in order to move on, a "Tallyho, lads! Onwards and upwards! Don't mention the war!" kind of approach that has its roots all the way back to Freud at the turn of the twentieth century. We only have to look at the clinical models for dealing with grief of the past to see that we are only just finding our way home with the more compassionate model for healing trauma and living with grief.

In 1996, Klass, Silverman, and Nickman shed light on an important bereavement concept in the book *Continuing Bonds: New Understandings of Grief*. Their work questioned the previous linear models of grief which viewed behaviours that promoted a continued bond with deceased loved ones as pathological or unhealthy.

I took comfort in discovering that Klass and his colleagues disagreed with the earlier "get over it" views on grief, instead suggesting a paradigm in which it is normal for the bereaved to continue their bond with the deceased. In their work, they observed many cases in which remaining connected to the deceased provided comfort and support in coping with loss and adjustment.

And so, I followed my heart once again. What came next wasn't the end of my grief, but a deeper understanding of what it meant to live alongside it. My writing, my rituals, my connection to my boys—all of it led me to a truth I could live with: that grief doesn't demand closure, it asks for presence. That love doesn't end with death, it only changes form. And that healing doesn't mean forgetting, it means remembering with love, with reverence, with grace.

Because the body remembers. And the heart always knows the way home.

This is the grief model that I uncovered naturally. Why? Because it made sense to me. It was the natural process that my brain and heart took to begin to heal: Follow your heart and what feels right.

So, no, I wasn't crazy and yes, it was normal and healthy to want to stay connected with my boys after they were gone, whether it be saying goodnight or good morning, kissing their urn, or creating art together after they passed. Journaling gave me the portal to the communication I'd always wanted with my boys. I'd write them a question or two about our life together and ask them, "What message do you have for me today, William? What do you want me to create, Hamish?" I don't think about the answer, I just let the pen write the first words and observe them as they come out and onto the page:

*Mummy, we love all you have done for us*
*So please take time for you to rest*
*Our souls are here to care for you now*
*Listen for us, because angels really do exist.*

I've been told believing in angels and things that can't be seen, things that aren't physical, is foolish. For most of my life, I believed those voices. But there is an unspoken energy and an angel can be many things. When menopause and grief wanted me dead, and I almost succumbed to their misguided fate, something beyond this realm saved me. Immortal wisdom of my heart and soul ensured I stayed here until my job was done and I completed my purpose. It felt like a call from the same heart-knowing that had stirred so often before, that sacred inner compass I'd followed through my depression, grief, and daily writing ritual. And maybe that's what the heart's wisdom is—a quiet, unseen force that some might call spirit, higher self, or angel. But whatever name we give it, it is what reaches across worlds to hold us and anchors us here in the physical realm when we need it most.

The keepsakes

So, maybe it's possible to cross time and space and forge a connection. To maintain a relationship past the grave. I keep the communication lines open in order for my boys and me to stay connected. I can communicate with Hamish and William now, though I suppose it's not always when I want to, or as strongly. I can't recreate that feeling I had when I created art with Hamish during his last days, or with William right after he died and I helped usher him to the next stage. When I first lost my boys, I thought I lost all of them. But now I know I lost only their bodies. Those imperfect perfect bodies. I found my boys again through another dimension, one much more spiritual and heartfelt than this limited, physical world. Perhaps all of us would be better if we learned new-old ways to connect again.

The way I view death is important to how I view life. As soon as I accepted my boys could cross into this earthly realm, and me into theirs—when I became comfortable living between two worlds rather than fighting to live in one—my desire to die ceased. I didn't have to choose one world, physical or spiritual. I could exist in both as everything exists in both. I could still be alive and be with my sons. That idea feels so much more comfortable to me than a sudden stop and separation. That's how I choose to grieve.

It may strike people as unusual, but when you're grieving you'll do whatever it takes to find solace and refuge from grief, like keep a room made up for boys who will never again play with the toys in it. The silver pendant I had made from a mould of their fingerprints when William was six and Hamish was four—I wear that 24/7 on a silver snake chain around my neck. But I couldn't bear to walk into my kitchen every day and confront my losses in the images covering the fridge. I had to strip things back. Regain a little control of the things that trigger. So I collected the rest of my sons' things from around the house and made a space in Hamish's old bedroom across the hall from mine to hold all the keepsakes, like a subtle shrine. The photos were arranged on Hamish's dresser. Many more photos in frames are now stored in boxes under my bed. Will's Swans scarf still hangs on the back of the bedroom door and his tartan kilt and sporran are now worn by Catherine's favourite teddy bear that she gave to William when he was a baby. Hamish's silver heart urn with the piece of him that isn't with Scotty and his brother sits next to Will's Tigger, also on the dresser, along with Hamish's frangipanis. I gave much of William's Tigger-related things away to other children who would love them—I donated a beautiful painting of Tigger done by my friend Jan to the VSK hospice William and Hamish stayed at frequently—but I will always keep the Tigger teddy who has William's last kisses.

I never expected to learn or know what has now helped me process my grief. I am no longer scared of the nonphysical. No longer scared of my emotions. They open the door to eternal wisdom, presence, and love.

Every night before bed, I walk into my sons' room and for a moment I'm a mum again. The walls are covered with their art. The bed's nicely made. I stand in the quiet space and I say goodnight to my boys. "Goodnight, Hamie! Goodnight, Will! See you in my dreams!" I'll pop in and say good morning when I wake up. Again, I imagine they hear me and will respond when the mood strikes them.

Pregnancy, birth, caring, death—nothing can take those experiences away from me. I will always be the mother of two beautiful souls. I am never truly alone. William and Hamish are with me—always have been, always will be.

Namaste.

*Epilogue*

# A LEGACY STILL UNFOLDING

IT'S ALMOST CHRISTMAS AGAIN AS I FINISH THE FIRST DRAFT of this book. Christmas Day—Hamish's birthday—now carries the weight of his passing, a bittersweet marker of both beginnings and endings. Yet this year, for the first time since he died, I find myself softening into the season. I'm saying yes to festive catch-ups, reaching out to friends, and quietly celebrating the year that was. I even managed to put up my Christmas tree. Just last week, I reconnected with my old running girlfriends—something that was once very triggering was actually so uplifting.

In these small steps back to life, I'm reminded that healing doesn't come all at once. It's a quiet, continuous weaving. Each time a significant traumatic event happens in our lives, it's as if someone walks straight through the delicate web we've spent years spinning. You're left standing there, staring at the wreckage. What was once a beautifully crafted life now reduced to torn strands fluttering, disconnected from the centre, which is you. My life was just like that—a web of people, communities, routines, and meaning—all of it held together by William and Hamish at its core. When they passed, it was as though the centre was ripped out, and the spokes and silken threads that once gave my life shape blew loose and directionless in the wind. How do you even begin to rebuild something so fragile and intricate after such a loss?

It took a few years. But thread by thread, I've started to rebuild a new centre, knowing this web will never look like the old one, yet honouring that it's still mine to weave. The only way I could see forward was to give myself permission to discover what I had long denied myself—to strip back the old, limiting beliefs and ask: *If I could do exactly what I want now, what would it be?* Forget money. Forget the expectations of others. Forget the ties to relationships that no longer fit. *What do I truly want the outcome of my life to be?* I knew I wanted to heal, not just survive. I wanted to meet my traumas with compassion, not judgment, and give myself space to become whole again. More than anything, I wanted to feel that my boys left me better than they found me.

As I reclaimed parts of myself, I began to see that healing didn't end with me, it extended outward. The more I softened into my lived experience, the more I felt called to transform it into something that could support others. My boys had given me more than memories; they had given me a message. Just like in William's poem: *"When we connect, accept and care for each other the world will be a better place."* And I knew the next step in my journey was to share that message—so no family would ever have to feel as alone as we once did.

Awareness of Adsl Deficiency is slowly but surely expanding across the world. More paediatric specialists and metabolic teams are recognising the condition, and with that, more families are receiving a diagnosis. Each month, a new parent finds the Facebook community I founded back in 2014, "Our Journeys with Adsl Deficiency," and sends a request to join. We are now connected to over one hundred thirty families, spread across countries and cultures, connected by a rare condition, and an even rarer kind of love.

Our group and its families continue to raise awareness and funds for scientific research, alongside new initiatives like the Rare Birds Foundation, founded by another devoted mother, Nicole Lytle, who's also walking this path along with her husband, Justin, and two children, Flora and Jonah, who both have Adsl Deficiency.

I've written this book to serve as a conduit—a way to connect and expand awareness of Adsl Deficiency, and to honour the stories of our families. Their lives matter. Their voices matter. And it's important that they have the opportunity to be heard.

To continue this mission, I started a podcast called *Back to Life and Beyond*, a space where I explore meaning, purpose, and how to find joy after significant life events. As part of the podcast, I began a special interview series with rare mothers like myself, women raising children with rare and complex conditions. I've also begun including rare fathers in these conversations. While it's really about rare parents, naming them specifically feels more personal and powerful. By giving voice to our experiences, we're not just sharing our truths—we're breaking the silence, building connection, and reminding one another that we're not alone.

Sharing our stories is powerful—not just for connection, but for change. Every family that opens up about their journey with Adsl Deficiency helps light the way for those still searching for answers. These stories do more than raise awareness; they drive the need for faster diagnoses, more research, and better systems of care.

That's why I continue to advocate for the Bratton-Marshall test, which detects SAICAr in urine, to be included in the recommended genetic screening for inborn errors of metabolism, particularly for children with undiagnosed developmental delays, seizures, or infantile spasms. I also support making in vitro pregnancy screening for Adsl Deficiency more widely available. In Australia, access to these screenings is slowly improving, a small but vital step towards fewer families being blindsided by symptoms they don't yet understand.

Prevention also means recognising risk. I believe it's time to expand metabolic testing before routine childhood vaccinations. While I am not an anti-vaxxer, I do believe some rare metabolic conditions, like the one my boys had, may be contraindicated for a regular vaccine schedule, which could increase the risk of further neurological damage. I hope future research explores these intersections so the lives of children like William and Hamish continue to inform science and protect others.

And just as we work to protect our children, we must also care for the ones who care for them. Carers often carry their grief, exhaustion, and love in silence—and too often, in isolation. Through my own journey, and conversations with friends, I've come to realise that supporting families goes beyond medicine and diagnosis. It's about building community, tending to our nervous systems, and creating spaces where we feel seen, heard, and accepted.

That's why I'm creating retreats and online offerings designed specifically for caregivers and bereaved parents, to give them a place to breathe again. These retreats will combine self-care practices like Pilates, TRE (Tension and Trauma Releasing Exercises), and gentle movement, with honest conversation, social connection, and emotional restoration. They're for those of us who've lived through the unimaginable and who need support from others who truly *get it*.

Of course, I know affordability can be a barrier, which is why I hope to raise funds each year to offer sponsored retreat spots, a way to pay it forward through the kind of random acts of kindness that carried me when I needed them most.

Whether it's gathering in person or connecting online, my hope is to bridge the deep loneliness that often comes with caregiving and grief. Because healing often takes time and space—and that journey can feel long and isolating when walked alone.

Movement has been one of the ways I've found my way back to life, and I now share that through one of my greatest passions: horses. Through equine-assisted movement therapy and Pilates programs tailored for riders, I offer a playful, grounded, and empowering way to reconnect with the body and restore balance, control, and confidence, to begin again—both in and out of the saddle.

In addition to this memoir, I've written several resources to support families, carers, and individuals navigating both rare disease and personal healing which are available on my website and online store:

- *Adsl Deficiency Simplified—A Parent's Guide to Navigating Scientific Insights, Therapies and Complex Care Strategies*
- *Unstuck: From Stuck to Unstoppable*—a how-to guide for releasing stress, restoring inner peace, and breaking free from the habits that hold you back, using TRE, journaling, and somatic self-care
- A collection of guided journals with prompts for deeper insights and connection

And at the time of this book's release, I'll be in the thick of writing my next one: a self-care guidebook to complement the journey shared in these pages. It will offer both the theory and the practical programs to help you start over, come back to life, and return to your authentic self gently and in your own time.

I warmly invite you to stay connected through my social channels and by subscribing to my monthly newsletter, where I share updates, reflections, and resources to support your path forward. You can scan the QR code at the back of this book to learn more.

Thank you for reading these pages and walking alongside me. My hope is that somewhere in this story, you found something that resonated—a moment, a feeling, a quiet reminder that we are bigger than our bodies.

This memoir has been my way of weaving a new web—one thread at a time—through loss, advocacy, healing, and hope. And if I leave you with anything, let it be this: *William and Hamish were here.* Their lives mattered. And the ripples of their existence will continue reaching far beyond what any diagnosis could define.

Their legacy is still unfolding.
And so is mine.
That's all of it.

# ACKNOWLEDGMENTS

THIS BOOK WOULD NOT EXIST WITHOUT THE LOVE, PATIENCE, and strength of the many people who stood beside me as I made something meaningful out of deep loss.

To my mum—thank you for your love, your quiet compassion, and your gentle guidance. Thank you for sharing this journey with me and holding space for both my grief and growth.

To my dad—thank you for giving your all for our family. I'm so glad we've had more time together over the past couple of years. It's meant more than words can say. Thank you.

To my brother, Bill—a man with a big heart. As a child, you inspired me more than you'll ever know. Your incredible work ethic, passion for life, and ability to balance hard work with fun and adventure have always stayed with me. And to Kirsty—my favourite sister-in-law—thank you for bringing out the best in this man.

Together, you helped me start to dream again. I'm so grateful, and I can't wait for our next trekking adventure.

To my sister Linda—thank you for being my big sister, always looking out for me as a child and for sharing your love of horses with me. Your generosity reaches deep into my heart. Your can-do spirit, presence, and encouragement helped nurture me when I needed it most and for that I love you, thank you.

To my sister Julie—thank you for your big-sister wisdom and for always looking out for me, even from afar. Your empathy and quiet strength gave me space to begin healing my broken heart. I love you now and always.

To my eldest sister, Catherine—my best friend, my wingman/chick, my rock. Any time I needed help, you were there without question. Thank you. I love you deeply and endlessly for everything you've done and everything you are.

To my niece, Emily—you are the reason I'm still here today. Thank you for being you, beautiful girl. Never give up on your dreams. You're capable of more than you know.

To Maggie—my second mum—thank you for being a caring and loving role model to me and so many others. I'm sorry for the loss you've endured, and that we now share the unimaginable grief of losing a child. I hope your heart finds peace. I also want to thank you for the love and care you've shown my dad over the years.

To my cousin, Chris—you've been a distant guiding light, quietly teaching me so much about compassion, friendship, and embracing difference. Thank you, cuz.

To Andrew—my dearest friend. This book simply wouldn't exist without you. Thank you for showing me who I am, gently and with such kindness. Your unwavering support—your time, your care, your attention to detail—gave me the space I needed to bring this story to life. You inspired me to rise above my limiting beliefs and reach for more. Thank you.

A special thank-you to Libby, Michelle, and Kelly—my closest friends for the longest time. Your presence, laughter, and unwavering loyalty have carried me through seasons I never thought I'd survive. I'm so grateful to have you in my life.

To my friend Sammy—thank you for your friendship and the beautiful way you embraced motherhood. You were, and always will be, a mother I admire. Your friendship in those early days gave me deep comfort and hope, something I'll be eternally grateful for.

Thank you to Will and Hamish's carers—Ruby, Karen, Donna, Karlie, Carly, and Carla. Six of the most beautiful, caring people I've had the pleasure to know. Your gentleness, dedication, and love for my boys touched our lives in ways I'll never forget. You gave them safety, comfort, and joy, and you gave me peace and laughter in moments when I needed it most.

To the Adsl Deficiency community—every parent, every child, every advocate. Thank you for your courage, your honesty, and your willingness to share your journeys. We are stronger because we stand together.

Thank you to the disability advocates—past, present, and future. The reason we've continued to evolve inclusion for minority groups is because of those who bravely shared their stories, warts and all. Without sharing our truth, nothing changes.

To the parents and carers who came before us—thank you for speaking up, for challenging outdated systems, and for demanding better. Your courage has helped shift perceptions, improve care, and show the world that it's not only okay to be different, it's something to be understood, supported, and respected. Your voices paved the way, and will continue to embrace difference with acceptance.

To all the staff and teachers at Bendigo Special Development School—thank you for walking this journey with us for so many years. Your compassion, patience, and unwavering support changed our lives in ways you may never fully realise. You helped create a safe and supportive space for my boys to learn and grow, and for that I am deeply grateful.

To our early intervention therapists, Bonnie Gutteridge and Paula Morris—I know you were just doing your job, but what a gift you both had, and what a gift you gave to us. Your support during those early, uncertain years gave us strength and guidance when we needed it most. You helped lay the foundations not only for my boys' development, but for my own growth as their mother and advocate.

To Carla Mullins from Body Organics Pilates—thank you for inspiring me to bring my Pilates studio home before the pandemic and for always encouraging my growth as a Pilates practitioner. Your passion for learning, teaching, and movement continues to shape my path. You inspire me.

To my earliest Pilates instructors—Jessica Morley, thank you for the random act of kindness that truly changed my life. And to Steven Charles, thank you for helping me transition from student to teacher. I'm so grateful for the body wisdom, clarity, and inspiration you both shared so generously.

To Sandi Simons—thank you for taking my hand and showing me how to regain my confidence, not just with horses, but with life. You are a remarkable woman whose wisdom and energy transcend far beyond the arena. Your guidance reminded me of my strength, even when I'd forgotten it myself.

To my spiritual mentors—Andrea Rae, Intuitive Heart Coach; Carmel Glenane, Spiritual Healer; and Sally Urokohara, Kinesiologist, thank you for teaching me the wisdom of the heart, for guiding me back to my inner knowing, and for encouraging me to trust it fully. Your teachings were not only supportive, but life-changing.

To the amazing women of the Gazelles—Aida, Maree, MaryAnne, Megan, Trinity, Bronwyn, Lou, Mel, and Jac—thank you for being such an inspiring and uplifting bunch. Your energy, encouragement, and shared laughter have been a true gift. I'm so grateful to run beside you—not just on the trails, but in life.

To my clients—past, present, and future—thank you for allowing me to walk beside you in your wellness journey. It's all for nothing if we don't learn from each other. My life has been deeply enriched by working with you, and I'm honoured to be part of your path towards movement and vitality.

A heartfelt thank you to Richmond Heath, founder of TRE Australia and a grounded yet dynamic TRE master practitioner. In 2016, you gently introduced me to the practice of tremoring, and it changed everything. Your wisdom and the way you speak about trauma helped me make sense of what I was holding inside. You showed me there was another path—and you continue to lead the way as a mentor towards healing.

To Dr. David Berceli, founder of TRE and the Trauma Prevention organisations—thank you for your pioneering work and vision. Both you and Richmond Heath have offered me a path back to my body and a way forward in my healing journey. Your teachings have been lifelines—not only to me, but to thousands around the world.

A special thank-you to all the not-for-profits and charities that helped improve the quality of life for our boys and many others like them through generous donations, time, and care. Your support made a huge difference to our lives.

To the Steve Waugh Foundation, Variety the Children's Charity, Make-A-Wish, Anglicare Bendigo, Lions Club of Victoria/Bendigo, The Kuene Foundation, Paul DeAraugo, Very Special Kids House, Royal Children's Hospital, Royal Institute for Deaf and Blind Children, and Scope Australia—thank you from the bottom of my heart. Your generosity gave us moments of relief, and joy.

To the dedicated staff of the Children's Ward at Bendigo Base Hospital and the palliative care teams at the Royal Children's Hospital—thank you for your compassion, care, and unwavering support during the most difficult moments of our journey. Your kindness will never be forgotten.

To the professionals at Scribe Media who helped me give voice to this story: my publishing manager, Jamie Cappelletti; cover designer, Anna Dorfman; and editor, Amanda Hoppe.

To Pauline—the best hairdresser in my world—thank you for planting the seed and saying, "You should write a book." Well, here it is. You were right, it was healing. And I'm so grateful for your friendship through it all.

To my dear friend Debbie—thank you for your steady support and heartfelt friendship over the years. Walking a parallel path with you has been comforting and has given me the strength to do this for us rare mothers. Your beautiful children, Connor and Keely, have left a lasting imprint on my heart. I'm so grateful our journeys have intertwined.

To Stacey and Georgia—thank you for inspiring the opening chapter of this book with your heartfelt encouragement. I hope these pages answer the questions you so bravely asked. Your kindness and willingness to reach out when I needed it most meant more to me than you'll ever know.

To Jan Henderson—thank you for sharing your time and your barn with Hamish, Shadow, and me. In that space, I rediscovered something I hadn't realised was missing. Your quiet compassion opened my heart to new possibilities and continues to shape my life. Thank you.

To the quiet readers—the ones I may never meet—thank you for opening your heart to this story. If even one sentence helped you feel seen or less alone, then this was worth every word.

To dear Scotty—thank you for being the father of our beautiful boys. For all that we shared, and for walking part of this journey with me. Your place in their story—and mine—will always be honoured.

And finally, to the part of myself that kept me writing, even when it hurt—thank you.

We did it.

# ABOUT THE AUTHOR

**NATALIE WATSON** is a Pilates movement therapist, holistic health coach, and advocate for caregivers, bereaved parents, and trauma survivors. Her journey began as a mother to two sons with a rare metabolic condition, which led her to become a certified Allied Health Assistant and immerse herself in therapeutic care.

She is the founder of Back to Life Studio, where she offers somatic-based Pilates and Trauma Release Exercises (TRE) to help people manage stress, release tension, and reconnect with their bodies after significant life events. Her approach is deeply personal and grounded in both professional expertise and lived experience.

Combining her lifelong love of horses with her professional skills, Natalie has also created specialised Pilates programs designed to improve riding posture, body awareness, and overall equestrian performance.

A gifted writer and poet, Natalie uses storytelling as a path to healing. Guided by curiosity and a conscious approach to self-discovery, she shares her ongoing blog, self-guided workshops, wellness journals, and *Back to Life Portal*—an online space she created to hold and teach the practices that supported her own healing. In this memoir, she shares her raw, personal journey through grief, transformation, and an unexpected spiritual awakening.

Natalie divides her time between the Gold Coast Hinterland, Queensland, and Bendigo, Victoria, where she nurtures her own well-being through nature, horse riding, mountain biking, and writing with her beloved Boston terrier, Stevie, by her side.

Credentials:

- Certified Health Coach
- Level 3 Pilates Practitioner & Movement Therapist
- Certified Allied Health Assistant & Disability Support Worker
- TRE® & Neurofeedback Provider

More at www.nataliewatson.com.au
Blog: https://nataliekwatson.substack.com/
Studio: www.BacktoLifeStudio.com.au
Scan here for more information.

www.ingramcontent.com/pod-product-compliance
Lightning Source LLC
Chambersburg PA
CBHW070239090526
44586CB00035B/1004